My dearest [illegible]
and d[illegible]

How can [illegible]
enough for your amazing love,
friendship and help all these
years and especially the last
few days? You are so
amazing to me and to say
that I love, cherish, honor
and respect you, would be
a gross understatement!! I
truly look up to you and
have so much love for you
and all you do for so many.

please accept this book
from the bottom of my heart.
May God bless you with
everything that you need
and may He continue to
show you His grace, favor
and mercy.

With my love, respect
and eternal friendship,
Your Sister,
Christine xxx
xx
X

Christine Mercy Nerton

50 Things I've Learned From 50 Years Of Life

5 Decades of "Ah-Ha!" Life Learning Lessons

Christine Mercy Overton, D.D., Ph.D.

BALBOA.
PRESS
A DIVISION OF HAY HOUSE

Balboa Press books may be ordered through booksellers or by contacting:

Balboa Press
A Division of Hay House
1663 Liberty Drive
Bloomington, IN 47403
www.balboapress.com
1 (877) 407-4847

Printed in the United States of America.

ISBN: 978-1-4525-9865-9 (sc)
ISBN: 978-1-4525-9867-3 (hc)
ISBN: 978-1-4525-9866-6 (e)

Library of Congress Control Number: 2014920035

Balboa Press rev. date: 12/02/2014

This book is dedicated to my beloved precious son Geoffrey who has sacrificed the most in order for me to fulfill God's will on earth

It is written for the glory of God and our Savior Jesus Christ

"My home is in heaven. I'm just traveling through this world." Rev. Dr. Billy Graham

Contents

With a Foreword by Jeff Boxen (1943-2014)

Since I first met Dr. Christine Overton 32 years ago, she has taught me more about life than any other person I have ever met since; and as a seventy year old man, who all my friends, family and business associates refer to as a man of "Infinite wisdom," that is truly saying something.

I have had the privilege to know Christine in a personal, and work capacity, and she has proven to be the rarest of human beings. I can say without question that Christine is the most remarkable woman I have ever met, and consider it an honor that she came into my life. In all the years, I have known her, she has proven to be not only brilliant at every level of her work, but also she has shown unswerving loyalty to me since we first met. I may have started out as her mentor, but I don't believe that anything could have held her back or prevented her "Star," from eventually shining through. Everybody she met noticed her skills, abilities, determination, amazing positive attitude, and the sheer ability to get the job done.

I have watched this amazing woman survive events that killed thousands and her faith to recover, combined with her tenacious courage left me humbled and proud. In respect of all these qualities, you have to add Christine's amazing empathy with her fellow man, and her vibrant, dynamic and larger than life personality. I can only liken her to Princess Diana, as people of every color, race or creed are drawn to her warm heart like a magnet.

In respect of her working prowess, the first thing I noticed about her was her natural ability in public speaking. She was always the first to stand up and do a presentation, and all the other sales people marveled at the ease and confidence she showed. The number of her audience never frightened her, in fact the more people present, the more she shined. It comes as no surprise to me therefore to know that she has conducted over 3000 interviews, had her own radio show, and made award-winning films for TV.

It would take many pages to highlight all Christine's talents, but whether it has been in events planning, sales and marketing, leadership, communications expertise or the rarest of qualities to just make it happen, Christine has always been at the top of her game. If you add to this, her multi-cultural knowledge, you have the complete package.

Knowing Christine has enriched my life.

Preface

I literally thank our father God for my life every day, and I praise him for who I am becoming. I find that the closer I get to fifty years; I seek more for others than myself. I seek less razzmatazz, and a more meaningful relationship, vocation and faith. I think before I act now, as I am aware of the consequences of my actions. Thus, I feel more evenly balanced. God has brought me to a wonderful place in my life.

The book that you are about to read comes from my heart to yours with love and it is written in such a way that you can almost hear me speaking to you. I would like to offer it to you with sincere and loving humility, and with the hope that you may find some semblance of encouragement and empathy within its pages and stories.

People are often shocked when they hear about my life story. Certainly, my life has been one of highs and lows, much like you and yours. However, few people have had to face such extreme lessons as I have. I suppose those who know about my life are shocked to find that I am very down to earth, loving, forgiving and well balanced. I genuinely love every man, woman and child with a passion that is impossible for me to conceal; you can feel it and see it in everything I do or say.

Throughout the last five decades of my life, I have attended schools, colleges, universities, seminaries, monasteries, institutes and even a law enforcement academy. I have taken the usual classes of languages, art, science, history and geography, as well as leadership, business administration, counselling, marketing, public speaking, communication, sales and theology. I have studied and compiled political agendas for lobbyists and congress for consideration. At the citizen's police academy, I learned about forensics, firearms, bomb squad, domestic violence, substance abuse, dispatch, K-9 unit, homicide, traffic enforcement and patrol procedures. I have been a United Nations representative and I have sat on many influential committees around the world.

I have been most fortunate throughout my life with the presence of many academic, religious, political and professional teachers and mentors. I thank God for them every day, for when I am pondering over an important decision, I can recall their advice to me. Thus, more often than not, I can make a decision that is wise and right for my positive wellbeing. Then there are the classes that come in forms of behaviors like forgiveness, patience, compassion, kindness and selflessness. I am equally grateful for those lessons. Overall, you are about to read a book about the earth classes I have attended thus far.

I do not see life on earth as my home. One day soon, I will take my last breath and go home to my father in heaven. God sent me to this school to learn about life, and to be a humble servant and pilgrim. As Reverend Dr. Billy Graham once said, "My home is in heaven. I'm just traveling through this world."

Complete strangers often seem to track me down and even at work, people would wander in off the streets saying, "I know this will sound odd, but I had this urge to come in here; yet I don't know why?" The receptionist or my colleagues became so used to this that they would smile and say, "Let me take you to see Christine."

I can safely say that if you were to spend a few days with me, you would see things that defied explanation and witness love expressed in ways that few can comprehend. You would find wild animals behaving like pets as I walked passed and touched them, and tearful strangers reaching out to touch me. God moves through me in an amazing way. You will quickly deduce that he is the center of my life in a mature and well-balanced way and I am not ashamed to declare that I am a daughter of the King of Kings and Lord of Lords.

We really cannot fathom growing old when we are children can we? We look forward to parties and holidays, and groan with frustration that the time seems to go by too slowly. A month seems ages. Yet now, in my fiftieth year, time seems to be passing by very quickly. I am finding that I ask with an earnest heart, "What can I do for others? Please show me how to serve you today almighty God!"

Part of his answer continues to be, "Have the courage to write this book and teach my beloved daughter. Many men, women and children will be blessed by your words." Amen.

Lesson 1: Life is precious

So let us begin. How do we define the beginning? Is that at conception or is it after birth? Is it a near death experience, or a move to a new part of the world? Could it be a major event that completely changed your life, or a painful love affair, that broke up unexpectedly? How we define the start of our life is always an interesting topic of discussion and I have found that the vast majority of people I speak with believe that their birth is day one for them. Others, like me, believe I began when God created me, which was a long time before my mother and father had even met.

Let us talk about birth. As Mark Twain commented, "The two most important days in your life are the day you are born and the day you find out why."

I was born on September 28, 1965 in Penzance, Cornwall in the United Kingdom. My birth was right by the ocean on the southwest of England. This is where the pirates of old would dock and store their stolen treasure. Some say that if one is born by the ocean in Penzance, one is doomed and destined to roam the earth forever more. That is my excuse for the being the black sheep of my family, and I am sticking to it!

A working class man and a woman from a respected middle class family, who did not expect or want a complication to their romance, conceived me. My father was a married man who saw the relationship with my mother as an extramarital fling. She on the other hand was apparently in love with him, but her feelings were in no way reciprocated. His solution to the prospect of my birth was to give my mother money to abort me, with the understanding that she would leave him alone from that point forwards. My mother was twenty-one years of age and wanted to attend Art College. She did not wish to bring shame on her family by announcing that she was pregnant by a married man.

I was born underweight with several dislocated joints and shrouded within an atmosphere of great sadness. Few knew about my birth, and those who did were not happy about this child's entrance. There was no rejoicing or smiles, no visitors and nobody to offer me comfort or love. In short, my arrival caused grief and embarrassment.

My father continued his life, oblivious to the fact that my mother had not aborted me. My mother returned home and soon met and married her now wonderful husband of over forty-nine years. She went on to have four other beautiful children, and I met her later on in my life. She had written a letter that accompanied me to the orphanage, and when I read it over two decades later, I came to understand how painful it was for her to give me away; yet she wanted a life of which I could never be a part. I am so grateful that she did not kill me, but instead gave me the opportunity to live.

Conclusion

Firstly, all life is precious to God, as he does not make mistakes with his creations. One must be responsible in one's sexual relationships, for a child can be conceived and this life is precious and not to be discarded like trash.

Secondly, please have the courage to allow your child to be born, trusting that social systems are in place to find a home for that baby, giving him or her opportunity to fulfill his or her own destiny.

Lesson 2: Mission

My adopted parents were distinguished aristocrats who came from a long line of noblemen with generations of kings, barons and lords. Our family was part of the rich royal history of Great Britain with naval, air and military leaders. Having given a home to one girl, they decided that they wished to adopt a son. They made enquiries to a Cornish orphanage to select a boy, but instead came home with yours truly.

Years later, my adopted mother told me about that day. They had looked at all the babies and children, and yet not one of them felt right to her. When my parents came into my room, I was sitting silently in a cot. By my side was a brown leather suitcase in which was a dress, a toy bear and the Bible. The orphanage told them that I had neither cried nor attempted to move from the cot. They said I simply always lay or sat there without movement or expression. They said nobody had wanted to adopt me because I seemed too quiet. My adopted mother's heart moved with compassion. She all but begged my father to allow her to bring me home. Thankfully, he agreed.

My secrecy continued. It was not until my adopted father had suddenly died when I was seventeen years old, that the subject of my adoption was raised and discussed. My adopted sister would always introduce me as the child they, "Got." This never made sense to me until after my father had died. My sister had been a four-year old child when they brought me home. They had told her that they had gone to get me.

I was a secret child who had come from the poorest of the poor orphanages in England. As Obert Skyen so eloquently summarized in *Leven Thumps and the Gateway to Foo,* "He came into the world like a delivery that no one knew what to do with, and nobody wanted to sign for."

I was a secret to everybody except my father God. In Psalm 139 we learn, "For you formed my inward parts; you wove me in my mother's womb. I will give thanks to you, for I am fearfully and wonderfully made; Wonderful are your works, and my soul knows it very well."

I have always felt God's presence in my life. Never has a single moment gone by when I have not been completely aware of his guiding hand upon me.

My birth mother named me, "Tina Lorraine." Names are very interesting and important. When Mary was pregnant with our Savior, Archangel Gabriel appeared to her. He told her that the baby was to receive the name, "Jesus." His destiny was to encapsulate this sacred name. His name meant "Savior." It is symbolic to our Lord because he saves his people from their sins. This is his special role. He saves them from the guilt of sin, by cleansing them in his own atoning blood. He saves them from the dominion of sin by filling their hearts with the sanctifying Spirit. He saves them from the presence of sin when he welcomes the just into heaven in a glorified body at the end of time. He, who is the King of Kings and the Lord of Lords, might lawfully have taken some more high-sounding title. However, he does not do so. Those seeking salvation may draw near to the father with boldness, and have access with confidence through Christ. It is his role and his delight to show mercy. He is our father and as Jesus called him "Abba," which means "Daddy," or "Papa." We too, have permission to refer to him in this intimate way.

His name had purpose, and so does ours. We all sit pondering over what to name our children, for we understand its significance on every level. Moreover, many of us continue a family tradition by naming our children after our parents or grandparents. Often, we look through books to find the meaning of the chosen names. I also believe that God prompts us to name our son or daughter in a certain way, because he knows the journey that we are about to undertake.

What was I to undertake and fulfill in my life? What does my name mean? "Tina," develops high spirituality, as she has God's protection. She has an inherent courage and endurance to accomplish the impossible dream. With this power comes responsibility. She holds keys to the material world. With this gift comes high spiritual responsibility to be fair and true to others. She is philosophical and mature, determined and intense with a desire to endure.

Within days of bringing me home, my mother apparently had a significant dream. An angel told her to christen me, "Christine." Had my mission now changed with the new name? Christine is a derivative of the word "Christ," which is the Greek translation of the Hebrew word, "Messiah."

God marked me from the moment he created me. His plan was for me to live a life of service to others, and I pray always that I will never let him down. Later when I turned forty-eight years old, I took the confirmation name of, "Mercy." I chose this name because my wish is always to show loving kindness and mercy to all beings great and small.

As Hans Urs Von Balthasar said, "The Church does not dispense the sacrament of baptism in order to acquire for herself an increase in membership, but in order to consecrate a human being to God and to communicate to that person the divine gift of birth from God."

As an amusing side note, most people do not know that my name was once, "Tina." Even to this day, it does not matter how many times I say that I am "Christine," people still insist on calling me, "Christina."

Conclusion

To those of you, who are not able to conceive, please look upon this as a different kind of gift from God. Perhaps you are to raise a baby or child that is unwanted by the ones who were its egg and seed vehicle to earth. Those of us who were given away need good homes, and I assure you, as much as we are grateful to the ones who gave us life and chose not to kill us, it is you who raises us that wins our hearts and lifelong loyalty. If you choose not to adopt, then understand that every single child of God needs love and kindness.

Perhaps he intends for you to be the favorite aunt or uncle of ones around you who need that loving support. Everybody needs a cheerleader, in order for him or her to grow and thrive.

When it comes to giving your child his or her first name, spend time in meditation and prayer. Ask God to come to you and tell you what you are to name the child. Remember that this name signifies far more than just a signature on a future form. This is how others will identify your child, and there is a deeply spiritual significance to the mission surrounding these vowels and consonants.

Lesson 3: Family

I have had the honor of traveling all over the world during my life, and I have lived within diverse cultures who have always welcomed me into their homes with loving kindness. If I have learned nothing else from these experiences, it is the great importance of family life with an extended community of people to aid in the raising of the children contained within its boundaries.

At the end of the day, the most precious thing that we can give to all children is the gift of a stable, loving, well-balanced and peaceful upbringing. The clothes, toys and gadgets are nice to wear and play with, but they are not what establish the confidence within that child to excel and prosper. It is the love and the genuine interest in what the child is thinking and feeling that counts. It is the time when the family comes together and prays before sharing a meal that counts. This nourishes the child and helps them to feel part of something that is strong and sincere.

When members of the family have been out all day at school or work, the home is where they return to each evening. Thus, the home is more than bricks and mortar. It is a place of sanctuary and love – or at least it should be. As George Moore says, "A man travels the world over in search of what he needs, and returns home to find it."

Sadly today in the western world, the family unit is fast disintegrating. The divorce rate is increasing; the social and economic pressures are forcing families to move away from their support systems; and what was once a certain solid foundation for a child, has rapidly become a battle ground of anger, misunderstanding and outright hatred. Parents worry about how to make ends meet. Debt collectors call at all hours demanding payment for utilities and things bought with credit cards. Children either sit in their rooms drowning out the shouting with loud music, or worse still, disappear into the cyber world of strangers who lift their spirits with goodness knows what flattery or sinister propositions.

Her Royal Highness, the Princess of Wales, (our cousin) was a passionate advocate for family and children amongst all her other loving charities that so consumed her heart with compassion and love. She always said that family was the most important thing in the world to her. One thing I know for sure, Princes' William and Harry have no doubt that the love of their mother surpassed anything else in her life. She was adamant that they were raised to know the truth about life and to always extend their arms of kindness to everybody they met.

I was born and raised in the 1960's (anything goes) era. My adopted parents were in their fifties and were from the Victorian era, (which was strict and focused on protocol). They instilled the same values to me. It could be difficult at times because my classmates had younger parents who lived very modern lives in comparison to me. We had help to run our home, yet my father was very strict about us (well me) learning to do things independently.

My life was different from my sister. My mother told me years later that my father had often felt that I was significantly different to any other person he had ever known. He felt a need to protect me and knew that I would be a world traveler and not the typical stay at home woman. My sister learned to cook and make clothes, to be a wife and mother, to dance and to be the social butterfly at parties. I was educated in music, law, business, sports, driving, economics, world religions and serious conversation. My sister was educated locally, whilst I went away to boarding school.

Frankly, mealtimes were the most stressful part of the day for me and I developed a phobia for eating. Mealtimes meant silence and disgusting food, which I neither liked, nor could bare to swallow. It was not that I was spoilt. On the contrary, people protested that my life was much tougher than my adopted sister's was. I had many food allergies that were unknown back in those days. A child instinctively knows when something is making them feel ill. In hindsight, I wish that my parents had been open minded enough to realize that there was a problem and take the time to discover what I needed to eat opposed to what was being served each day. After the majority of mealtimes, I would be in the bathroom vomiting or creased over with severe abdominal pain. It was the exact same thing at school and I spent many an afternoon in detention for being late back to class.

Regardless of how many children a couple may raise, understanding that each child is an individual with his or her own needs is an important requirement to their mature development. Even twins are separate people with an individual purpose and mission on earth. You cannot assume that they will like the same things and you should never expect a child to assume your role. What was fun and easy for you to do when young, may not necessarily be something that your child wishes to spend his time doing today. One must know ones child and when recognizing a certain gift or aptitude, one must do all one can to encourage and foster that occupation and skill. Every child is a gift from God. Every child needs to be encouraged positively. As David Ogden Stiers so rightly said, "Family means no one gets left behind or forgotten."

All families have traditions that include essential skills that keep the community or tribe safe and alive. They include respect for lineage and customs, stories, ceremonies and elders' wisdom that marks the transformation of a child into adulthood. My prayer is that elders never fail in these responsibilities or I worry about what be left for future generations.

We simply cannot allow the, "Who cares!" mentality to take its hold on society. Please raise your children to respect all beings and to be polite at all times. Please teach them to care about the environment with its creatures, plants, trees and water that sustain all life. Help them to understand that education, health, medicine and engineering are things that matter in order for the world to continue.

Our homes must be places of dignity, humility, strength and truth. Our homes must be beacons of light to all those who sleep within it or walk passed each day. Our homes must embody the love of God, who opens his arms to all those in need.

Confucius wrote, "The strength of a nation derives from the integrity of the home."

I have had the honor of working for and living on a number of Native

American Indian nations in North America. My former husband is one of the chiefs of the Hopi Nation. This nation is the oldest tribe in North America, and tourists with cameras and other recording devices are excluded entry. As such, I am not at liberty to discuss my life there. My step children and grandchildren are very dear to me. I am so proud of who they are today and for the fact that they have never lost their traditions. Each of them is dedicated to transmitting the sacred traditions to the younger ones. Despite modern pressures to disregard ancient ways, they have maintained their dances, music, language, food and dress. Furthermore, their highly sacred religious ceremonies continue today in exactly the same way as they were hundreds of years ago. No elder or child there goes to bed hungry. Every child is as an extended and protected family member. The beloved dead lay with dignity and honor and all life is valued and revered above modern thoughts and ideas.

You see brothers and sisters - for that is what we are to each other - we are all family. Therefore, wherever I roam on this earth, I always feel that I have my family around me. We are all the same. Cut my skin and you will see that I bleed the same color as you. Watch my eyes and you will see that when I am happy or sad, I also cry like you. I sleep like you, need food and water like you and my child is as dear to me, as yours is to you.

Please let us realize this fact and instead of planning how we can exclude others from our lives and kill those who think or look differently to ourselves, may we stop for a moment and really see that the person we claim to hate, is the same as we are inside out.

Conclusion

Most importantly, please never forget your child's birthday. There is nothing worse (and I speak from experience) for a child to wake up to indifference, go to school and then lie in bed at night on that special day in which nobody wished him or her a happy birthday.

If a family is too poor to give a gift, then at least give a special kiss to them whilst offering up a prayer. It is unforgivable for a person to feel ignored on this day. It deeply saddens me when friends say, "Oh, it's no big deal. I never do anything on my birthday!"

It *is* a big deal! God chose this day to present you to the world and he does *not* make mistakes. Even if nobody is around to wish you a happy day, at least thank God for this gift of life. Please do not waste this day, for by doing so, understand that there are others in the world taking their last breath and wishing to God that they could be on this earth for longer.

Part of my daily routine (which I love) is to go to Face-book, Twitter, Google and LinkedIn. I have thousands of friends in my network from around the world and every day some of them are celebrating their Birthday. I like to go to his or her individual pages, post a beautiful picture and write, "Today, I am here to join everybody who cares for you in wishing you a very happy birthday my dear friend. My prayer for you is that the year ahead will be your best ever. I pray that sincere friends and trustworthy business partners will surround you. I pray that your health will sustain you with the energy to complete every task that you set out to do and that you will continue to help others with compassion and kindness. I pray that you will learn a new skill or find a pastime that brings you joy. I pray that you will be happy and at peace, with a contrite heart, a wise thought process and a peaceful soul, free from danger. Above all else, I pray that you will find a renewed closeness to God, and that this precious relationship with him will help you fulfill what he created you to do. God bless you on this very special day - the day you entered our world and began to bless us with your kind and loving heart."

Lesson 4: "Speak up!"

My father was a respected professor (amongst many other aristocratic responsibilities) who blessed me with guidance throughout my childhood. I could read and write before I went to school, and I knew my twelve times tables inside out, and upside down. My father felt that as long as you could add, multiply, divide and subtract in your head, you would be able to balance your checkbook later in life. My father wanted me to have a well-rounded education, which included music, languages, chemistry, physics, biology, art, history, geography, social studies, economics, world religion and literature. In his opinion, a thorough understanding of etiquette training and public speaking finesse was of paramount importance.

From an early age, I grew to be polite and to know my place in society. My mother taught me how a woman should conduct herself. My father had professional teachers train me in elocution, body language and stage presence. He would often say to me that regardless of what profession I chose to enter, or what charities I chose to volunteer and represent, there would be occasions where I would have to stand up to present or to speak to others. He felt there was nothing worse (and I agree) than an inarticulate speaker with poor stage presence.

My mother always dressed and behaved as a refined woman. In her opinion, there was no excuse for foul language or a disheveled appearance. To this day, although they have both gone to heaven, I am incredibly conscious of how I present myself. Whether we like it or not, the fact is that people do judge us within seconds based on our appearance, body language and manner of speaking. You can be the sweetest person in the room, with the most intellectual brain amongst the crowd, but if your clothes, stance and accent are so contradictory to your message, people will shun you.

During my professional life as an executive and Chamber of

Commerce president, I have had to make hundreds of speeches and presentations. One simply cannot rise in the ranks of the corporate world if you cannot string a sentence together with finesse and confidence. I have sat in meetings where executives were to give what we call an "Elevator pitch," which is to say a two-minute overview of their company, product and service. I have observed some people literally sweating and shaking with fear at the mere prospect of speaking in public.

Currently, although we have texting abilities, we do still have to speak over the telephone, especially in business. One tip to pass along is to close your eyes when you are speaking to somebody. That might sound a little odd, but the advantage of this includes being able to concentrate and listen to any sounds that might be giving you a clue that your listener is bored with you. If you hear tapping on the table or a key board from the other side, you might conclude that you are boring this person or that you called them at the wrong time. One can also detect if their chair is moving backwards and forwards, which tends to suggest you are either boring them or fascinating them if the movement suddenly stops. It is an art. However, once one has truly mastered the intricacies of telephone technique, it really makes you highly successful and beneficial to a company. For anybody in the sales or human resource profession, this is a crucial lesson to learn.

Having hosted hundreds of live radio shows in Phoenix, Arizona and other forms of media including documentaries and television, I have had to put all my childhood training into play. These lessons included mastering the techniques of pitch, pace, pause, power, passion, practice and "POW!"

With this technique, you can stand and read from the Bible at Church, talk about your company or team, and converse over the telephone in such a way that you are, quite simply, an enthralling people magnet.

"Do you mean me?" I hear you saying with a nervous laugh. Yes, even you! I mentor hundreds of students and teach public speaking classes to political, religious, corporate, nonprofit and educational leaders around the world. With the seven "P's," mastered, one is able to enter any room and speak to an unlimited number of audience members from one person in an interview, to a thousand people and beyond in a hall. I could write a book about this technique or you might choose to sign up to come to my classes.

Can I humbly claim to be able to take you (or anybody) from a nervous wreck, to a confident speaker, within one month using my personal guidance and seven steps? One hundred percent yes!

"How?" many ask.

Think about this next question for a moment. Are you attracted to people who smile, or frown? Is a friendly looking face easier to approach than one that is obviously displaying anger and aggression? Do you prefer to listen to an interesting news anchor or a public speaker that exudes confidence or arrogance and cruelty? Do you enjoy listening to those who can weave a story that encompasses drama with humor, adventure with intrigue and a balance of personal experience that makes us gasp, "Whoa, I didn't see that coming!" Do you enjoy listening to a story that is monotonous, dishonest and dull? Do you ever check the time wishing the speaker would stop talking, sit down, and put you out of your misery?

The accomplished operatic soprano, actor and guru, Dorothy Sarnoff once said, "Make sure you have finished speaking before your audience has finished listening."

We are attracted towards people who appear dignified and friendly, who speak with respectful authority and who engage us with their warmth and positive attitude of grace and clarity. We feel safe listening to somebody who has experience in their subject matter and who is able to share that message in such a way that we can understand, relate, empathize and then gift to others.

What I am about to teach you will literally transform the way others see you. This is the best advice you will hear today.

The key to success is to talk about what you know and what makes you feel excited.

"That's it?" I hear you exclaim.

Yes. Quite simply, if you can master the seven "P's," and then go out and talk about a subject that you feel incredibly passionate about, you will have an enthusiastic audience who will hang on to (and drool over) every syllable you utter.

This is crucial and I cannot emphasize it enough. If a TV camera was to suddenly appear right now and ask me to speak with authority about global warming for instance, I would look like a complete idiot. I do not know enough about it to sound credible. However, if the same TV company asked me to speak about meditation, death, leadership, business, domestic crime, inspirational people who have influenced my life, or traits such as loving kindness and forgiveness, I could speak for hours with no notes by my side, because I have experienced these things. I have interesting stories and practical examples to back up my statements with passion.

Conclusion

The most important extracurricular classes that you should send your children to are either acting, elocution, voice coaching, public speaking or drama. It is cute to see our children taking ballet lessons or playing softball and soccer. I am certainly not advocating you replace those with speaking. However, you are doing your child a major disservice by not having them taught how to give public speeches. Throughout their academic years, (which include college and interviews) your child will have to present him or herself to peers, professors, boards, and prospective employers. If their communication is ineffective, they lose to a candidate who has the finesse and public speaking confidence to convey his or her prowess.

It is never too late to begin. I have helped people as mature as sixty years (and older) to confidently speak. Within a few weeks, they have spoken with powerful authority and have even marched onto podiums and won political elections.

There is no need for you to feel nervous when you must communicate.

Give yourself the gift of public speaking classes and you can gift the world with your wisdom and life mission message. Every single living person has a story to tell. Learn to tell it with confidence and learn to be an effective telephone participant.

Speaking with eloquence is a jewel in your crown that everybody will admire.

Lesson 5: Faith and grief

The greatest gift in my life is my unshakeable faith. From the moment I came home from the orphanage as a small child, mum took me to church. My family is part of the Church of England. Having parents who put God first in their lives, was a strong foundation with which they built their marriage and life. I went through Sunday school from the age of four, which educates children in the basics of the Bible. As I matured, I became a chorister and a lector.

Many can vividly recall the day they made a conscious decision to give their lives to Christ. This is what we call our, "Testimony of conversion." Their story is typically a dramatic moment that moves the congregation to tears and roars of delight. Although I have always known him (God) and his presence in my life as a constant and loving father, there was a day when my faith came alive to me in a very profound way.

My faith has been a life long journey and I always describe myself as a pilgrim. My earthly father sensed early on that I would be a world traveler. He decided to encourage me to understand faith in terms of how everybody on this earth practiced and related to it. As my parents were in their fifties, it meant that many of our relatives died during my childhood.

I can easily recall rushing to school one morning in late September when I was eight years old. I had no clue that my grandmother was ill with cancer and had somebody told me; I think that I would have been much quieter and more careful. I nearly knocked her over in my mad dash to get out of the house. When I came home, she was not there to greet me. With every passing day, I felt more and more agitated. Questions were swirling round in my head and yet nobody would tell me the truth. It was not until six weeks later that I overheard my parents discussing a funeral.

At that tender age, I had no knowledge of what that word meant. I heard them talking about death; but again, I did not know what that entailed. I heard my name mentioned. "Audrey, I think we need to sit Christine down and tell her what has happened."

My ears pricked up. To this day, I can easily recall how my heartbeat increased as I sensed something terrible was about to happen. The tone in their voice told me that this was not going to be a good story with the ending, "And they all lived happily ever after."

I cannot recall the exact words they used, but I know it was to the effect of my beloved granny was sick and she had to go to hospital. The hospital could not save her life and so she had died.

There was that word "Died," again. I sat thinking about this for a while. What is death? Is it a place? Where is it? How long do you go for? When will you be back?

"When will granny be back?" I innocently asked.

"She won't be coming back darling," my mother gently said.

"Can I go to see her?" I asked.

"No darling," my mother answered. "You see, when we die, it is forever."

"How long is forever?" I gulped.

"Forever, means there is no end," mum said with a distinct tone of uncertainty.

"Why did she go?" I continued.

"Darling, granny was very old, it was her time. When we are old, we will die too," mum replied.

"But I thought granny loved us. Why would she leave without saying 'goodbye,' or at least telling us how we can see her?" I did not understand and felt confused and hurt.

"Christine, look here," my father interjected with annoyance. "We never know when we are going to die and go to heaven or hell. It just happens. I am sure if she had of known, she would have explained to you. However, she was ill and it was her time. You will see her again one day, but it won't be until it is your time to go there." My father was a strict man who did not throw sentimental emotions around easily and British decorum (stiff upper lip) insisted on bravery. "Run along now and get ready for dinner," he muttered.

Granny was in either heaven or hell dad had said. I worried about this and posed two questions to myself. Firstly, did we have a choice of where we went? Secondly, if I chose the wrong place and granny was not there, did they have cars to drive me to where she was staying?

"Can I call her? Do they have telephones in heaven and hell?" I continued disregarding the order to leave the room.

"Christine, when you are dead, you are dead. You cannot communicate with anybody. It is the end! Let us stop talking about this please." My father was getting very irritated with my questions and unsure of what to say to calm me.

"She has gone and that is that. You will not see her again. Now leave this room," he angrily concluded.

My mother recalled this scene during the last few months of her life. She said that the sight of my eyes full of tears and my bottom lip trembling with grief almost broke her heart. I had never once cried before.

"Tony," mum whispered to my father. "Look, she's crying!" she gasped.

"I know Audrey," my father worriedly acknowledged. "Oh damn!"

I fell silent for months and did not speak a word to anyone. I contracted shingles and went into a very sad place for over a year. I can clearly remember struggling with her death. I vowed to find her, as I could not imagine the prospect of never seeing her again until I died. There had to be a way to get to her. I was sure God would tell me how, if I remained silent.

Even as a toddler, I would be on my knees in church. I loved being there for it felt so safe and quiet. I was unsure of what I should be doing except silently listening. My mother often told me the story of Samuel and promised me that if I learned to be still, I, too, would be able to hear God when he spoke to me.

I prayed, begged, bargained and shouted at God before becoming quiet. I promised to be a model child in exchange for a glimpse of granny. Days turned into weeks, weeks into months and months into years. I could not hear God speaking to me in the way Samuel had. I was afraid to break that silence and no amount of professional counseling worked to convince me to speak. Understanding death became my only mission. I could not care less about any other subject. I had to understand all about God, including where he was and what I had to do to get there. Mum had told me that good people went on the journey to heaven. Every journey I had been on required us to buy a ticket. I wondered where these tickets were and I wondered how much they cost. Granny was a very good person and so I was certain that she had gone on the journey to heaven.

Thus from a very early age, I studied the Bible word for word trying to learn where the ticket was found. I felt sure that the key to granny's whereabouts were within this book. Mum had told me the Bible told you everything. Therefore, I began to read from Genesis and when I got to the New Testament, I found my answer. I saw it in John's Gospel a few days before my eleventh birthday. The disciple Thomas said to him, "Lord, we do not know where you are going, how do we know the way?" Jesus said to him, "I am the way, and the truth, and the life; no one comes to the Father but through me. If you had known me, you would have known my Father also; from now on you know him, and have seen him."

That was it! Jesus was the ticket to heaven. Heaven is his home. That was where granny was!

I was so excited because for the first time, I truly understood that she was in a place, not suspended in goodness knows what. It was something tangible to me. There was a tugging within my soul. (I feel it to this day). God was clearly saying to me, as Jesus had told his disciples in John 14: "In my Father's house are many rooms. If it were not so, would I have told you that I go to prepare a place for you?"

I can clearly remember the still small voice of the Holy Spirit within me that gently, yet firmly said, "Christina, Jesus is - not was. I am alive! I am with you!"

God spoke to me!

I ran home and excitedly told my mother what had just happened. I was so giddy that I could barely get the words out of my mouth. My mother looked both happy and relieved, if not somewhat confused. I can still see the expression of her face in my mind. For years, I had been so quiet and sad, yet unexpectedly it seemed, I was back.

From that day on, I studied the Bible with clarity and care, rather than with irrational urgency. I shed the skin of grief and despair and put on the coat of peace and calm. I had great joy and hope again and I decided that I was going to devote my life to earning a place in our heavenly home where I was certain that granny and I would reunite.

Conclusion

Death is an inevitable part of life. Every one of us will die one day. How a child will deal with this fact of life depends upon how you, their parent, explain it in such a way that it is not a frightening experience.

Your faith will have its own traditions and beliefs when it comes to funerals and the afterlife. Far be it from me to instruct you on such practices and rituals. However, my plea to you is that, (considering age appropriateness) you do not leave a child wondering where a loved one has gone. Rather, (if possible) allow the child to see the person before death and explain the process gently. They will ask you questions. If you give a flippant answer at best, your child will have mixed emotions that might cause significant confusion.

Be honest with your children and allow them to grieve *with* you.

Lesson 6: Beyond abuse

I had four godparents including Lord Louis Mountbatten, (the Earl of Burma) who was the last Viceroy to India, Queen Victoria's great-grandson and a close friend of my father. My other godparents included a cousin and friend of the family on my mother's side and a long-time colleague, (Edward) who was my father's closest friend.

This is a very difficult part of my life to write about, so I ask for your kind understanding in advance. Just recalling this fills me with trepidation and I find myself stopping and starting as I try to find the wisest words to use.

My mother told me that I was about two and a half years old when it happened. Edward worked with my father. I can see him perfectly in my mind's eye. My parents trusted him and had no hesitation in asking him to babysit for us on occasion. All I can remember is seeing him through the glass panels in the front door and feeling afraid. I can see him taking me upstairs to my bedroom and the rest is a blank.

My parents came home to find me lying in a pool of blood that was seeping out of my anus. I remember the instruments inserted into my bottom at the hospital along with the pain, and that is it. It is a complete blank after that. I never did know why he had been there or what honestly happened to him afterwards. Nor did I ever saw him again. It became a family secret and I was not to speak about it to anybody. Maybe that is why I am struggling to write about it now.

Children can be very cruel and the bullying I received was merciless. Unlike them, I could not easily to sit down. It was and continues to be sheer agony to use the toilet. Those who have lived with me throughout my life have witnessed me in the restroom, as I spent hours trying to go and crying every step of the way. I have had to wear sanitary pads to soak up the blood with most of my restroom visits, and I have spent many an hour curled up on the floor or couch trying to deal with the pain that nothing seemed to relieve.

Doctors suggested to my parents that smoking would stimulate my body to relax the muscles, which would subsequently aid in me defecating more easily. This began a lifetime of smoking cigarettes for the nicotine. With a few puffs in the morning, I was able to go to the bathroom and defecate (albeit with pain). Without one, my body would not cooperate at all.

Naturally, you cannot broadcast such a thing, so I learned to hide this habit for years by washing my teeth, wearing clothes over my clothes and washing my hands frequently. I became good at hiding the smell and few knew about my guilty secret. I accepted that this was my life and I prayed about it often. I asked God to help me to heal. It is interesting how he answers our prayers and sometimes you have to go through darkness before you can ever hope to reach the light.

On December 23, 2010, I had just arrived home after a very stressful day at work. I was walking across my living room when the worst pain of my life hit me. It made childbirth look easy and for those of you who have given birth, you will know that this means the pain was unspeakable. I fell to the floor and began bleeding profusely from my anus. I felt a strong urge to push and with no control over my muscles, the rectal tissues fell out. I had suffered a complete prolapse with the entire wall of the rectum sliding out of place. To say I was terrified would be a gross understatement.

I cried out to God, "Father, help me!"

My phone was on the other side of the room and I literally crawled towards it. With having several doors locked to my home, I decided to call one of my closest friends who had a key. I tried to explain what had happened and she rushed over. Police escort took us to the hospital and the emergency room doctor took one look at my injury, gasped and (unnervingly) shed tears. He gave me morphine to numb the pain. My friend just sat crying and it was a bit disconcerting to have medical staff rushing in and out shaking their heads and quietly discussing my case.

Over the next few weeks, I went through eight excruciating surgeries to push the tissues back inside my body with glue and stitches (and goodness knows what else). The tests and scans showed the extensive scars from the childhood abuse and revealed the obvious problem with defecating. The muscles required to contract, (in defecation) were so tight that they were off the scale in terms of this function being possible. The muscles that should retract, (stopping the urge to go) were so loose that there was no way my body could function normally. The doctors and surgeons confirmed that it was the result of the sexual abuse. They felt that after the surgeries, with a disciplined approach to my care, I could lead an easier life.

The positive part of this episode was the simple understanding of why my body had been unresponsive all these years and why I had always suffered so much pain and humiliation. The damage was clearly permanent, but I began to study and change my diet to alleviate some of the issues. This knowledge would in turn help to get me through the rest of my life more holistically.

Those surgeries were horrific because I elected to have them done with little anesthetic. The thought of having anybody near to my rear end terrified me, thus I needed to feel in control. I used to lie on my side with a rolled up towel between my teeth, and with each needle inserted, I would try not to scream too loudly. We went through three nurses during those surgeries. The first one was so upset that she could not stand to even look at me (bless her). My friend wept when she saw my face afterwards. She said on one occasion I looked like a holocaust victim in shock. It took several minutes to heave myself to the car, as each movement was agony. When we got to my apartment, I had to walk just as slowly to my couch, where I literally spent several weeks. My company insisted I continue to work as we were in the countdown to a congressional dinner and I needed the money. This meant that I lay on my couch making telephone calls and as I needed to be on my game, I could not take any painkillers during the day.

You cannot imagine the pain. My friends Gulzar, Thakor, Jan, Carol and Roger were so kind to me and there was a twenty-four hour watch at my home. I even had friends fly in from India to help care for me because I could not move to cook or shower. The simple act of going to the bathroom was long drawn out and agonizing. My dear Gulzar Singh never left my side and he held me in his arms day and night.

At the end of April in 2011, I was well enough to travel to India. To be honest, my doctors were horrified at the thought, but I had promised to fulfill a request to go and film at a hospital in Pune who did free eye surgeries for the blind. I felt strong enough to travel and I was determined that my body would not slow me down any longer. I was reassured that there was little chance of a relapse if I was careful, so I left America and flew to India.

There is good news with this story you will be pleased to know. God is faithful, merciful and mighty. For years, I had prayed earnestly about my health. I wanted to stop smoking (for obvious health reasons) and I wanted to stop taking the sleeping pills I had needed since childhood. Once I had taken these pills, I had no memory of my actions until the following day. I would eat at night (unknowingly) and sleep walk, talk on the cell phone and drive. I was also taking several other medications that caused my hair and teeth to fall out. When men and women would tell me that I was very beautiful, I would laugh to myself when I knew how much I was struggling to look publically presentable.

I sat down with a spiritual elder in Mumbai, India and asked his advice on how to realign my body. I explained the ins and outs of my medical problem and asked for his wisdom. You see, I believe that one of the greatest things we can ever pray for is wisdom. It says in the book of Proverbs, "Get wisdom! Get understanding. Do not forsake her, and she will preserve you; love her and she will keep you. Wisdom is the principal thing; therefore get wisdom. And in all your getting, get understanding. Exalt her and she will promote you; she will bring you honor when you embrace her."

The elder told me to meditate with a clear mind and to pray for a healthy body. He told me to set my mind on being drug free. He asked me to visualize a positive life without unnecessary medication. We meditated together and from that day, I ceased to take the sleeping pills (and three of the others) with no adverse reactions of withdrawal.

Let us fast forward to the beginning of Lent in March 2014. I was in the bathroom during another one of my painful (nature calls) sessions. Rather than feeling afraid, I became empowered with the Holy Spirit. For those of you who have never experienced this, the easiest way to describe it is to ask you to imagine a feeling of complete peace, combined with a strength that tells you, "Anything is possible!"

I came out of the bathroom and never touched a cigarette again. God helped me to visualize exactly what I was to eat and drink. He assured me that if I had the discipline to eat these things, excruciating pain in the bathroom would cease. I began to lose weight and by the end of September, I had lost over fifty pounds of weight. I began to swim and walk. My mind began to see positive visions of the future. I felt alive and extraordinarily healthy.

Saint Matthew's says, "The woman came forward to Jesus, trembling with fear. She told him everything that had happened to her, and why she had touched him. Jesus smiled, held out His hand and helped the woman to stand up straight. 'Daughter, your faith has saved you. Go in peace and be cured of your affliction.'"

For those who have known me for many years, my healing has been nothing short of a miracle!

Conclusion

Abuse is a terrible and evil thing: be it sexual, physical, professional or emotional in nature. It causes long-term problems that can lead to an accumulation of unhealthy crutches to aid in the coping mechanism of recovery.

Abuse stunts the growth of an individual and it robs them of light and laughter. Trust and respect is harder to gain and it leaves a sinister mark upon a family, which never truly disappears.

Abuse is the secret world of shadows and lies; a place that is too unspeakable to recall. Yet by faith, the ugliness of sin can disappear with the sun at dusk and the healing light of hope and recovery can rise forth when the dawn of day approaches.

I believe we should protect our children from anybody who might wish to harm him or her. My mother and parents-in-law accepted the responsibility to babysit our son and we knew that we could trust them completely. After my situation, I never wanted our son alone with anybody other than his immediate family. You might consider this with your own children.

In my opinion, after a child has reached fourteen, he or she has learned enough to speak up if they feel uncomfortable. The challenge in teenage years shifts from sexual abuse to rape. Empowering our children to protect themselves and others is a precious gift that cannot be underestimated.

To those of you who were the victims of abuse, I can give you three pieces of wise advice. Firstly, people will encourage you to recount the story of the abuse with counsellors. My advice is to avoid this if the abuse happened to you when you were very young. The imagination is very powerful and constant recalling can cause the mind to invent scenes that did not actually happen. In addition to disturbing you, it can potentially cause immeasurable damage to a family. My advice is to recall it once and then to let it go.

Secondly, if your injuries are similar to mine, it is crucial to have extensive examinations, tests and scans to determine the obstacles and to find procedures, medications and helpful hints. I have always found doctors and surgeons to be very kind, and it is worth noting that after forty-six years, I finally found a specialist who was able to diagnose my issues precisely with scans and intricate tests. When I was a child, these tests were unavailable because they are not yet been invented. Today, we have access to improved equipment, so please do not suffer quietly when then are things in place to help.

Finally, it is important to be honest with your sexual partner. If a particular word, act or position causes you to feel fear; you must find your voice and be candid. I have heard of victims who could not (would not) tell their partner that each time they touched them in a particular place, it brought back memories of the attack.

I know it might seem easy for me to say, "Forgive those who hurt you, for by releasing them of the hold upon your past, you will be free to lead a beautiful forever!" I assure you that it took decades for me to have the strength of faith to speak those words and wholeheartedly mean them. The courage to forgive has taken time, especially when I am reminded of my attacker with every trip to the bathroom.

I mourn for the child. I mourn and feel sad for little "Christina," who did not have the protection she needed or the understanding from anybody around her. "Christine Mercy Overton," is a woman who has learned to stand boldly in life. This ability to separate the two facets of me has significantly enabled me to recover.

Lesson 7: First love

The last chapter was a tough one to write and possibly a hard one for you to read, so with that in mind, let us move on to happier days. I have some amusing stories to share that bring back hilarious memories to me. Suffice to say, Lionel Richie's song *All Night Long* has a dear memory in my mind and heart.

John (to protect his identity this is not his real name) was my first love. My parents had sent me to a very strict all girls' private boarding school when I was fourteen years old. It looked more like a prison to be honest with you. The thought of three years in that place was quite horrifying and when they gave me a very big book of rules that I was expected to follow, I was mortified. I leafed through the pages with the eyes of a doe in headlights. There was only one thing to do with such a book: master each rule, by breaking them systematically. I felt this was a good way to protest my sentence (which is what it felt like) and would get me expelled. I wanted to go home, until I went to church the following Sunday.

John served at the church where I was a chorister. I loved singing, and this was a way for us to leave the school during the week, and twice on Sundays. We would walk in pairs like animals into the Arc, clothed in formal uniform, adorned with hideous straw hats and itchy gloves. How anybody could find us attractive looking that way, is simply a tribute to his or her ability to see underneath the garb and into the soul of the breathing mannequin wearing it.

John was gorgeous. He stood at over six feet tall with dark brown wavy hair, deep brown eyes and rippling muscles. He had the Scottish build of a sturdy romance novel hero and was twenty-four years of age, I later learned. His voice was magical and although he was profoundly deaf and wore hearing aids, this affliction gave him an endearing way of speaking which we were all adored. The moment I saw him, I fell in love.

I would follow him with my gaze whilst he served during the Mass. Every waking moment in between would be spent dreaming of our next encounter. He ignored all the other girls. It was not a foolish notion on my part, for he watched me as they giggled and flirted with him each week. He would search for me and smile at every opportunity, but in a very respectful and refined way. He did not know my age, but knew I was not in the sixth form yet. This meant I had to be between fifteen and seventeen years old.

This went on for two years until we finally spoke. John asked me if I was permitted to ever leave the school alone. I confess that I lied. I told him that I could come and go and wondered why he had asked me that question. He described the new club in town and wondered if I would like to go with him the following Saturday evening. Of course, I jumped at the invitation, wishing to appear a sophisticated woman who could make her own decisions.

When I told the girls in my dorm, they were as excited as I was. Immediately we began to plan my escape, making sure we crossed every "T," and dotted every "I."

Finally, the day arrived for the date. One of my friends had managed to borrow a sparkling black mini skirt and boob tube, which was the signature outfit in those disco days (think of the pop group Abba). I even had the sparkling silver hat and platform shoes to match. I carefully applied lipstick, eyeliner and blusher, which we had borrowed from one of the kitchen staff when she was not looking one morning, and with my hair up, a squirt of perfume behind my ears and on my wrists, I was ready to go on my first date.

Imagine starched white sheets carefully knotted to act as a rope. Envision yours truly climbing down a drainpipe, whilst grasping the sheets between my hands and hoping the clothes would not rip. Once I reached the ground, I looked up to my friends and waved both excitedly and reassuringly at the same time. I hobbled over the sandy beach and met John by his shiny truck. Off we went for an amazing night of dancing and laughter. The last song was Lionel Richie's, *All Night Long*. It was wonderful and I experienced my first kiss.

I did not care what the time was. It had not occurred to me for a moment that my friends would have gone to sleep by the time I got back. After John had kissed me goodnight, I discovered the sheet rope was gone, and the gates locked. I muttered under my breath, "*Uh oh*!"

The headmistress opened the gate (much to my horror) and without saying a word, pointed to the dormitory entrance. I knew that a severe punishment was going to be enforced. You are probably wondering if this blatant disregard for the rules got me expelled. I was there for another year.

Once inside, I sat in her office as she telephoned my father and I had to explain to him why I was in permanent detention for the rest of the term. He was completely calm after I finished telling the shortened and less graphic account of the events. I could hear the disappointment in his voice as he told me that in addition to deliberately letting everybody down, I had let myself down and should be feeling great shame. I did feel guilty, but I would be lying if I said I felt ashamed. I was too happy to care.

You might be wondering if John ever heard about my escape plan gone wrong. Truthfully, I did tell him after I had left school and he laughed until it hurt. Until then, my friends found equally creative ways to help me sneak in and out to see him. I thought I was in love with him and that nobody understood (or cared) about how important he was in my life. After being informed I was continuing to sneak out, my father, being a shrewd man, calmly told me to invite John to our home for the summer. I cannot recall how I told John, but whatever the words were, he accepted the invitation. Once John arrived, my parents met with him privately. Even today, I have no idea what they discussed. Suffice to say we had a wonderful few days of romance and love.

I chew my nails. I always have. Nevertheless, I wanted to look beautiful for John, so I bought some false nails and stuck them on with glue. Hand in hand, we walked through an enchanting forest, gazing into each other's eyes and snatching the occasional sweet kiss. Each moment was perfect and you could almost hear an invisible orchestra playing a romantic symphony.

However, with every good love story, there has to be a twist and mine was no different to any other affair. The unthinkable happened. As John gently lifted my hand to his lips to kiss, one of the nails came off in his fingers. He was not sure what it was at first, and then when I explained, he did not say much at all. He was the perfect man and masked any smirk that wished to form. I wanted the ground to open up and swallow me with shame. He gave the nail back to me and suggested that once home, I could probably glue it back into place. The rest of the walk was a combination of me praying the others would not fall off, and worrying about what he was thinking.

Later the next day, we were walking into our old parish church and I was wearing a ridiculously high-heeled pair of golden shoes. Still embarrassed by the nail incident, I kicked my leg out, which sent one of the shoes hurtling off into the air, where it landed abruptly in front of the vicar's feet. This was the last straw for John, as I stood mortified and blushing; he laughed aloud and did not stop for the remainder of the evening. I do not recall the service at all, just the sight of John and my mother laughing. You may have seen the movie, *Bridget Jones Diary*. That film could have been a depiction of me I swear. I felt and looked like a complete fool. I expect you are laughing just reading this. I am happy to amuse you. It *is* funny today!

Sadly, the vacation ended and I had to go back to school. I had one more important year left there, and as I had promised my father I would concentrate and not sneak out, I did not see John for that entire year. He transferred to London, and kept his promise to my father that he would not communicate with me. At the end of that year, my father had a heart attack and died. John sent me a lovely card, but I did not see him again until a job interview, when I bumped into him by chance. We went out for a few weeks, but it was different.

A couple of months passed and my mother gently sat me down one morning to tell me the news that John had just got married. I was naturally a bit upset. Occasionally I would sit and look at his photographs and imagine what might have happened if we had continued dating, and I had not been so young. I have never forgotten John, and I realize he must be close to sixty years in age. He might be a grandfather and I have always prayed that he has had a wonderful life.

Conclusion

Your first love is significant. This is the initial glimpse into adulthood, where childish whims slightly overlap into the possibilities for the future. It is not a rational feeling that runs through your heart. Your mind seems incapable of thinking of anything other than how you can quickly grasp onto that fix, which first love gives you. This first love is dramatic and intense. It has the potential, if handled incorrectly, to turn into a scene from one of Shakespeare's (*Romeo and Juliet)* plays. If unprepared or ignored, the consequences can oftentimes result in an unwanted pregnancy, or with the young couple running off together in a bid to make a statement of unbridled love, which they feel their parents cannot understand.

Our first love experience can actually be a positive stage in a life if you can help him or her to understand the biological, legal and spiritual consequences of their actions. Underage girls have the ability to look in their twenties with ease, and yet seldom have either the experience or maturity to deal with the passion of a man's libido or the funds and stamina to co-exist in the adult world of employment and social etiquette.

Sex is natural and does not require much of a spark to flame a fire of great passion. As adults, we know that loving, healthy relationships take time. They require maturity, patience, forgiveness and the practicalities of employment with a stable income to sustain them. Teenagers do not understand this, which is why conversations about protection and abstinence must occur at a very early age today.

Keeping the lines of communication open between you and your teenager is essential. There must be respect for him or her. When you show them respect, it is far more likely that you will receive it in return. There is no point in shouting at your child about underage sex, when you are only fourteen or fifteen years older than they are. Teenagers do not respond well to hypocrisy. Therefore, one can use one's own mistakes as a means to explaining how best to avoid the same errors. Honesty with calmness is always a great way to communicate. An open dignified relationship between parent and child enables those early romantic years to be building blocks for a healthy marriage in adulthood.

How you choose to live, will affect how your child relates to you and others. Young people learn from you and the community. Therefore, please guide them wisely.

Lesson 8: Loss of father

My adopted father was a formidable man. From day one of bringing me to his home from the orphanage, he prepared me for adult life with every tool I could possibly need to succeed. Psalm 103 says, "As a father shows compassion to his children, so the Lord shows compassion to those who fear him." This was my father.

When I was a child, I was not like other people. I was introspective, reserved, observant and aristocratically British. When one says "British," it means that you know your place in society and you remain dignified and well-mannered at all times. One gets on with life and does not complain and it is a mindset that I am certain has helped me to stay gracious and strong. I preferred to be around elderly people or in church where I felt safe. I had a mischievous side to my personality, but when I tried to express it, my father would engage me in conversations where we dissected the decisions that I had made. Instead of mocking me though, he either praised me for attempting the lesson or remained quiet until such time I realized my error and apologized. I respected my father highly. He was a politically powerful and regal man who was well educated. He could have boasted about dozens of awards and medals for bravery and yet he was modest about his success.

At six feet four inches tall, he walked with strength, dignity and purpose. People admired him. We all knew that he would always hold us accountable for our actions, just as his father had expected him to take responsibility for his deeds. He was a loving husband and my mother adored him for their entire forty-five year marriage.

Although we were quite affluent, my father made us walk the three miles to school each day. He insisted on me cleaning my shoes and maintaining the day-to-day- aspects of bed making and cleanliness. We were to marry aristocracy or at least British professional men of good standing who could support us. However, my father also recognized that

I had an independent (Christopher Columbus) aspect to my personality that liked to wander and he knew that I was unlikely to remain in England after I had left home. Therefore, I was educated in foreign and diplomatic affairs, world religions, international etiquette and survival skills, which he knew would give me the confidence to travel around the world safely.

I loved to go on nature walks with my father. His knowledge of birds, trees, plants and insects was enthralling. On one particular day, we happened to come across a small rabbit that was clearly dying of some disease or other – probably myxomatosis. As is my way, I wanted to go and stroke it to offer a kind presence. I was seven years old and clueless to the harm such an injured creature could inflict upon me. My father yanked me away and shouted at me with a furious tone in his voice. The more I tried to pull away from him to go to the rabbit, the more he shrieked at me. To this day, I can see the image of that poor creature in my mind. I felt so helpless, and I was very angry with my father for what I saw as a heartless gesture from a man that I thought cared about nature. He refused to discuss it with me and I went to bed that night without supper.

My father saw great potential in me and subsequently insisted on me learning to play musical instruments including the cello. My sister was very feminine and cute with a bedroom covered in pink flowers and full of dolls with houses and other cute toys. I went into that room twice during my childhood and I can still recall the wonder I felt when I sat on her bed and scanned the magical ambience. My sister was proud to show off her room, and although I could not touch her things, it was special for me to sit and admire. My room was small, white and stark in comparison. I do not know why that was the case, so anything I might choose to write would simply be based on theory.

I always yearned to be outdoors. From a tender age, I was quite obsessed with Native American Indians, which was surprising as I lived in England and had never seen one in my life. Yet I have photographs of me sitting on the ground constructing a headdress made out of feathers, whilst sitting in a meditation. Creatures were my friends. My parents would often recall accounts of all manner of birds and animals sitting next to me when I meditated. I was able to calm wild animals within seconds, just with a mere look of love. I also loved Asian Indian things, especially the sitar and old movies we would occasionally watch. I dreamed I would marry an Indian man one day. I did not obviously know that both these aspects of my childhood would play a significant role later.

When I went to boarding school at the age of fourteen, it felt like a punishment. One morning, I stood shamefully in the headmaster's office after refusing to sit down in class. I had had a particularly painful trip to the bathroom and sitting was not an option for me. As it was a secret, I could not tell the teacher why it was impossible for me to sit in her class. My silence was mistaken as blatant disobedience. I remember the headmaster being very sarcastic. He threatened to give me a caning on my bottom if I continued to refuse to explain my rudeness. I was already in dreadful pain and the thought of being hit in the same area was just too much for me. In my frustration, I blurted out the reason for me not being able to sit. The more details I gave, the more his face turned from red to white. He was completely shocked to hear of the sexual abuse and gently told me to stand in the hallway. Within minutes, my father was also standing there and I was very afraid. He went in to see the headmaster and although I could not hear the conversation, I could hear the angry tone. When my father came out, he looked at me with utter rage.

"Why did you tell him about this? " My father said between clenched teeth. "We agreed to never talk about it. Do you want to bring more shame to this family?" He nudged me towards the door and took me home. I was never to return to that school.

For the remainder of that month, neither my mother nor my father said more than a few words. The silent disgust I sensed was punishment in of itself. I remember feeling confused by the whole episode. I inwardly vowed that regardless of how much pain I was in, I would never tell another living soul. Clearly, I had disgraced my parents by my lack of courage. I had broken their trust it seemed and every day I wondered what would happen when I went back to school after the summer vacation.

When that time arrived, instead of walking to school, I found myself on a train bound for boarding school in the south of England. My parents would not discuss it with me and I had no idea what was about to happen.

My mother just told me to trust them and reassured me that this new school would be a safe place to study.

I felt fear as I walked through the huge metal gates and looking up at the building ahead, I wondered what on earth was about to happen. We passed girls who looked gaunt. There was no laughter and I felt like I was in an absurd dream.

My mother told me that I would be spending the next three to four years in that place, with only a few weeks leave of absence. I fell to my knees (This is a very hard thing to talk about) and literally begged her to take me home. I pleaded, begged, cried and bargained with her. I promised I would not speak about the abuse again and I promised that I would be an obedient daughter who would do anything they wanted.

I know this sounds very cruel, but in hindsight, I think they were trying to protect me from any more harm, and perhaps trying to protect our family name too. Mum explained to me that my father had insisted that for my welfare and education, this school was the best place for me. She told me to be a good girl, to work hard and sit at all times. With that, she turned and walked out of the office without looking at me. The room became silent for a moment.

The silence was abruptly broken. I looked up to see the headmistress clapping her hands slowly and laughing at me. "Well, well, well…what do we have here?" She sneered with a menacing tone. "A proper little royal princess I see. Well, as you now know that nobody wants you and nobody cares about you, welcome to your home for the next few years. I am looking forward to watching you beg again. You grovel so well!"

She has been the only person in life to spit in my face. As I wiped away the saliva, she pointed to the door and yelled at me to go to my dormitory. I can vividly remember saying two things repeatedly. One was, "Oh my God," and the other was, "Lord Jesus, help me."

It was a very difficult (sadistic) three years and yet my friends and I spent considerable time figuring out how to have relief regardless of the utter hellhole we were living in. Those three years passed by very slowly, and I rarely saw my parents. I wrote to my father one week asking him if he had forgiven me and if he loved me. He never responded. His lack of reassurance told me that I had disrespected him and even up to the day he died, I never heard those words of forgiveness and love, which I so longed to hear.

With our examinations over, we had a concert and award ceremony, which our parents were invited. I did not know whether mine were coming and I was so thrilled to see them both there sitting on the front row of the theater. I played my cello and recited a piece of comedy that had won me first place in a competition earlier that year. My friends gave me a standing ovation with cheers and whistles. They were always so supportive, perhaps because more often than not I had accepted their punishment to spare them. After two of my friends had committed suicide, I was determined not to let the younger ones suffer anymore.

I turned to look at my parents and caught my father's eye. He placed his hands together and bowed to me. I reciprocated with a bow and telepathic message of gratitude. My mother looked at him, glanced at me, and wiped away tears from her face. I knew they were very proud of me. Sadly, I did not get the opportunity to see them. After the ovation, the headmistress grabbed my arm and literally dragged me backstage. By then, I had learned that fighting back was futile and I did not want the younger ones punished for my defiance.

On the last day of school, I stood in the headmistress's office. My uncle had arranged for me to go home by train. She gloated that my father had just had a major heart attack and was about to die and as she stood laughing within a foot of my face at the prospect of me being orphaned again, something snapped inside of me.

As I walked out of her office, I turned and calmly said, "I only have one thing left to say to you."

"Oh? And what would that be?" she mockingly laughed.

"I hope you like very hot places because you will rot in hell for what you have done to me and my friends!"

"Excuse me?" she sneered.

"You heard, you piece of shit," I snarled. "Even God will not show you mercy for the evil that you have done here."

God forgive my language. I could have used a different word whilst recounting this story, but that would not have been the truth. I used the curse word and it stands as it is. I had never sworn before and I rarely utter a profanity today. It takes a great deal for me to explode.

I have deliberately not gone into graphic detail about the violent incidences that occurred at that place. My family took matters into their own hands and the school shut down within months. I remember it every day when I look at my feet and arms. However, rather than feeling like a victim, I feel empowered by the resilience within me. That woman contracted cancer within a few weeks and was dead by the end of the year.

Our French teacher, who had always been very kind to me, immediately drove me to the station. He was the first to express his condolences and assured me that this would be the last time he would see me. "I am very sorry for all you have suffered here," he remarked as he helped me. Mr. Sims regularly competed with the Duke of Edinburgh and owned several horse drawn carriages. "We do know what is done to you girls."

"If you know, then why don't you do something to help us?" I questioned him. "It is hell here Sir."

"I can't speak for the others," he continued. "But I need this job."

"You would work for a school that abuses its students like a Nazi camp?" I said in astonishment.

"I am sorry," he said with his head held low.

"Well let me tell you something Sir," I defiantly announced. "I will not rest until this shit hole is closed forever. I'll not sleep until everybody is held accountable and if it is the last thing I ever do, that woman will never be allowed near another child!"

"I'm so sorry," he repeated.

"You know, I actually believe that you are sir. However, if you will not stop this evil, then I will. How many more girls have to take her own life before somebody will investigate? This is finished!" and with that statement of affirmation, I walked into the railway station and climbed on board the train for home.

I stripped to my underwear and replaced my school uniform with civilian clothes. I opened the train widow and victoriously threw out the garments with a cheer of, *"Woo-Hoo!"* I took my straw hat and jumped on it before discarding it out the window and I *whooped* again with utter joy. I realized that I was finally free from the hell. In less than a month, I would be eighteen years old and legally an adult with rights.

When I arrived at our local station, there was nobody to meet me, so I walked home with my heavy cello and suitcase. Nobody was at home either. A driver took me to the intensive care unit where my mother, sister and some family members met me. My father was lying in a room, hooked up to machines and drips. He was quite simply a shadow of his former self.

I have always had a gift to see auras and to date it has never given me false readings. It is difficult to describe because I have read many articles on what others see, yet what I perceive is different. When I look at people, I can sense the nature of their illness. If they are dying, I know when that will approximately occur. I can even see when somebody is being dishonest. I can remote view with ease and I am very telepathic.

I looked at my father's aura and knew that he would be dead within three weeks. Within a few days, although he was sitting up and laughing and the doctors felt that he would make a full recovery from the cardiac arrest, I knew differently. The following week, his energy had turned white and I knew then that he did not have long to live. My family was distraught and yet, I felt unusually calm. There was so much that I wanted to ask him, but it was obvious he was not in the right state for such selfish enquiries. I knew that I had to remain peaceful and silent. This was his experience and my thoughts were irrelevant.

I was the last person to see him alive. The diabetes had overtaken his resolve to counter attack and he was being barrier nursed to protect everybody from infection. The smell in the room was deathly and as I sat next to him, I took his hand in mine and began to pray. I heard sniffling, and when I opened my eyes, I could see tears falling down my father's face. He looked like a little frightened child and my heart felt so much compassion. This once tall and mighty man looked more like a little lost boy. I reassured him that I would take care of mum, lead a good life and fulfill our family responsibilities. I expressed my gratitude for everything he had taught me and I assured him that we would meet again one day in heaven.

"I love you dad," I tenderly told him. "Oh gosh, this is so sad. I wish I could do something to help you," I gently said stroking his face.

A nurse broke the silence. "It is time for you to leave. Visiting hour is over."

"I wish to stay with my father," I told the nurse with a tone of insistence.

"No you must leave," she replied. "Hospital rules do not allow people to stay here."

"But my father is dying," I continued. "I do not want him to be alone."

"Nonsense," the nurse retorted. "You can see your father tomorrow. Now please leave." She insisted.

"But, it's doubtful he will be here tomorrow," I continued.

"Please leave now!" she all but shouted at me and it was obvious I had no choice.

"Has he seen our Vicar?" I asked.

"That is none of my business," she replied. "Now, you must leave or I will have you removed!"

I glanced into my father's eyes and noticed he looked profoundly sad and as I walked out of the room, I turned to look at him one last time. As I closed the door, I knew I would not see him again until I had also gone to heaven. I felt very, very sad.

The hospital telephoned us at three o'clock in the morning to inform us that father had passed away. Mum took the call and waited until morning to tell us. I had an overwhelming sense of deep regret and sadness for I felt that I should have stayed with him until he had died. To this day, I feel very sad and guilty about not being strong enough to insist I stay with him to the end.

Father's death was not the only shock we faced. Our uncle sat us down the following morning and explained that we were not his biological children. My sister was very angry and hurt. She refused to believe this news and insisted that there was only one outsider in the family, and that was yours truly. I sat in a state of complete shock and the information took a long time to sink in.

Much to the disgust of family and friends, my sister went out to our garden and destroyed every single rose and carnation that bloomed there. This ensured that I had nothing personal to place on my father's coffin. The funeral and memorial services were attended by hundreds, including heads of state and other dignitaries. My sister sat next to mum and insisted that I sit several rows behind. I never did find out who sat next to me at the funeral and to be honest the whole service was a blur that I can barely recall.

My sister and I remained cordial until after mum died. After her funeral, my sister felt there was no reason for us to speak again and that is exactly what happened. She pulled away from my son and his family and I closed the chapter with a shaking of my head and a shrug of my shoulders.

Conclusion

An unknown author once wrote, "To become a father is not difficult, but to be a father is."

Most of us had mixed relationships with our father, but overall, we can look back and know that he raised us in the only way he knew how. My birth father had wanted me aborted, and when I saw him one day later in life, his response was, "In my opinion, I paid for you to die. You do not exist to me!"

Thank you to the man who was my father in the way that mattered, for he gave me a life that my seed had rejected.

Lesson 9: "You're hired!"

I was to study Law at Oxford University. However, with my father's death those plans changed overnight. Our uncle announced that he had died without making a Testament. Family members received many of his possessions and the estate went into probate leaving mum as good as destitute. To this day, I refuse to believe there was no legal Will. Family members had gone through his things before and during the funeral and I know my father, he was a stickler for formality. Perhaps I am being naïve, but I doubt it. It infuriated me to see how my mother was treated and after a short time, she and I had to move. Mum had no income and with my father now dead, she was penniless. My sister immediately moved in with her boyfriend whom she married a few months later. I remained with my mother taking over the role of my father, as I had promised him I would do on his deathbed. It was disgraceful to me when I considered my father's aristocratic heritage. I could not believe he had left his wife in this way and I honestly thought that his family would step up to the plate and treat her with the respect she deserved. However, nobody was particularly kind and my respect for the immediate family was gone.

One morning I sat reading the classified section in the local newspaper. There was an announcement for a competition posted near the top, with an unspecified prize. The advertisement claimed the winner would have the potential to become very rich. That grabbed my attention. I telephoned to get the information.

Two days later, I sat in the showroom of a replacement window company. I had taken the bus to the interview as we had lost our car and I was not able to drive legally yet. Fifteen others sat there as eager as I was to win. A confident looking man entered the room and excitedly told us about the company and its many benefits. I can recall that day as if it were yesterday, for what was about to happen became one of the most important turning points in my life.

The speaker cleared his throat and enthusiastically announced the arrival of Vice President Jeffrey Boxen. He gave us a brief overview of this remarkable man and by the time he had finished, I honestly wondered what kind of a mighty leader we were about to meet. We all enthusiastically applauded. I was sitting at the back (my normal positon so I can observe the entire room safely) and when I noticed that this man was going to come from behind me, I draped my left arm across the top of the chair and turned to see who this distinguished person could possibly be.

The door burst open and in walked Mr. Jeff Boxen in the flesh. He was astonishingly debonair and stunningly eloquent with the kind of confidence that is rare and impossible to describe. He proudly talked about his family and said they were the most important thing in his life along with his faith. Jeff was Jewish, but later converted to Catholicism after meeting Saint Pope John Paul II. He spent several minutes talking about his career and I sat mesmerized by the positive energy he exuded. He emphasized that he had been searching for somebody very special and he wondered if that person was sitting in the room. He explained that the prize was significant. "The winner will be an extraordinary candidate," he declared. "The recipient of this prize is hungry for success and I can smell that determination and courage from this platform," he continued. "The winner of this challenge is a man or woman whose mold was broken after they were born," he concluded. I noticed everybody was excitedly grinning from ear to ear.

Prior to our interview, we had completed an extensive questionnaire. Jeff Boxen went from one person to the next and systematically asked a series of noteworthy questions pertaining to what they had written. When my turn arrived, instead of asking me a question, he simply stared at me for several seconds before moving on to the young man to my right. After a few minutes, everybody had spoken with the exception of me, which I found very odd. He asked if we had any questions and I raised my hand. He indicated to me that I could speak.

"Excuse me Sir, but everybody was asked a question except me. I was wondering if you had received my questionnaire," I gingerly enquired.

"I did," he replied with a smile. He walked towards a board and began to discuss the competition. I felt embarrassed and confused. When the others all sniggered at me I could not help but think, "Please God, don't let the business world be as petty as school."

We received the rules of the competition. The next day we were to carry a heavy window sample around neighborhoods and walk from door to door. We were to persuade people to agree to allow our vice president to visit them to discuss buying replacement windows and doors. The winner of the competition would be the candidate who brought back five leads. These leads had to be viable. If the homeowner did not agree for a visit, the lead would be invalid.

Despite feeling somewhat disorientated with recent events surrounding my father's death and from the harrowing years at school, I had not lost the fight of that student in my belly. I was anxious to win this competition because I knew mum needed the security that a solid income would provide. I sat up straight and concentrated on learning product knowledge that afternoon, determined to win.

As I was leaving the showroom to catch my bus home, Jeff Boxen touched my arm and said, "I'm expecting you to win tomorrow Lady Christine. Don't let me or yourself down."

"I won't Sir," I replied.

The following day, I woke up bright eyed and bushy tailed, ready to get those five appointments and win my prize. I still had no idea how much money I could win, but when you hear that it is going to make you rich, you assume it is a sizeable amount. It was a sunny morning and I glanced in my wardrobe to find something suitable to wear. I took one final look in the mirror, kissed mum goodbye and headed out to catch the next bus.

When I arrived at the showroom, nobody else was there (or so I thought). I felt worried that perhaps I had misunderstood the details and arrived late to discover the horses had already left the starting gate. I was certain that we were to arrive for an eight o'clock start and I had subsequently arrived at seven forty-five. My father had always taught me to be early. Eventually the others came, laughing with excitement. I had not noticed that Jeff Boxen was standing in the showroom window watching us and when he came out, one of my competitors flippantly remarked, "How long have you been watching us?"

"Long enough to note manners and professionalism," he replied. He divided us into several groups and indicated that he wanted me to ride in the back of his car. "Shouldn't the lady sit in the front seat Mr. Boxen?" one of the sales managers asked. By this stage, the entire management team was watching.

"Ordinarily, yes," he replied. "However, today she can sit in the back." I shared the car with three others who chatted about how they were going to spend their prize money should they win. I remained silent as we drove to the competition site. I noticed Jeff Boxen glancing into his rear view mirror to see my face. When I looked back at him, he instantly looked away.

We arrived on Ivy Road, which was an upper middle class neighborhood. After picking up our window samples and checking our pockets for lead forms, identification and brochures, Jeff Boxen told us to, "Go!" It really did feel like the Epsom (or Kentucky in USA) Derby when the gates open to release the horses.

I figured the task would only take me an hour at the most. I was wrong. Doors slammed in my face. I barely had an opportunity to introduce myself, least of all discuss replacement windows before the homeowner would say, "Not today thank you." In addition to the misery of rejection, dark foreboding clouds began to accumulate across the sky. I glanced up and muttered under my breath, "Uh-Oh, it's black over Mabel's." When I was growing up, there was a very old woman called Mable who lived in the creepy looking mansion atop the hill above our home. Whenever it was going to rain, my mother would look out of the window and say to us, "It's black over Mable's!" I was convinced this declaration was a technical weather term until she told me the story of old Miss Mabel. Thus from that day to this, whenever I see black clouds, I know it is going to rain and I say, "It's black over Mable's."

As I walked up and down the driveways, it was getting *very* black over Mable's and then it began to rain. I had managed to persuade four people to give me their information and just needed one more. The rain was so heavy, that you could say it was, "Raining cats and dogs." Thanks to those cats and dogs, I was rapidly beginning to look like a drowned rat. I was cold, tired, drenched and thoroughly frustrated. Apart from anything else, those window samples were extremely cumbersome (and heavy) requiring two arms to carry them.

As I looked down the street, I noticed my fellow competitors were back in the car. They had obviously beaten me and I felt disgusted with myself. I saw absolutely no rhyme nor reason to keep flogging a dead horse, so I shamefully returned to the car, feeling undeniably dejected. As I approached the car, Jeff Boxen wound the window down and asked me how many leads I had secured. I told him that I only had four, but as it was obvious that I had lost, I wanted to concede.

He refused my request by saying, "I told you to bring me back five leads, not four. You can get back in this car when you have brought me the other!" I was horrified and asked the others in the car how many they had collected. In a pathetic exchange, each one admitted to either none or one lead at best.

"Pardon me Sir," I replied. "With all due respect, I'm soaking wet and freezing cold. I have just admitted that I realize I have lost, even though four leads are not exactly shoddy. Won't you please let me in before I get ill?"

"No," Jeff responded. "Go and get that fifth lead."

"No?" I exclaimed. "But these others haven't brought you five leads either and yet you expect me to stay out in this treacherous weather? Can't you see that I'm soaking?"

There was another lightning strike followed immediately by a thunderbolt that was plainly right above our heads. The candidates sat in the car with their heads in their hands and one shrieked when the thunder boomed. The rain that followed was even heavier. I was mortified.

"I didn't ask you for a weather report," he angrily replied. "God knows I can see it is raining. I told you to get me five leads, and until you do, you will stay out there and work!" With that, he wound up the window, turned on the radio and deliberately looked away.

"I'll show him!" I muttered under my breath.

The next house I came to was smaller than the others were. I noticed a woman run past her living room window as I knocked on the door. She pretended to be out. I knew she was there and so I continued to knock. Eventually, a cute little girl (possibly three years old) opened the door.

"Mummy told me to tell you that she isn't in," the little girl said. I began to laugh.

"OK. Can you ask her when she *is* going to be in please?" I responded gently. The little girl went into the house and shouted, "Mummy, the lady wants to know when you *will* be home!"

A very embarrassed woman came to the door, but I could not convince her that replacement windows and doors were an important investment anytime soon. However, she felt so sorry for me that she agreed to give me her information. I went back to the car with my fifth lead assuming that I would now be able to get into the warmth. Wrong! The only thing that assuming does, is to make an *ass* of *u* and *me*.

"So, is this a real lead, or is it a Mickey Mouse lead?" Jeff responded sarcastically. "In other words, if I call this number right now, am I assured to be able to go in there tonight and sell our products?"

"Uh-Oh," I thought to myself. "This man is smart!"

I mumbled under my breath that it was not likely to convert into an appointment. The window was wound up in my face and the music became blaringly loud. As I looked through the windows to see the others were laughing at me, my mind was racing with rage. Who did this man think he was? Would he leave his own daughter out in the rain walking up and down the streets? I had never been a quitter before and I would show him that I had the guts to endure this outrageous behavior.

The next house was at the end of a very long, dark and sinister looking driveway (the thunderstorm made it feel like a horror movie) and I nervously knocked on the door. I almost expected a grotesque hairy creature with the stench of death upon it, to answer with a creepy, "You rang?" I was relieved when a normal looking elderly man opened the door to greet me. I would like to say that I spoke with calm eloquence, finesse and style. but that would be a lie. I explained my story with desperation and frustration and blurted out the entire tale of why I was there. I wept as I told him about my father's death and I sniveled like an idiot when I told him that I desperately needed money and I was in a competition that assured me wealth. He patiently listened to my story and then agreed to let Jeff go back that night to sell. Incidentally, he ended up purchasing a significant number of windows and made Jeff promise to share any commissions with me. That conversation earned me close to four thousand dollars, which back in 1983, was a great deal of money.

I marched back to the car and presented my lead. The door opened and Jeff indicated that I should sit beside him.

"Aren't you going to call the lead?" I challenged him.

"There's no need," Jeff replied. "I know this will convert."

He knew that I had come by bus that day, so after dropping the others off at the showroom, he proceeded to drive me home in silence. I was glad he did not speak because I was cold, wet, and feeling miserable.

As we sat outside, he switched off the engine and turned to look at me. "Well Lady Christine, you are exactly who and what I thought you were." I was half expecting him to conclude that I was rude, sarcastic, and lazy, not to mention a failure.

"I know you're very angry with me right now, but let me explain something to you," he continued. Actually, I was not feeling as angry at him as I was with myself. I felt weak and stupid for letting the weather get the better of me. I was exasperated with how everything always seemed to be complicated and stressful. Surely, life had to be easier when you were an adult and not a continuation of the humiliation of youth.

"Christine, there are winners and losers in life," Jeff Boxen continued. "A winner is not necessarily wealthy or famous, but whatever happens to them, they will always survive because they have the determination to succeed. A quitter will always fail in life. Any small success he or she gains will be quickly lost due to lack of effort, arrogance and laziness. It is easier to be a quitter and to make up excuses for failure. A winner has to work hard, think smart and constantly study to improve. A winner shares their wealth with others and is able to duplicate it for the entirety of their life. When life throws dirt in a winner's face, he is able to use it to reach heights of distinguished accomplishment. However, when life throws dirt at a quitter, he suffocates and dies a slow and pitiful death. Lady Christine, you are a winner and you have won this competition. Many congratulations!"

"I've won?" I said with complete surprise. "Is there a prize?" I laughed.

"Yes," Jeff said with a huge smile on his face. "The prize is unique and I hope you will understand its value."

I was confused and shrugged my shoulder.

"Your prize is wisdom and knowledge," he announced.

I was still confused and wondered how these nouns were going to equate to the money that I badly needed to support mum and me.

"Christine, in order for you to be successful and rich, you need to have information and skills. You can acquire this education or experience by learning the facts available to anyone who has the right resources. You need to learn how to make sensible decisions and give good advice. It is not enough to have knowledge about a subject unless you have the wisdom to utilize this knowledge effectively. You can gain knowledge by educating yourself but you can only gain wisdom by experience. Do you understand?" he said with a tone of great admiration.

I nodded that I did understand his point for this was exactly how my father had explained education to me since early childhood.

"I have run this competition for over ten years and have never had one person succeed in bringing me five leads until you achieved it today. This is an extraordinary accomplishment and I suspect it will be the first of many more to come. You came early today, which is exactly what a leader should always do. Despite the horrific conditions, you bravely continued to work. Yes, I could have let you give up, but I did not want you to quit. I deliberately ignored you at the meeting the other day and I am sorry that the others laughed at you. However, I wanted to ignite that fire of passion within you. Passion fuels success. Do you understand?" he asked.

"Yes," I nodded. "Thank you for your not letting me give up Sir," I replied.

"I'm going to send you to the Dale Carnegie Institute. They will teach you everything you need to know about sales, marketing, business and the psychology of human beings. Furthermore, for the rest of my life, I will be your mentor. Every week I will send you either books that we will discuss, or inspirational quotes for you to learn. I will send you on every course that I feel will help you grow. I will guide you, encourage you, and inspire you to be greater than you dare imagine."

He took my hand in his and continued, "When I look at you, I see a girl who has the potential to be an inspirational leader who thousands will pay to hear her speak. I am certain that one day you will be one of the wisest and most beloved women in the world and your story will inspire generations to come. It is a profound honor for me to know that I have you in my life and I'll not let you down!" After shaking my hand he continued, "You will report to the office tomorrow morning at eight o'clock. Over the next few weeks, you will learn to drive a car and you will go to the Institute in six weeks. Your income will come from working with me and together we will take care of your mother." I was speechless.

Conclusion

For the next thirty years of my life, until his death in January 2014, Mr. Jeff Boxen kept his promise to me. Such was his complete devotion to teaching me everything he knew, that indeed, wherever I was in the world, we would communicate every day, in one way or another. Every Friday he would send me a book or inspirational quote and I graduated from the institute with excellence.

As I was completing that competition form back in my teenage years, the last question asked us to name six things we would wish for, if offered anything in the world. Everybody had apparently said they wished for a sports car or a million dollars, not to mention boats, motor bikes and exotic vacations. I named the six most important things to me. They were the wisdom of King Solomon, the courage of King David, the vision of Nehemiah, the compassion of Joseph, the forgiveness of Jesus and finally, the blessings of Abraham. I knew these answers were unconventional and I was quite prepared to defend my thoughts. As much as I needed financial abundance, I was wise enough to know (even then) that money alone was not the answer to my long-term security.

I cannot adequately express my respect, love, admiration and gratitude for this truly inspirational human being. I met him when I was as a grieving, angry young girl and I grew to know him as a confident, loving young woman. Over the years, I have received far too many awards to mention here with humility. However, none of them can top the greatest prize of guidance by an extraordinary leader.

Please permit me to ask you the same question as I was all those years before. If you could have three things right now that would transform your life, what would you request?

Lesson 10: Adoption

Discovering after eighteen years that you are an adopted child is a very unnerving feeling. All that you took for granted up to that point disappears as you sit and think about the situation from every angle. I saw my adopted parents as my mother and father. Yes, I did want to know why my birth mother had given me away, but more importantly, I wanted to know if there were any genetic diseases on either side that could influence my life, or the future of my children's health and wellbeing. I meant no harm to anyone in my search. I did not expect or need a relationship outside of my immediate circle, but I did have unanswered questions that I wanted clarifying honestly.

As a matter of respect and privacy to my biological families, I have chosen to be deliberately vague. I had no wish back then, nor do I have a desire now, to cause undue pain or suffering to anybody. This is an important subject to discuss however, and I will do so with wisdom.

Finding my birth mother was easy. She had left her information with every social services department in the country. I could have gone straight to her with the information that was on my birth certificate, but I decided it would be better to have a social worker approach her first, so that she had time to think about whether or not to speak with me. We met and formed a decent relationship. I look like my father, and just seeing the resemblance brought her tremendous pain. It became obvious to me that my presence in her life was not in her best interest, nor was it helping her children. Everybody was very nice to me and I learned about our family history from India to Canada to the United Kingdom. I sadly walked away from the situation to save them all from the upset and embarrassment that my presence obviously brought. Mum was able to have a relationship with my son and for that, I am very grateful.

Social services also traced my birth father. He was outraged when they called and explained that I wanted to meet with him. He immediately slammed the phone down and told them not to call him again. Several months later, I was the lead contralto in a choral concert. One of the other soloists attracted me immensely and to cut a very long story short, we chatted and discovered that he was my half-brother on my father's side of the family. That evening I came face to face with my biological father. When he realized who I was, he stormed out of the room cursing me and refused to speak about me to a living soul. I decided to tackle this from a different angle. I needed to know the genetics of the family.

My half-brother arranged for a meeting with his uncle. We spent an evening going through the family history and he gave me a couple of pictures, but asked me to please leave the family alone, as nobody knew about me, and it was better off that way. I was at a business meeting several months after that, and again my father and I came unexpectedly face to face. He came right up to me and sneered, "Listen to me very carefully. In my opinion, I paid your mother to abort you. You are supposed to be dead. You do not exist to me! This town is not big enough for the two of us, so you have to leave and never come back. I'd better never see you again, Capiche?" I sadly agreed and just quietly walked away without ever looking back.

When I heard that he had died, I felt sad to be honest. My half-brother had always stayed in partial contact with me and so I had a good understanding of whom they all were. How sad that my father, who was a very gifted stain glass window artist, saw his own baby girl through the eyes of so much hatred and malice.

Conclusion

Many adopted people imagine that their birth family will be very happy to meet them one day. They fail to understand that their appearance may be unwelcomed in the lives of those who have moved on. The best advice I can give to those of you who may be considering looking for your biological family is to caution you to conduct the search calmly, with great respect and tact. Prudence is necessary in order to protect the sensitivity of both your adopted and biological parents' feelings and lives. Courtesy requires you to tread carefully and it is crucial that you do not undertake this emotional journey alone.

You must consider two things. Firstly, your adopted parents were the ones who invested their time, money, energy and care. They nursed you through illness, sorrow and disappointment. They cheered you on and encouraged you to be the person you are today. My adopted mother felt hurt by my wish to know my background and although both mothers met one another, I regret the pain they both felt by my decision to search.

Secondly, one cannot know the circumstances surrounding the decision to give you away. My advice to those people searching for their roots is to go through a trusted mediator like a social services counsellor or a family attorney. It saves both sides from being unnecessarily embarrassed or hurt.

An adopted person must realize that they cannot just barge into what is primarily a stranger's house and expect an enthusiastic welcome. Our lives are not always like movies with happy conclusions. Life has often moved on for everybody concerned. Although it may seem almost outrageous to be rejected and dismissed, the truth and reality of the situation is that your mother and father may have thought about you, prayed for you and wished you well, but with needing closure, they dismissed you from their conscious minds as they moved forwards with their lives. Thus, trying to unearth details that maybe shrouded in great sadness and even violence can potentially hurt you in ways you may not be able to handle. Sometimes you may just need to wish everybody well and keep living your life without them.

Having said this, I still believe it is very important to know your genetic background and I believe it is the right of an individual to know as much about family medical history as possible. If this information were to be on the adoption forms, a meeting with biological family may not be necessary. If not, then biological parents must be prepared to face their child one day and expect to offer this information.

One final piece of advice that I have to share on this subject is important. There are many television shows these days, (we all know exactly which ones) who invite you to reveal dirty secrets, take paternity tests and reveal outrageous secrets including the identity of your biological mother or father. It turns into a disgusting circus for the amusement of the viewers. Do not go on a show like this! Let me emphasize that again - do not go on a show like this! No good can ever come from publicly parading your most personal and potentially painful life in public.

Adoption means that one or both parents made the decision to let their child go. No parent does so from a mindset of happiness and celebration. On the contrary, this decision can be terribly painful and you will understand why when you become a parent yourself. Keep this part of your life respectfully private, for by doing so, you are maintaining your sense of dignity.

I firmly believe that almighty God does not make mistakes. I believe he gives you the opportunity to live and grow through other parents, if needs be. You are who God made you to be.

Do you remember the advice I gave to you earlier? Fulfill your name! That is the conclusion I had to come to myself.

When the deck of life shuffled its cards one day, it dealt me a sickening hand of spades, clubs, diamonds and hearts. However, at least I had a hand to play. I learned when to hold those cards in my day-to-day experiences and I knew exactly when to stand up and walk away. I had a heavenly father by my side who loved me deeply and whenever I felt alone, sad or in pain, he would say to me, "Christina, you are my child and I will never leave or forsake you," and he never has.

Lesson 11: "I do!"

I was not very lucky when it came to intimate relationships or marriage in my twenties and thirties. My first marriage was when I was twenty-one years old and he is the father of our beautiful son. My other relationships sadly ended too. I loved these men very much indeed and I genuinely tried hard to be all they needed. Unfortunately, other women loved them as well, and they were far more adept at winning their hearts than I was. Their identities are irrelevant because each of them happily remarried and I genuinely wish them all much happiness and peace. I have maintained *very* positive relationships with most of them and with all their wonderful families. You will never hear a bad word from my mouth about any of them.

I deliberately chose to remain unmarried in my forties, vowing to dedicate my life to others. I wished to strengthen my own sense of worth and maturity and to live alone. I wanted to break the negative patterns that had dominated my previous years of life and I wanted to spend time in monastic retreat and religious education without the drama of personal relationships. It was after a significant year in isolated retreat that my life significantly changed, and I slowly began to implement God's instructions in my fortieth year.

Younger people often ask me for marriage advice and although I am happy to listen to their woes, I am reluctant to speak about it when I do not have a successful one under my belt. I usually encourage them to spend significant time in prayer before making any conclusive decisions. I should have done that when I was younger instead of presuming that I knew best. I am very careful not to give advice often, but rather, I encourage people to go to their pastor, rabbi, swami, minister or priest who will be able to guide them through the process with maturity and untainted wisdom.

Probably the number one question that I am frequently asked is,

"When is a good age to marry?" In addition, others often ask, "Is it better to marry later on in life when your career is settled and you have financial stability?" Relationships can be difficult and marriage is tough. When we join with another man or woman, we cease to be one person. Two people who have joined in marriage become one flesh. Many women have a tendency to fight their husbands on every issue and wish to stamp their independent personalities on every decision made. A huge mistake occurs when some seek outside counsel (from so-called friends) on decisions that are between the husband and wife.

When we are younger, we beautify ourselves and fret about our outward looks as we actively seek to attract a mate. I can confidently tell the younger ones who read this, that one of the wonderful aspects of growing older is the shedding of those concerns. Age calms you. Maturity injects a sense of peacefulness into you. You think before you jump when experience has taught you that one must be more discerning of people and (so-called) opportunities. Relationships change and deepen. You realize that distance, and even death is no reason to fear a loved one being out of sight. You seek less to impress and more to understand. You wish to help others calmly and quietly, rather than shout from the rooftops and demonstrate with passionate appeal and anger. You seek a peaceful and purposeful life, with the understanding that the world does not revolve around you. You seek a mate who is supportive, reliable and decent, rather than dashing, daring and oftentimes womanizing or flirting with other men.

Moreover, by far the most beautiful thing about growing older is the deeper relationship you have with father God. Please understand that time gifts you the wisdom to appreciate the opportunities of life. It enables you to see the gift of his greatness, perseverance, forgiveness and unconditional love.

One of the most important pieces of scripture to read and digest when one is contemplating marriage at any age can be found in 1 Peter 3:1-6. "Likewise, wives, be subject to your own husbands, so that even if some do not obey the word, they may be won without a word by the conduct of their wives, when they see your respectful and pure conduct. Do not let your adorning be external—the braiding of hair and the putting on of gold jewelry, or the clothing you wear— but let your adorning be the hidden person of the heart with the imperishable beauty of a gentle and quiet spirit, which in God's sight is very precious. For this is how the holy women who hoped in God used to adorn, by submitting to their own husbands, as Sarah obeyed Abraham, calling him lord. And you are her children, if you do well and do not fear anything that is frightening."

Conclusion

I have prayed a great deal about my past relationships, and I take full responsibility for my failures. Over the last ten years, I have grown to see men and myself in a different way. Consequently, I feel more able to contemplate a future marriage without the crippling fear that this subject would fill me with before. I have studied scripture in preparation and I would like to share it with you as you pray about your own relationships and possible marriage proposals. The book of Genesis says, "It is not good that a man should be alone; I will make him a helper fit for him." The book of Corinthians chapter two says, "Do not be unequally yoked with unbelievers. For what partnership has righteousness with lawlessness? Or what fellowship has light with darkness?" In other words, God will send the right man or woman to you in His time and one must discern those who come into your life with great wisdom and care.

Finally, my three best pieces of advice are as follows. Firstly, always pray for God's guidance before you say, "I do!"

Secondly, I would encourage both parties to be completely candid about their current situation. Some feel it is better not to discuss past relationships and to a degree, I agree. If things are in the past, there is no need to bring them into the present unless a child is involved. However, if there is a current love affair, (which will not disappear in a puff of smoke just because a ceremony has taken place) everybody involved must be aware of each other. That may sound horrifying to a person who is involved with a friend (with benefits). To be candid, one should not be getting married if he or she intends to continue a sexual relationship with another person, regardless of whether that other man or woman is married. I am sure you would not wish to be halfway through your ceremony when another person stands up and declares their love for you or your future spouse. We laugh when we see this in a movie, but the reality is far from humorous. Equally painful, is the realization that the other person will continue to stand in the wings offering their love when you are away. Call me old fashioned, but I would like to think that my husband's heart, soul and mind is set on only God and me.

My final piece of advice is to marry your best friend. As you walk together through life, there can be nothing better than to face it with your trusted companion.

Lesson 12: Children

Children are a precious gift from God. All over the world, men and women are praying for the blessing of a newborn baby. There are women in clinics right now who are undertaking specialized procedures like artificial insemination and in vitro fertilization, whilst others are preparing themselves to be surrogates. The dichotomy of birth is profound. Whereas some women are delivering their children with the help of qualified midwives and doctors at home, in hospitals or at specialized units, others are alone in dirty back alleys or crouched in remote fields and jungles. Young girls are giving their babies away for adoption, pregnant women are preparing themselves for surgical abortion and families sit weeping with the sadness of a miscarriage or stillbirth.

A healthy woman has a few years of fertile possibility. For most, childbirth is a glorious celebration where a woman can feel wholly accomplished. A man is able to stand proudly amongst his peers, confident that his seed and name will live on through another generation and the community sees it as an accomplishment. A newborn baby is adorable. Their innocence and vulnerability pulls at the heartstrings. When we hear an infant crying, there is an immediate, almost animal-like emotion, which tugs at us deeply and causes us to reach out to comfort and protect.

However, there is an emotionally harrowing side to childbirth, which many feel too uncomfortable to discuss. This subject is taboo. When one dares to approach it, there is horror. I am referring to the miscarriage of a baby. People tend to react in one of two ways. Some say "Well don't worry, you can always have another," whilst others will cross the street rather than have to face the mourner in question.

God eventually bestowed a beautiful, healthy baby boy upon me, who is now twenty-six years old. He brings immense joy and happiness to everybody he meets and when I think about him, I call him my "Miracle baby," for his siblings did not have the same opportunity to live.

I was newly married and ecstatic to be pregnant. It never occurred to me that I would have a miscarriage a few weeks into the pregnancy. I awoke one morning with a dreadful pain in my abdomen. I lifted up the sheet, looked down between my legs and was horrified to see I was bleeding. I gave birth to my baby girl in the restroom at the hospital. As I looked down at her fully formed body, (she was the length of my palm) I felt tremendously sad.

A nurse came in and handed me a transparent plastic trash bag for my baby's body. I thought she was joking, but she explained to me that at twenty weeks, my baby was too premature to qualify for burial. She mumbled some outrageous comment that she was not a fully formed baby yet. Through clenched tears of grief and outrage, I demanded to know what was going to happen to my daughter's body. With absolutely no kindness or hesitation, she told me that my baby was, "Clinical waste." In a matter-of-fact tone, she told me that she would be piled with the other waste and burned later that day, so I did not have to worry about what to do with her myself. I all but fainted. There was no further discussion and I had no choice. There was not one single comforting word - as God is my witness.

I walked out of that hospital numb and deeply hurt. Nobody knew what to say to me. Everybody knew that I was pregnant because it had begun to show. As news spread around the community about my miscarriage, nobody could look at me. Not one single person ever said they felt sorry. I am sure that they were not trying to be cruel. In hindsight, the women had probably had their own children die, and mine was a reminder of their own disappointment and grief. My husband would not talk about it either and we decided to try for another child immediately.

A few weeks later, I became pregnant again. After fourteen weeks, I lost him in the bathtub. My mother heard me shouting and ran in to find the bath water red from the blood loss. I did not know what to do and I literally sat in the bath crying. Eventually I managed to climb out of the tub and wrapped my baby in a towel, but I did not know what to do next, so mum called the doctor. A nurse asked her how big my baby was. Her advice was to flush him down the toilet or bring him in if he would not go down the drain. With clenched teeth of anger, mum explained that he was far too big for that. She then suggested that we either wrap him in a bag and put him in the garbage, or bring him to the hospital when I had my checkup and surgery to scrape away the fetal mass. I am sure you do not need me to tell you what I was feeling.

A few months later, the pain began again. This pregnancy had seemed to be going very well with no complications. After two miscarriages, there is a tendency to be almost paranoid about pain and whenever one goes to the bathroom, one finds they are looking down there to see if there is any blood. If you have experienced a miscarriage, then you will be able to resonate with that observation.

I had my son at the hospital. As with my other babies, he was trash. The nurse promised to bring him to me for a final moment, for by this stage, I knew exactly what they were going to do. An hour or so passed when the nurse finally returned with my son. His body was in a jar and he looked like a science experiment. I literally shrieked profanities as she dropped the jar on the floor. I sat staring at his remains in shock. The doctor suggested that there be tests done to determine what had happened to our son and to discover why I kept miscarrying. He coldly told me that once the test was completed, our son would be officially clinical waste.

I know that as you are reading this, you are gasping and saying, "Oh my God!" Perhaps you have never thought about this subject before. Yes, it *is* horrifying!

One might wonder how we managed to find the courage to try again. I had a dream one night where I felt the Holy Spirit upon me. I woke to know that the next baby would be healthy and strong, with no complications. Nine months later, Geoffrey was born. He was and is a most wonderful blessing.

Some of you may not find this an easy story to read. Others might be thinking that this cannot possibly happen, as it sounds almost medieval and barbaric. Few ever think about what happens to their child once they have left the hospital from a miscarriage or the clinic after having an abortion. It is as if our minds cannot comprehend such an overwhelming tragedy. Pushing it to the back of your mind is futile, for with every monthly period you remember the loss and feel a sense of failure for not being pregnant. Every time you see a baby on the television, in the shops or at church, the pain of your loss and the sense of desperation are overwhelming.

When I had a radical hysterectomy in 2006, I was ecstatic. I knew with that procedure that I would never have to experience another depressing monthly period. If I had realized how fantastic I was going to feel both emotionally and physically, I would have insisted on having that surgery back in my twenties. We hear so many horror stories about hysterectomies. In my case, it has been fantastic and it gave me a new lease of life!

I am a realist. I have always asked the questions that few dare to have the guts to utter. It is my nature to seek the truth and defend the weak. I am a strong woman and can deal with anything life chooses to throw at me, and it is difficult to shock me to the point that I am angry beyond words. On August 5, 2014, a documentary aired in the United Kingdom. Investigations found that the remains of 15,000 or more aborted and miscarried babies were incinerated as clinical waste, with some even used to heat hospitals. Ten national health trusts admitted to burning fetal remains alongside other trash, while two others used the bodies in "Waste-to-energy," plants that generate power for heat. Twenty-seven other NHS trusts over the last two years alone had treated our babies (our children) in this way.

It is staggering! It is evil! It is almost impossible to know what to say! I was enraged, and yet relieved that this barbaric behavior was public knowledge. Mind you, I doubt much will change sadly.

Can you imagine the tens of thousands of deceased babies who are being used to heat facilities around the world and crushed in landfills?

Our children deserve to be shown dignity and respect. Mothers and fathers need to be treated with compassion and understanding. If we sit idly by and allow this monstrous behavior to continue, then nothing will change. Most women and their partners do not know what happened to their baby or the remains of their pregnancy. The law states that burial or cremation should occur for babies who are stillborn (born dead after twenty-four weeks of pregnancy in the U.K) or who are born alive, but later die. For babies who die during pregnancy before twenty-four weeks (miscarriage or spontaneous abortion) the situation is different because there is no law that governs what happens to these children. After a late miscarriage, most hospitals offer a simple funeral with either burial or cremation. Some hospitals offer this respectful funeral for all babies, regardless of their gestation.

Hospital practice is improving all the time, but shockingly some hospitals may still treat the remains of an early loss as clinical waste. I would personally recommend you call around the hospitals to find out their procedure just in case. When faced with this traumatic event, you are not thinking rationally. A man does not go into battle to lose the war, any more than a woman becomes pregnant thinking that her baby is going to die. Having a dignified plan in place should your child die early, will be spare you all a great deal of suffering.

If you miscarry at home or somewhere else, that is not a hospital, you are very likely to pass the remains of your pregnancy into the toilet. You may look at what has come away and see a pregnancy sac or the fetus – or something you think might be the fetus. The hospital might suggest you flush the toilet. I cannot imagine flushing my baby down the toilet like a dead goldfish and I know many women who have done this with deep regret.

You might think about taking the remains to your physician or to that compassionate hospital, perhaps for them to confirm that you have miscarried or because they may be able to do some tests. You might choose to ask the hospital or your doctor to dispose of the remains of your pregnancy. Alternatively, you may decide to bury the remains at home, in the garden or in a planter with flowers or even a shrub perhaps.

Although there is no legal certificate after a pregnancy loss before twenty weeks, some hospitals provide a certificate for parents to mark what has happened. For many parents, this is an important memento. If you have not been given a certificate but would like to have one, contact a nurse or midwife on the ward or unit where you were cared for or the hospital chaplain.

Conclusion

A few years ago, I helped organize a memorial service for the lives of these babies and to offer closure with comfort to those people who had experienced a major loss in this way. Some sang beautiful songs, whilst others read touching memorial poems. We lit a candle for each child lost, gave them each a name, and prayed for their eternal resting peace and grace. Everybody left with a sense of unified grief.

I would like you to consider organizing this service within your own communities. You can hold it at a church or in a chapel, perhaps at the hospital. Be imaginative with who you invite, and do not assume that people are oblivious to this shared experience. I assure you; most women have miscarried and a few opted for a termination. Some men and women may have chosen not to talk about their loss. Yet, when they hear of this service, they may finally find the courage to walk forwards and admit, "This also happened to me."

A memorial service is a comforting way to say, "I know you are gone my precious baby, but I still think about you. Rest in peace little one."

Lesson 13: The squatter

I sat watching the BBC news in 1989 feeling tremendous compassion for the thousands of men, women and children who were passing on from the worst flu pandemic that England had experienced in decades. People within our city were dying and an outbreak of meningitis hit the community. It was my son's first birthday when I began to feel unwell.

I was as fit as a fiddle in the morning when I arose to go to sing at church. By the end of the service, I began to feel a severe headache coming on. My sight was blurry and I was succumbing to a fever. I thought that perhaps I had a migraine approaching, as it did not occur to me that it was any more serious than that. We were living with my mother at the time and she cared for our son, in order for me to go to sleep for a while. Within an hour or so, my neck began to become unusually stiff. Light, sound and the bedclothes were becoming increasingly irritating and I had a low-grade fever. My husband called the doctor for advice. He suggested that I should just continue to drink sips of water, swallow some fever reducing pills and rest. By the end of the afternoon, I was in excruciating pain and developing a rash on my chest and neck. It felt like my head was about to explode and any movement, however slight, was agonizing. When the doctor came to see me, he immediately diagnosed Meningitis.

Emergency services transported me to the intensive care unit at the county hospital where they conducted a lumbar puncture test, which confirmed bacterial meningitis. My family and pastor were called to the hospital and I can vividly remember everybody crying before I fell unconscious in the quarantine room. During that time, other members of the community (including a boy I knew very well) also contracted this illness. Within days, they had all died. Later, you will read about my near-death experience as I lay fighting for my life.

The recovery took a long time and I relapsed again a few months later. The illness had left me profoundly deaf, with significant short and long-term memory loss. My kidneys were malfunctioned, my bladder permanently damaged and my limbs were weak and constantly painful. The tinnitus in my ears was loud and irritating and when I tried to stand up and walk, I felt constantly dizzy, weak and clumsy. I did not recognize anybody around me and nothing was familiar anymore. I developed frequent seizures and experienced vivid nightmares that would leave me in a cold sweat night after night. My mood swings were extreme and the depression was almost uncontrollable for the first few weeks.

God had told me that I would recover. However, trying to convey that message of reassurance to those around me was impossible. When I would try to stand up, I would fall to the ground in a heap. I had limited control over my bladder or bowel for several years, which meant depending on others to change my diapers, until I was able to do it myself.

The meningitis opened up a Pandora's Box in my brain. One minute I was watching the television and the next I found myself in a hospital room. The memory of the childhood attack had surfaced when I saw a man who resembled my abuser, and it was, to my brain, as if it had only just happened. The seizures increased in duration and severity. With each episode, I fell into a deeper and blacker hole that seemed almost impossible to comprehend. My body was incapable of cooperating. One month I was healing then the next I would relapse.

I went from one hundred and thirty pounds to over two hundred and eighty pounds in weight from the medication and lack of movement. My marriage ended and my husband took our son to his parents' home. Overall, it was a very sad and frustrating situation. I was just twenty-four years old.

I liken the meningitis to a squatter. One day when we were out, he broke in and refused to leave. I did not invite him to enter and despite demanding him to leave, he was adamant that this was where he intended to stay, with or without my permission.

It took years to rehabilitate, and in many ways, I am still coping with some areas of that recovery process, although thankfully, the battle is now under control. I learned over the years that pain is not necessarily something we can avoid, but suffering is an option.

Many people have played a significant role in that journey from the blackest of holes to the great light of renewal. I will always be grateful to the physicians, rehabilitation teams, social services and other medical professionals who over the years have rebuilt me, much like the seventies television series *The Six Million Dollar Man.* I will always be grateful to my son's father who courageously carried on without me and raised our son to be the fine young man that we see today. I am even grateful to those who consciously injured me, for their unkindness was a reminder of how far I have actually come in my recovery.

To look at me today, twenty-five years after this terrible illness, you would never know that the squatter had paid me a visit. My recovery is nothing short of a miracle. The great heavenly physician himself gave me his healing grace. Amen.

Conclusion

One-day a farmer's donkey fell down into a well. The animal cried for hours as the farmer tried to figure out what to do. Finally, he decided the donkey was old and not worth retrieving. He invited all his neighbors to come over and help him cover up the well. They all grabbed a shovel and began to throw dirt into the well. At first, the donkey realized what was happening and cried horribly. Then, to everyone's amazement, he quieted down.

A few shovel loads later, the farmer finally looked down the well. He was astonished at what he saw. With each shovel of dirt that hit his back, the donkey did something amazing. He shook it off and took a step up. As the farmer's neighbors continued to shovel dirt on top of the animal, it continued to use it to take a step up. Soon, everyone was amazed when the donkey stepped up over the edge of the well and happily trotted off!

Moral

Life *is* going to shovel dirt on you. The trick to getting out of the well is to shake it off and take a step up. Each of our troubles is a stepping-stone. We can get out of the deepest wells just by not stopping and never giving up. Shake off the dirt and climb higher!

Lesson 14: Heaven

I have told this part of my life to thousands of people for many years and the story never changes, nor will it. I do not need to embellish it, defend it, understand it or convince you. I hear cynical people who roll their eyes and tut with sarcasm when they hear such stories and it is as if they wish somebody would tell them something different from the usual accounts. Skeptics have scoffed that the patient simply had a dream, and sadly, these survivors of death have always felt a need to insist that they did die and go to heaven.

To be blunt, the very fact that thousands of us have seen the same thing is an indication that there *has* to be some truth to our shared experiences. Survivors have seen deceased loved ones and sometimes without ever having met them (or heard about them) during their lifetime. Others suggest the devil is playing with our mind. Yet, I doubt he would be so keen to fool a person who in turn has a deeper faith and love for Christ as a result. If nothing else, those of us who do return to life after this holy experience are significantly affected.

I conclude therefore, that if it *was* a dream, I am grateful to God. That dream changed my life forever and it gave me framework to build my second chance, so to speak. I cannot prove I went to heaven and nobody can prove that I did not. May you find comfort from what I am about to share with you. Those who have seen the miracle of my life have certainly been touched by my time with almighty God.

I lay in that isolation room struggling to survive the grip of the meningitis, which had already taken the lives of people I knew. I was close to death and everybody around me was crying and praying for a miracle. Nurses and doctors came, went, and cautioned my family that I was probably going to die. The pain was indescribable and I was afraid. I can vividly remember asking God to help me before I became unconscious, and then my world went black.

I came out of my body. The *"I,"* that is my soul. I did not realize that it was my soul until later and even then, I only call it that because I do not know what else to say. I could see this huge being standing right next to me, surrounded by light and warmth. I looked up at him, and then down at my body. As I tried to touch it, I realized that I did not have hands or the ability to feel, thus my energy just brushed through the body. I was very confused.

I knew this being! It was my Guardian Angel. The last time I had seen him was when the man who abused me as a little girl, was leading me up the stairs. I wondered why he was standing there with me.

I was pulled towards this bright white light. Everything accelerated and I can understand why some people describe it as a tunnel, for in truth you are moving so fast that it feels like you are in a suction tube. I was not afraid. I felt very peaceful, safe and completely free from the pain.

I passed through a black area, which I have always referred to as the, "*No-thing* space." It felt very sad, cold and separate from life.

My Guardian Angel did not speak in audible words, but did transmit the meaning of this blackness to me in a way that I could comprehend. When we are alive on earth, we sometimes say to people, "You are nothing to me!" or, "This means nothing to me." The word "Nothing," fills us with a sense of rejection, as if nobody could care less if we lived or not. This is, in many ways, an aspect of hell. Although there were no obvious souls floating around, there was a distinct impression of loneliness and despair. This dense isolation felt torturous because it never seemed to end. There was no light at the end of that tunnel.

Immediately after that, everything suddenly stopped with the biggest and brightest light that you could ever imagine. It was the most beautiful thing that I had ever seen, and I could hear musical instruments being played and songs of praises being sung, which I could not understand as the language was unknown to me. I have since come to learn that these hymns of praise were Aramaic. It sounded like holy worship. Nobody had to tell me where I was. I knew I was at the entrance to heaven. It was glorious!

You cannot begin to imagine how beautiful the entrance is to heaven, and I could only imagine how majestic it would be once I had gone through the gates. Nothing that anybody ever writes about it can describe the magnificence. You would have to see my face when I talk about it to have a sense of the profound beauty that has never left my face when I recall that gift. To utter the word, "*Wow*!" would still not describe it adequately.

I wondered what was about to happen, as my energy suddenly stopped moving. It was as if I was in a movie theatre sitting in the best seat of the house. The screen before my eyes began to play the film of my life. They say your life "Flashes in front of you," before you die. They are correct about the *seeing* your life, but wrong when they describe it as rapid. Some say that you see "Every part of your life," and they are right too, with a *major* exception. You do see your life, but not as you remember it at all. You see it moment-by-moment, frame by frame and from the point of view of everybody else's experience of how you influenced their lives.

For example, a person may make a comment, which the group thinks is foolish. They sarcastically mock rather than listening to the person with politeness and an open mind. When replayed, if you were part of that group, you get to feel and hear exactly what that poor person heard and felt, as you and the others were cruel. It sounds humbling and it is shameful. Trust me; when you are accountable for everything you have ever done or failed to do during your life, sadness overwhelms you and you feel terribly ashamed!

You cannot hide from this examination of your life. The credits do not roll until you have seen the works and deeds of your life. You see your compassionate acts that may have included smiling at the child on a bus, or giving food to the hungry man as he lay on the sidewalk. Every word, gesture and act of kindness is significant to God. Every blasphemous insult, pathetic excuse, deliberate lie and broken law which is contrary to God's will, (however big or small) is put right in your frame of understanding. You hear, see and experience every single aspect of your existence from the perspective of all those other people and creatures whose lives overlapped yours, in the intricate tapestry of what we call, "Life."

Moreover, to those who cruelly mistreat God's animals contrary to his laws are made to feel exactly what that creature suffered; every gruesome and terrifying moment at a time.

You might recall that I mentioned earlier in the book about a walk I had taken with my father during childhood, when we came upon a rabbit with myxomatosis. I had wanted so much to offer that animal comfort and healing. Yet instead of permitting me to run over to it, my father had angrily pulled me away. I was hurt and furious with him for his lack of compassion for many years. Now, as I had my life replayed, I could clearly see things from the perspective of my father and the creature. I saw that my father was concerned about the rabbit, but knew there was nothing he could do to end its misery with me there. His responsibility was to keep his child safe, as there was no way to explain nature and disease to an infant. He knew that I was angry with him, but what else could he do? I saw dad silently praying that this poor creature would die quickly and I saw this same scene from the rabbit's perspective. It definitely sensed positive energy and although it was in pain, shock and fear, it died with a prayer over it that secured its place in heaven. To those who do not believe that animals go to heaven, I will respectfully beg to differ. I know that some do.

Finally, God brought me to the moment of my death. It was then that I became completely aware of the presence of Christ. It was as if he had been waiting in the wings to this point, but now was happy to step forward as his father revealed the most important lesson that I needed to learn. I was to see the tragic scenes of my life and as much as I wanted to shout, "Please don't make me relive those again!" I had no choice but to trust that there was a positive message in them for me.

I saw those times when I was discarded at birth, sexually abused, beaten at school, abandoned and left, grieving at the loss of my grandmother, feeling guilty when father had died, holding my dead babies and other significantly painful events. Rather than being alone, God was happy to show me his presence with every breath I had taken. Moreover, my Guardian Angel had stood next to me as well and at no time was I ever alone. It was awe inspiring to say the least.

Many people have asked me what God looked like. With every scene, that God showed me, he was with me. He was in that doctor who gave me treatment. He was in that social worker who handed me to my parents as an orphan. He was in that kind nurse and encouraging teacher. The Holy Spirit was within them.

His angels, (specifically created) accompany us on our journey through life to eternity. I did not see God as himself. You cannot see his Majesty and live, for even the seraphim's wings cover their faces from his mighty power through reverence and awe. I felt him. You cannot make yourself low enough to pay him homage. You simply know that you are in the protection of your creator, king and master. His majesty is beyond comprehension.

Jesus Christ has a similar presence and for those of us who know what he endured on the cross to pay for our sins, it is impossible to be in his energy and not feel a combination of shame and gratefulness for his sacrifice. However, instead of condemning me, our Savior enveloped me with a blanket of forgiveness and love. You see, even those who reject him on earth, have him as their main witness during this final examination. I have met other near-death survivors who were not Christians. Even they saw Christ at the end of the tunnel, but he did not know them.

Jesus told his father that he knew me. He told him that I was one of his own. Those two admissions were the admission ticket I needed. If you recall the story of my grandmother, I knew she had gone to a place after death and I knew that you had to go on a journey to get to that place. I also knew that a journey required a ticket and I had surmised that Jesus was that ticket. Here I was at the gates of heaven being told that my Lord "Knew," me and by him admitting boldly, with authority, that I was one of his souls, I could now walk in through those mighty gates. I knew that my grandmother was there on the other side of those gates and I was within seconds of seeing her again.

I realized that earth is not our home, but rather a special place where we learn our lessons by developing an enthusiastic, loving, patient, sharing attitude, with a contrite heart. There is a final examination, which you will either pass or fail. Your graduation takes you up and into the light of the heavenly realm with God or down to the hellish existence of separation from him.

If you could truly wrap your head around this today, your eternal life would be secure. I have met many people who did not know either where they were to finally rest or who could not care less to contemplate the end. In their opinion, when they are dead, they are dead and buried in the ground and it is over. For those who have given our lives to Christ, our final resting place is with him. For those who do not care to think about this next part of their journey, the end can be a frightening wakeup call. I cannot imagine facing my trial to hear my *only* witness saying, "I cannot vouch for this person. I do not know him or her. She or he was not one of mine." Screaming, pleading and bargaining will fall upon deaf ears as you go away to eternal damnation, which is separation from God. I do not know about you, but there is no Hollywood movie frightening enough in my opinion to convey that horrific image.

A man stood and challenged me at a seminar I gave several years later. He sarcastically asked, "Are you deliberately trying to frighten us?"

I looked him straight in his eyes and said, "Yes, I am."

He was shocked and asked me, "Why?"

"Because brother, you need to realize that once you have left this fleeting earth there are only two places that you can go. One is heaven and the other is hell. The moment you die, trust me, your soul leaves your body. Your soul has to go somewhere and I would prefer it to go to him," I replied.

The audience nodded their heads and cried aloud, "Amen!"

The man said, "I don't want to go to hell." I walked over to his seat, hugged him and said, "Brother, then give your life to Christ." He did.

You might recall the two criminals that hung on either side of Jesus at Calvary. One mocked him (he did not recognize who he was) and the other (fully acknowledging him as Lord) asked him to remember him in heaven. Perhaps the former went to hell, we do not know. However, the latter definitely went to heaven because Jesus assured him that he would see him there. Such was their *sin*, but such *is* his grace to *forgive* when we recognize who he is and ask for mercy.

I wanted to go through those gates into heaven and my savior presented a good case for me; yet I did not feel ready. After watching my life, I wanted to come back and try to lead it better. I was torn. I loved my baby son so much that the thought of him growing without his mother was just too sad to imagine. I had promised my father that I would care for my mother. The thought of her struggling to live was unimaginable. How would she survive with no job or money? She could not drive. I did not want to appear arrogant or ungrateful, but at the same time, I wanted some more time on earth.

It is hard to explain the great mystery of the soul. For those who think that we are all a mass of energy when we die, are correct in the sense that all matter becomes one in God, and yet, you are an individual energy within it. God made each one of us creatures separately and our experiences are mystical and unclear until our death. We are so much more than just "Creatures," and now I understand this completely. Some religions teach that there is no God and that we return to earth in a new body, or cease to exist entirely. It would be foolish of me to say that I know the answer to this. I can only speak to what the Bible teaches and to what I have seen for myself. We read that there are many rooms in our father's mansion. For all I know, the other room could be symbolic to mean a new body on earth or an entirely new world. I do not know.

There was an agreement for me to return to earth as long as I obeyed the instructions. God gave me the vision of key events and lessons that would be signposts to indicate which direction I needed to travel. The Holy Spirit would fill me with an inner knowing of which path to take at each juncture. Amongst many other events, I was to come to America as an able-bodied woman, be around Native American Indians, work in India as a humanitarian and study in monastic retreat. Along the way, I was to teach, share wisdom and love all people. I was to immerse myself in media technology and write inspirational books. Anointed with specific tools, which included gifts of healing and prophecy, I was to comfort the sick and pray with the dying. I was to teach kindness and demonstrate love.

Finally, I was to fulfill my calling in only a few short years before it would finally be my time to go home. Yes, I did see approximately, when that would be. I agreed.

My Guardian Angel accompanied me back to my body on earth. I had a clear mission to fulfill and I can humbly say that I am fulfilling it as I write the book that you are currently reading.

Conclusion

There is a Native American Indian legend about the youth's rite of Passage. They say that his father takes him into the forest, blindfolds him and leaves him alone. He is required to sit on a stump the whole night and not remove the blindfold until the rays of the morning sun shine through. He cannot cry out for help to anyone. Once he survives the night, he is a man.

He cannot tell the other boys of this experience, because each lad must come into manhood on his own. The boy is naturally terrified. He can hear all kinds of noises. Wild beasts must surely be all around him. Maybe even some human being might do him harm.

The wind blew the grass and earth, and shook his stump, but he sat stoically, never removing the blindfold. He knew that this was the only way to be a man within the tribe.

Finally, after a horrific night, the sun appeared and he removed his blindfold. It was then that he discovered his father sitting on the stump next to him. He had been at watch the entire night, protecting his son from harm.

We, too, are never alone. Even when we do not know it, God is watching over us, sitting on the stump beside us. When trouble comes, all we have to do is reach out to him.

Moral of the story

Just because you cannot see God, does not mean he is not there. We must walk in faith, not by sight.

Lesson 15: Great news!

One cannot go to the gates of heaven, return and sit silently on the sidelines, as if nothing has occurred. Yes, when I came back to earth much to everybody's amazement, I was a physical mess and it took many years to recover. I was too sick to speak with clarity and I struggled with profound deafness. God had instructed me to take his teachings out into the world, and with every passing month that followed, that message transmitted with more eloquence than I ever dared to imagine.

To have witnessed firsthand the glory of the Lord is a mighty event for sure. Beloved, when we have great news to share with others, we turn to social media, our cell phones, and of course word of mouth, newspaper, TV and radio. We are so excited, that nothing can contain that burning desire to let others know of our wonderful news. We celebrate. We throw parties. We all but stand on our rooftops to declare to the world that our life has just changed for good and we testify. We declare and we summon others to hear and partake in our joy.

So why is that so many people have a major problem in spreading the news of the greatest gift in their lives, that being of our Lord Jesus Christ, and the acceptance of him into their hearts, thus giving them eternal life through him and with him? Are they ashamed or perhaps embarrassed? Perhaps they are shy or poorly equipped with the right words to use to express this great event. Some may lack the knowledge to answer any rebuffs whilst others are private people who prefer to keep such matters to themselves. In some countries, people could be frightened that such a declaration could cause an imminent threat to their lives. Sadly, some churches are more adept at teaching their congregations to witness more enthusiastically than others. I have been to many a church that never instructs or teaches their sheep to go out into the world and openly testify.

You see brothers and sisters, we are not in our Shepherd's fold to sit there and bask in its security and love. We are not to graze on the good grass and meander around conversing with other like-minded sheep whilst ignoring those who need compassion and mercy. Neither are we shepherded into the fold to argue amongst ourselves.

God's fold is, "Love." Do we love one another? Do we extend that love? When people look at us, do they feel loved and welcomed, or do they see arrogance and discontent which makes them nervous to draw near to us.

Jesus did not say to his disciples and followers, (including you and me) "If you feel up to it, tell a few folk about me if you don't mind." Furthermore, he did not say, "It might get a bit heated out there if you mention my name, so perhaps it would be safer for you to just *do* good things. That in of itself will be the testimony necessary for others to come to me."

Jesus did not say, "Hide me." On the contrary, he said, "Whoever is ashamed of me and of my words in this faithless and sinful generation, the son of man will be ashamed of him when he comes in his father's glory with the holy angels."

Granted - some of us are rather shy, and some of us belong to branches of the Christian church that does not put great emphasis on going out into the world and witnessing verbally and boldly. Baptists for instance are wonderful proclaimers. We know that the Church of Latter Day Saints, Salvation Army and the Jehovah's Witnesses are wonderfully equipped with the materials and courage to go from door to door. I admire them tremendously. Whether you agree with their philosophy and doctrines or not, these men and women are bold!

We are soldiers of the cross. I am not going to say which particular church is right or wrong here, for that is subject to individual interpretation. Your elders will guide you. Over the last eighteen months, Pope Francis has spoken about evangelism in a very passionate way stating, "An evangelizing community gets involved by word and deed in people's daily lives; it bridges distances, it is willing to abase itself if necessary, and it embraces human life, touching the suffering flesh of Christ in others."

In the first chapter of Acts, our Lord tells us, "It is not for you to know the times or seasons that the Father has established by his own authority.

But you will receive power when the Holy Spirit comes upon you, and you will be my witnesses in Jerusalem, throughout Judea and Samaria, and to the ends of the earth." These were his final instructions before he ascended into heaven.

Note that he said, "You will receive power." In other words beloved, we are full of the high-grade gas to go on the journey. Energized, we have the confidence to know that regardless of what might happen on that journey, we are safe, saved, and have truth on our side.

Note also that he said, "You will be my witnesses." A witness is not a silent onlooker. Rather a witness testifies truthfully and accurately. Even those who would rather be discreet voyeurs, still have the conscience within to know they must step forward and state their account. We will come back to that point in a moment.

A witness has seen, heard and experienced an incident that will undoubtedly have changed him or her forever. Witnesses seldom keep such things to themselves, for it is human nature to tell others, even if sworn to secrecy.

To return to an important statement I made a moment ago, a witness, when challenged, must be able to back up his claim. People may mock you when you declare you are a Christian. Others might ask you to put your principles aside to fit in with others who wish to lead you astray. Resist the temptation to deny what you stand for. Leaders may expect you to compromise your faith from time to time by engaging in illegal practices or unethical behavior. I have resigned when asked to do this in the past. Your life could well be in serious jeopardy if you openly praise your faith in some countries and yet many are prepared to die rather than surrender to tyranny.

Students ask me if it gets easier to declare ones faith with time. I assure them that with guidance, they *will* find a level that feels comfortable for witnessing and it may be as simple as how they lead their everyday lives. Some quietly speak about their faith whilst others shout it from the rooftops. Either way, a gift is next to impossible to keep hidden. Those of us, who know the horror that awaits the sheep outside the fold, reach out to share that gift as enthusiastically as possible.

Throughout history, our Lord's sheep have been persecuted, imprisoned, tortured, mocked, flogged, fed to lions, whipped in public, burned, crucified, shot, hung, and on a lesser level ignored, overlooked in promotions and slung out as eccentrics. Subsequently, some might suggest that one should simply live a good life, and discreetly live under the radar. Others might urge you to remain quiet by telling you that "God knows you are one of his, so don't rock the boat. You can do more good for longer, if you just lay low." I have heard people even retort with a, "How can you be a witness to him, if you are killed?"

Is living a good life enough, one might ask? Is it ok to go to church each Sunday, even to confess and pray with your family, but do no more than that? You are not harming anybody, you might think.

Admittedly, there are worse ways to be, but this is not what our father taught us. Is it enough to just go to church and not actively speak about or demonstrate our faith outside of the building? No, it is not.

Permit me to arm you with four powerful resources that I like to call, "Pit stops." Firstly, your first and most essential pit stop is to seek God's grace. I call this one, "Prayer." I cannot emphasis enough to you the importance of unceasing praise and prayer. God is all ears. He wants to commune with you as you are his child. There is no need to be well educated, bashful or afraid. Just talk to him about everything and he will give you favor and grace. When you accepted our Lord into your life, he enveloped, ignited and anointed you with the Holy Spirit. I hope that you joined a church thereafter. Your church is a home and she will pray with you, but you must also establish a relationship with God. There are formal prayers with structure that you can learn to recite including the *Our Father,* which Jesus taught us to say to God. This is a good start.

The second pit stop is equally crucial. I like to call this the, "Word." I am always stunned when a Christian tells me that they do not read or study their Bible. Some do not even have a Bible in their home. You simply cannot go out into the world and profess your faith, if you have not even read the handbook of Christian life. Admittedly, we are not all theologians. We do not all have degrees in divinity and you might not wish to study the Word in the kind of depth that I do. However, your church will probably have a study group for beginners, as well as for the more advanced members, and I wholeheartedly recommend that you join one of them. It can be comforting and enlightening to learn with others and apart from the fact that it is educational and even social; it keeps you safe in the fold. Very importantly, reading the Word equips you with the knowledge you need to talk about your faith openly and accurately.

The third pit stop is your, "Defense." God has equipped his leaders to help you. These come in the form of ministers, pastors, priests, evangelists, apologists and elders to name a few. If you are Catholic, you can learn much from your priests, bishops, and cardinals and of course, today, Pope Francis. For those of you who wish to listen and learn from some great teachers of God, you can go to YouTube. Here are some great teachers that I respect and admire. Pastor Franklyn Graham, Mother Angelica, Bishop Fulton Sheen, Pastor John Hagee, Pastor Joel Olsteen, Pastor Joyce Meyer, Reverend Dr. Charles Stanley, Reverend Dr. David Jeremiah, Pastor Benny Hinn, Dr. Ravi Zacharia, Bishop T.D. Jakes and Reverend Dr. Billy Graham. If you are ever in Orlando Florida and can come to the Basilica of the National Shrine of Mary, Queen of the Universe, you will be most fortunate to hear the profound wisdom of Monsignor Juanito Figura and Father Paul Henry. These leaders, depending upon the denomination you have joined, (and there are significant differences within their doctrine, although we are all believers), will be able to instruct you with the right words to say when you speak about your faith to others. This is a controversial aspect to our faith, I admit. I have stood watching men and women of God viciously battling over their doctrine.

The fourth pit stop is what I like to call the, "Gift shop." I am sure you will agree me that giving gifts is a wonderful thing. We take time to think about what the receiver would enjoy and maybe what we think they need based on experience or spoken intention. Some of our loved ones need food and water. Some need clothes, whilst others would enjoy something musical. A few might simply enjoy you spending time with them, whilst one or two would cherish a good book, which they might enjoy more if you would kindly read to them.

You see brothers and sisters, Father knows us. He knit us together in our mother's womb and he obviously knew us before we were human beings. He carefully created and designed us perfectly, with inherent abilities to develop over the course of our lives. Some of us are very musical, whilst others are practical and can build or construct amazing buildings and instruments. Many have a natural aptitude in sport, whilst others are scientific and lean towards medicine. Some of us are better at listening, whilst others are naturally persuasive debaters and organizers. Every single child of God has at least one gift. I want to emphasize that point very, very strongly.

Beloved, however useless you think you are in some areas (and perhaps you think in everything) I wish to make an announcement: God does not make mistakes. He has a job for you, which he specifically created you to do for his glory. "But I don't know what that is?" I hear you say. Look at your life, brother or sister and think about what you really enjoy doing. If you can then translate that into a service to help others in a healthy constructive way, you *are* doing his work on earth.

I had a wheelchair bound student who came to me a couple of years ago and said, "Dr. Overton, you know that I am disabled and pretty much house bound. How can God possibly use me?" I knew that this young woman was very softly spoken, calm and humble. Her personality was the epitome of gentleness. I put in her in touch with a telephone helpline and today she is one of the most confident and competent counselors on a suicide crisis line.

You might wish to play a role within your spiritual community. I can guarantee that your church has outreach programs, which include visiting the sick, dying, imprisoned or housebound and helping in soup kitchens, on the streets and in over-sees missions. Most churches have a crèche, Sunday school and choir. If your church does not have any kind of program in the community you can either start one or look for a church that is actively engaged in helping the less fortunate. I would be highly suspicious of a church that did nothing to help the community and if you were a student of mine, I would most humbly caution you to find another place of worship.

If you ask God to use you for his glory, he *will* lead you to a ministry, which you will grow in confidence and grace from being a part, by offering your talents to help others in need. This act of service will fill you to overflowing with joy and peace as you fulfill your destiny here on earth.

Conclusion

"Extra! Extra! Read all about it! Jesus died for our sins, rose again on the third day and ascended to heaven so that we can have eternal life!"

Beloved, there are many rooms in our Father's mansion and our Lord has gone to prepare a room for each one of us. When Jesus said, "It is finished," he accomplished his mission by dying for you and paying the penalty for your sins. That should be the best news you have ever heard and the best gift that you could ever receive and inwardly accept. In the grand scheme of things, I assure you that eternal life in heaven is all that matters.

There are those who enjoy a prosperous and exciting life on earth, with absolutely no sense of responsibility, regard, compassion or remorse for their actions. They rarely think about life after death. These same people often mock the mere notion of hell, by joking that it will be hot and fun down there. I have sat with such people like this in their last few minutes on earth. I assure you, demons were around and it was obvious they were seeing a terrifying vision as their souls prepared to make their final journey.

I was once with a priest in this situation and I will never forget the expression on his face when he took his last breath. That was a major wake up call for me and taught me that just because a person professes to have faith in the Lord, does not necessarily mean that is true. As you will learn later in this book, a man of God can very well be a wolf in sheep's clothing.

Lesson 16: The winner

The Winner Takes It All is a heart wrenching song of divorce, sung by the Swedish pop group known as *Abba*. It reminds us that more often than not, a breakup can produce a winner and a loser. Nobody stands there on their wedding day ever imagining that their blessed union is going to end in divorce. If the vast majority of us believed that, despite the statistics that speak very negatively to a marriage lasting beyond five years, I doubt we would invest the money, time or emotion into such a monumental decision that affects our entire family in one way or another.

Divorce is very painful. Many feel as though they have failed at the one thing that should be easy to achieve within their life. However, marriage is tough. You can awaken one day to discover that your partner has been unfaithful and wants to be with somebody else, or simply watch the relationship slowly disintegrate over time, leaving both of you feeling like a worn out dishcloth.

As a friend of mine once said, "There is nothing worse than lying next to somebody whom you know is in love with somebody else." I agree. It is soul destroying to know you are being lied to and it is emotionally painful to stand next to that person in public pretending that everything is happy and normal, when you know that nothing could be further from the truth.

With past generations, divorce was very rare. Many couples remained together within the confines of the marital home to save their reputation. Certainly, before the 1950's with the rise of females in the workforce, women could not just stand up one day and leave the marriage with ease. Men oftentimes took mistresses or became workaholics to find justifiable reasons to spend less time at home where they felt unaccepted or unappreciated. Women back then felt trapped in the façade of living the perfect life with the cute little cottage, white picket fence, station wagon, two children and a dog called, "Rover."

However, with the dawn of the 1960's both men and women said

"Enough," and divorce began to rise significantly. Children were born out of wedlock (including me) and the entire fabric of society began to unravel with shocking momentum. Modern technological advancements and the affordability of transportation meant families were additionally moving further apart. Women finally had careers outside of the home during the Second World War, with the understanding that when the men returned from the battle, they would resume their positions and the women would go back to their perceived humdrum lives. This changed in the 1960's and women could finally imagine long-term employment, which meant they could support themselves financially. For the first time in history, men had to compete for jobs and promotion. Children no longer had the idyllic family structure and they too joined the developing world of technology. As the decades progressed, the family unit unraveled and disintegrated with an ever-increasing number of children joining the "Stepfamily," statistic.

Most people feel that these advancements have been a very positive influence on society, by offering equality and choice. Many are excited to have the ability to send rockets and satellites to space and the exploration explosion has enabled us to go higher into the atmosphere and deeper into the oceans than ever before in history.

Today, we do not have to wait for weeks to receive notices or contemplate a vessel passage, which will take months to complete. Within seconds, we can send e-mails and text messages across the globe and within hours, we can physically visit loved ones via airplane or automobile. The machines that only the rich could once afford have become a standard household item for a wider social circle to purchase. Medical advancement has increased our ability to heal from wounds and diseases. Robots have become increasingly sophisticated and have the ability to replace man. Computers and televisions are valued as essential tools for men, women and children.

We have become accustomed to our lives being rapid and convenient. Everywhere we see fast-paced, fast-forward, fast-money, fast-sex and fast food. Even the romantic style of courting has become speed dating and computer matching. There was a time when *everybody* enjoyed the sacred church wedding ceremony. The entire family travelled to the church where God blessed the couple and united them in his holy ordinance. Today, the church has a formidable competitor in Las Vegas. Couples can join in holy matrimony within minutes at the Vegas chapels and some of them even offer a drive through quickie wedding for convenience.

You would think that in an age of such rapid convenience, we would have more time to spend together. Yet, this is not the case. Despite having technology to simplify our lives, we are using the extra time to cram in more activities and distractions. Humankind is facing a dichotomy. As the world opens up to us via technological advancement allowing us to observe the vastness of this planet and beyond, we are actually becoming increasingly immobilized and introspective. Our computers transport us to unknown destinations, which draw us into a private world of fascination. Television dangles a delicious looking carrot and occupies our attention with programs designed for every taste and age -programs that air twenty-four hours a day and repeat if we are nocturnal by choice or affliction.

The family structure has significantly changed. Instead of one close-knit unit who spent the evening together discussing the events of the day, today, we are all engrossed in our individual private worlds. Dad is downstairs watching football on the TV, whilst mum is in the kitchen watching a soap opera on her IPad. Fourteen years old Tommy is in his bedroom chatting to (goodness knows who) somebody on Facebook, who is engaging him in a new on-line addictive game or indoctrinating him into a (goodness knows what) cult, as sister Katie is in her bedroom texting a school friend or bullying a girl with cyber insults. Nobody has even noticed that sixteen years old Jimmy has sneaked out of the house to smoke a joint with his gang members down the street. Before you write to tell me that this is extreme, I assure you that I have witnessed this kind of a scene more times than I care to mention. I have yet to find a balanced family free of issues. People are switched *on* technologically, but far too many are turned *off* and tuned *out* to reality.

Families are crying out with the turmoil and tears of losing the one thing that truly matters in life - a secure, unconditional loving home. Men and women sit in their divorce attorney's office plotting and scheming to outdo their partner and to ensuring that they keep the house, car, gadgets and children, who the other must pay for, even if they are no longer part of the unit. Each shrugs their shoulders when asked why they think their marriage fell apart. The other partner is obviously to blame they believe. Their children sit frozen with sadness and fear. They turn to their computers and lose themselves in fantasy.

When a marriage ends in divorce, it bodes the questions, were all these advancements worth it? Is family time more precious than work, TV and the internet? Is my partner more important to me than any other man or woman? How could I have given more? Was God the center of our relationship?

Years ago, there were fewer women in the workforce and men, on the whole, only had access to female company through social gatherings or by discreet introduction via friends and confidantes. Affluent men had mistresses and some visited brothels to satisfy their sexual urges. Nevertheless, there was rarely a discussion of leaving his home to form a new life with these other women. If the wives knew, they did not dare speak of it to others. Today, it is very easy for men and women to have affairs. Statistics prove that many relationships begin in the workplace where colleagues are in close proximity to each other for several hours a day. In many corporations, management set rules forbidding these liaisons as they realize the destructive elements that arise including wasted time or the potential loss of a talented employee when the affaire becomes public.

People ask me, "Can affaires be avoided?" I always reply, "One cannot change the behavior of another person. One can only have self-control and decency. Why would you risk losing a beloved wife or husband, which will destroy many lives, just for the sexual rush of another human being? If your marriage has disintegrated and counselling cannot repair it, then why would you not have the decency to end it before introducing another person as a Band-Aid?"

Relationships are difficult today. You have to be the very best girlfriend, boyfriend, fiancé, fiancée, husband or wife possible and trust that your partner is a decent person who would not dare to sabotage your union. We will discuss this a little later.

Suffice to say, if divorce comes knocking on your door, how should you deal with it? You will find that many people will wish to give you advice based upon their own experiences and I guess that is what I will be doing as well.

Firstly, I wish to take you to the Word, for quite honestly, this should always be our first port of call. The book of Malachi 2:16: tells us, "I hate divorce, says the Lord God of Israel."

According to the Word, marriage is a lifetime commitment and as I said earlier, I believe we all stand at the altar as we say, "I do," with this sentiment in our hearts. Saint Matthew tells us that we are "No longer two, but one. Therefore what God has joined together, let man not separate."

The Bible has much to say on the subject of divorce and remarriage. In Matthew's Gospel, it says the injured person can only remarry when there was adultery in their other union. Some interpreters understand this exception clause as referring to marital unfaithfulness during the betrothal period. Jewish custom considered a couple married even when engaged and thus saw adultery during this engagement as marital unfaithfulness, thus allowing the other person to seek another mate; the Greeks understood the same marital unfaithfulness, to mean all forms of sexual immorality including fornication, prostitution and adultery.

Jesus understands that sexual intimacy is an integral part of the marital bond where two people become one flesh. He knows that the breaking of that bond by one or both giving themselves to outsiders, is destructive. Adultery is an allowance for divorce, not a requirement for it. Through God's grace and forgiveness, a couple *can* rebuild their marriage after an affair.

It is distressing that the divorce rate among professing Christians is nearly as high as that of the unbelieving world. The Bible makes it abundantly clear that God hates divorce and that reconciliation and forgiveness should be the marks of a believer's life. However, God recognizes that divorce will occur, even among his children.

I am fully aware that many of you reading this book may not be religious and so I will address the practicalities of how to cope with a divorce from my own experience. These suggestions are applicable to everyone regardless of religious persuasion.

- If you are divorcing due to spousal abuse, please seek the wisdom of law enforcement officer and an attorney. There are laws in place to protect you, which is particularly important in domestic violence.
- Keep calm. If you yell and shout, you will fail to hear the underlying reason for this monumental decision.
- Listen without blaming.
- Do not have this discussion where any children may be listening. Please allow me to emphasize this again. No child is ever responsible for a couple's divorce. One might have a volatile relationship with a stepchild for instance, but this is no reason to drag a child or teenager into the equation.
- Seek counseling from a divorce expert and a pastor or priest.
- Seek the wisdom of a good attorney. Sadly, divorce tends to deteriorate to resemble the trauma of a battlefield. Having your case represented by a strong attorney, who specializes in this area of law, is a crucial investment. If there are children, the court will usually appoint a Guardian Ad Litem to protect the interests of your children.
- Go to your bank. Understand that once procedures are underway, accounts are not accessible until such time that you both agree to the distribution of assets.
- Decide where you are both going to live. If you are going to remain under the same roof, you will have to discuss how you are going to live there as amicably as possible.
- Resist the temptation to confront your partner's lover if they have admitted to an extramarital affair.

- Mutually decide how you are going to explain the separation and divorce to your children. Remember, they are going to be afraid and terribly upset. You must reassure them that they have done nothing wrong. You must instill within them the knowing that you love them. You must ensure that they fully understand that you will both be raising them with the same amount of love however. You will need to explain to them that your locations may well change, which may mean a change in school. Reassure them that you will make sure they like their new surroundings and situation.
- If one of you has decided to leave the other for a new partner, it is very important that your child not face a stranger during this stressful transformation. Until the divorce is final and until you are one hundred percent certain that this new relationship will last, it is wise to keep your children away. Children will suffer greatly if they have to face two separations within a short period.
- It is natural for the slighted partner to wish to cause hurt. Fear and grief causes us to be irrational and emotionally unbalanced. Try hard not to do or say anything in the heat of the moment, which you might come to regret later on. This includes stalking the other mate and their new lover.
- Decide how you are going to tell family and friends. Please note that in most circumstances, they will all take sides. It is important not to paint your partner as a two horned devil who deserves little kindness or love. It is far better to encourage family and friends to support you both with prayer. It is essential for you both to keep all the intimate details of the breakup private.
- Resist closing the door. It is very important to keep the marital door open for forgiveness. You loved each other enough to say, "I do!" and despite everything that may have occurred up to that point, it <u>is</u> possible to repair the damage and continue the journey together.

- Pray. In many ways, I wanted to begin these fifteen points with this most important step. Remember, God brought you both together and knows you intimately. You cannot hide from Him. Adam and Eve tried doing that after eating the forbidden fruit, and we all know what happened to them. Nothing is secret. If you have conducted an extra marital affair and sighed with relief that you "got away with it," let me tell you right now, you did not! God was right there with you. He knows that you are both hurting and he knows every single thought within your mind, heart and soul. Go to him with your pain. Ask him to intercede and if it is possible, reconcile your differences and come back together in his love.

Conclusion

If divorce seems the only sensible option, ask God to bring you to a clear understanding of how to continue without your partner. There <u>is</u> life after divorce.

In order to heal from the pain of a breakup, you have to be gentle with yourself and others. Resist leaping into a new relationship too quickly and realize that you do not need another person to validate your worth.

You must strengthen yourself from within and release your partner with dignity and love. The healing process is much easier for all concerned if you can act with a calm and rational attitude.

Last, but by no means least, walk on the path to forgiveness.

Lesson 17: Two homes

The end of a relationship or marriage is a difficult phase in anybody's life, but probably the ones who hurt the most, are the innocent children of those divorces. Even if a child has witnessed the deterioration of the family home, there is always a dream within them that their parents will reconcile, and life will return to normal. Children have a tendency to blame themselves for a break-up and they constantly hope that at some point their parents will fall back in love with each other if they change their behavior. Sadly, this seldom happens.

If a child has come from an abusive home, they may have had to stay in a shelter for a while in secrecy, until such time law enforcement deems the situation safe enough for them to be re-homed. Family services could well be involved, and the court will appoint a Guardian Ad Litem, to serve the interests of the minors in the family unit. It is a very traumatic event in a child's life. Children simply do not have the maturity to understand what is happening in their world. Negative behavior from stress occurs when they cannot express their emotions in any other way than to act out aggressively.

Assuming there is no abuse to deal with, one of the parents has undoubtedly moved out of the family home. This leaves the children to cope with the two families. They have to adjust to shifting their books and clothes from one house to another each week. It may also mean that they do not see one parent for weeks or months at a time.

Today, divorce is sadly a common trend. Decades ago, children of broken homes were in the minority sector and had to learn to cope with the name-calling and embarrassment. Today, it is almost a trendy club. These same children discuss stepparents and stepsiblings as normally as they do the latest shows on TV. Naturally, each situation has its own unique characteristics. Each child, even one-half of a twin, has his or her own personality traits and needs. No two children express emotion in the exact same way. Great care has to shown by both parents by shelving their own anger and grief, to notice and respond to their children's questions, with honesty and calmness. A child must never me made to feel responsible for the end of their parent's relationship.

When I found myself in the divorce camp, I was battling with all the complicated issues of the meningitis. I was so ill with seizures and had no clue what was going on most of the time. I was not able to be the kind of mother that I had always wanted to be, but at least I was alive. My one regret in life is how our divorce affected my son. I missed so much of his upbringing as he lived so far away from me, and I could not travel to see him for a long time. When I did, I was too sick to be functional enough to play with him.

It was quite simply a horrible, tragic mess. I knew within my soul that eventually I was going to recover and I prayed to God daily that my son would understand and not hate me for the lack of activity from my side until then. I wanted to be the one that took him to school on his first day and to be his biggest cheerleader at events. I wanted to be the one that held him in my arms when he was sick and kissed his boo-boos better. I dreamed of being the one who read to him each night before he went to sleep, changing my voice with each storybook character. I wanted so much to be there to cuddle him and tell him how much I loved him.

Thankfully, he grew up with his grandparents who were simply amazing human beings. My son's father was also capable and when I look at my son today, I feel so much gratitude that he was deeply loved and well cared for by those who surrounded him with loving arms, and a dignified Christian home. His father remarried and I was thrilled for him. My only request and prayer was that his wife would be a kind and supportive stepmother to our son.

As the years have passed, my son and I have grown very close, thank God. We are more like friends than anything else and in addition to loving him so very, very much, I can honestly say that I really like him too. He is a man full to overflowing with compassion and kindness. He loves God, loves others and has the gift of humor and common sense. The divorce naturally did affect him, and I feel guilty for that. He was only a toddler when he and his father left. Perhaps that is a good thing, as he did not remember us together.

Who can say when is a good or bad time for children to experience this major change in their lives? I believe, overall, we are all doing the very best that we can with the cards we have to play with. There is one fact that will never change. Parents have a commitment to their son or daughter, even after divorce. Eventually you may both become grandparents within this circle of life. The more respect you show your ex-spouse, the easier those family functions will be. At some point, the anger and sadness of your divorce has to heal in order for the unit to find peace and forgiveness. Time heals if we allow. Before bringing other partners into the equation and expecting your child to deal with a new dynamic, it is always best to take a time-out from the distraction of the outside interferences. It is crucial to devote significant attention to the little human beings in front of you who are sitting wondering what has just happened to their world one day.

Conclusion

Children are emotionally vulnerable during a divorce or separation and they worry about what is to become of their lives. The responsibility of their upbringing, including education, health and spiritual nourishment, is a joint venture. The ideal scenario is for parents to forge an open communication policy, which is non-combative and honest in fact and detail. Last minute cancellations of plans, childish behavior in gift giving, accusations and deliberate intentions of belittling the other parent is damaging. If the intent is to hurt the other partner, the innocent child will undoubtedly feel the backdraft. Holidays, birthdays, graduations and other meaningful family reunions are special. Learning how to communicate peacefully will ensure that these cherished occasions continue to be happy.

The feelings of grandparents are important factors to consider.

Children need their older relatives, especially if their relationship has always been one of love to that point. If possible, all parties concerned must seek an agreement. Everybody should seek to resist the temptation to speak ill of the other parent in front of the child, or to display hostility that affects the child's sense of loyalty to one parent over another.

The family pet is important and should not be dumped, abused, discarded or euthanized. Children often feel able to talk to their furry, finned or feathered friends in a way they cannot to humans. The pet calms them, and in a world that is declining and changing, a child needs everything possible around him or her to act as a comforting buffer.

Listen to your child. Notice negative behaviors and if in any doubt, seek advice from professionals, including your spiritual advisor. Never assume that just because your child is quiet, they are feeling secure about the situation. If their personality changes over time, notice these warning signs and act accordingly. Let their school participate during the divorce and beyond. Be aware. Come out of your cocoon of hurt and focus on rebuilding life with your children by your side.

Eventually, life does settle down for most and the scars do fade. Divorce is not the end of the world. However, it does herald the beginning of a new chapter.

Lesson 18: Dating

Dating at any age is an experience we all engage in regardless of gender, race, culture, creed and country. Dating after divorce or a breakup from a significant relationship is tough. Depending upon how old you are when you get divorced and whether you have children living with you or not, dating can be a bit unnerving.

After my first divorce, I was not interested in dating because I was in the rehabilitation process. The others came after the gates of heaven, so I was able to compose myself and move on with grace and dignity, knowing God would lead me to where I needed to be to serve him. Therefore, I have never actively gone out looking for a man with a fishing rod over my shoulder and tasty bait in my purse. I have met some wonderful men at church and others through friends at social gatherings. I have had a few distinguished men approach when I have been giving keynote speeches and many others who send me messages through Facebook for instance. Unlike most of my female friends, I am not obsessed with finding Mr. Right. My life is one of service and I wish to help the less fortunate members of society. However, if I were to remarry, my companion will be a man helping the poor or leading his nation. He will be an intelligent man of God with distinction and humility coursing through his veins. I will know when I have met him.

Many men and women come to me for words of wisdom as sitting on the sidelines can give one a unique perspective. We all know that the world of dating has shifted these days. For many women, the tradition of sitting on the fence like a wallflower is gone. Today, women are more aggressive and actively going out to get what they want. This comes in diverse ways including the workplace, social clubs and the online world of dating profiles. Dissatisfied with meeting one man at a time, some join the latest craze in speed dating. I have never been to one of these admittedly, but I believe one gets to spend a minute or so with a succession of suitors, where you are able to glance at them and their attributes, much like an item on a menu. You then can select if you wish the waiter to bring you a taste of that item. I jest of course, but you get the idea and perhaps you have even attended such an event at some point.

Like you, I know of men and women who have joined dating sites and discovered quickly that the person they thought they were meeting from a profile turns out to be quite different in reality. If they have Skyped with each other, there is a better framework in which to ascertain the validity of the other person. This approach is much wiser in my opinion.

I have known people who have gone to restaurants to meet the online man or woman, only to find that the picture they were displaying on their page was in fact an image captured ten or more years ago. One could argue that it is still the same person so one might ask why that is wrong. Frankly, outward appearance does influence our choice and ten years or more can change the way we look significantly, whether that is mature or not. However, to counter argue that point, one must turn the table and imagine how you would feel if circumstances were reversed. I fail to understand why one would mislead in this way and feel it is better to present oneself in an honest manner knowing that you are being authentic.

There are numerous reputable sites geared towards marriage and there are as many, if not more, aimed at the, "Let's hook up tonight and have a wild naughty one-night stand baby." The latter fills me with horror as I imagine sexually transmitted diseases, affaires, rape, prostitution and all kinds of frenzied sex with goodness who.

I had one client a few years ago who had fallen for the *Russian Bride* dream site. He was so certain that the girl he was corresponding with was the love of his life that he booked a ticket and flew to Moscow. Prior to this, he had sent her money after a particularly emotional conversation when she described the horror of what she and her parents were experiencing. He was so concerned for her and happily wired her several hundreds of dollars. I warned him against this and knowing that he was a somewhat emotionally fragile man, I sat praying for his welfare when he departed American soil. A few days later, he called me frantically. After landing in

Moscow, there was no woman to meet him. Several phone calls later and a trip to her village, he discovered that she did not exist under the name she had given him. She was completely aware that he was on a plane coming to see her and maybe she was at the airport and did not like what she saw. Nevertheless, if a person goes to such effort to travel across the world, you should find the manners to be a gracious host. He never heard from her again. He was, as you can imagine, devastated.

I know of women who have gone to other states to meet a man they had met on-line. These men treated them appallingly. On one occasion, I had to arrange for one of my friends to leave a seedy club in New York to a place of safety before we could fly her home. The man had unchivalrously convinced her to travel to him, rather than him making the effort to go to visit her. Upon her arrival, they had engaged in erotic sex before going to a club where he ignored her in his drunken state and made out with another woman on the dance floor. Another one of my friends met an on-line man at a restaurant knowing only what he had spun to over cyber space. She was so enthralled with him during dinner that she agreed to go to his place for, "Coffee." The man brutally raped her that night. Sadly, I could fill a book with such stories – I really could.

However, it is not all negative. I have known a few of my friends, students and clients who have signed up with sites like E-Harmony.com. Within days, they have met the men and women to whom they are now happily married. Therefore, it is not that I am against such dating sites, but rather that I always encourage those I know to go gently with it and to take their time to get to know the other person before either leaping into bed with them or standing in front of the congregation saying, "I do!"

It is always interesting when men approach me on social media. Every single day on Facebook for instance, I have men sending me messages and propositioning me. I am staggered at how confidently they throw out their lines with bait, such as flowery compliments. Is it flattering to have dozens of men pursuing you every day? Maybe I should say it is, but I am also conscious of the fact that these exact same men throw similar lines to other women. At my age, I am no fool. With the exception of a few, most men who approach me are playing games and I am perfectly aware of this fact. Suffice to say, I am cordial but cool.

It seems like manners these days, have totally disappeared. Social media sites knock down certain inhibitions and I understand why emotional affairs are developed if one is not careful. Social media is very addictive and it affords one the opportunity to meet people you would never know existed. When I tell these men that I am not looking for a relationship, that I am not on Facebook to date, but to post my teachings and engage in humanitarian work, they are stunned. When I tell them that if their behavior continues I will block them, they are either angry or frantic to engage me more. It is like a silly playground game and one I refuse to play.

Many women come to me shattered after their divorce, particularly if their husband left them for another woman. I held a seminar a while back to discuss this very subject with a group of Christian women. I will state right now that the vast majority of my friends are men of God. Please note that I say, "Gentlemen," and not just "Men." There is a huge difference between the two that is somewhat influenced by the way they have been raised. I am not a, "Man basher." I respect everybody equally. Despite one or two unfortunate men who have crossed my path, the majority of those I socialize with are amazingly loyal, decent, hardworking, faithful, kind, loving, trustworthy, sweet, well-mannered, religious, educated, politically sound minded and any other positive word you care to mention. I count myself blessed to have a life full of wise men of God that I can turn to in need. We respect each other and offer a shoulder to lean upon with a nonjudgmental listening ear.

I stood looking out at over three hundred women of mixed ages and cultures at that seminar. They came armed with a long bucket list of questions, but as is typical, they really wanted to have one main subject answered. "Most men are losers. How do I get a man to treat me with respect?" All the women nodded their heads and cried out, "Preach sister, preach!" I knew that they were expecting me to give then tips on how to manipulate men or share advice on how to understand their personalities and quirks. In the past, some audiences have asked me to discuss women's rights and other conferences have expected me to discuss the bait in the box of dating tricks.

At the end of the day, we all know the *Catch me if you can* game. Magazines are devoted to giving us all the tip bits of trapping a man or woman with our looks. Therefore, the first thing I always caution when speaking about relationships is to ignore the advice columnists and authors that trot out any advice that is manipulative in nature. Their emphasis is on using your external bodies as bait, which we all know fades quickly with time and can transform owing to pregnancy, illness or a tragic accident.

What we have to understand when we are wishing to attract a mate, is that the key is not necessarily something they can visibly grab hold of in a tangible away like a lacy bra, short skirt, revealing top or a pair of high-heeled shoes. When you ask a man, why he chose a particular woman, more often than not he will say he was attracted to her smile or her confident laugh. The most common answer I hear from men is, "There was just something different and magical about her that I can't explain."

The attendees at the seminar were Christian women of all ages, which I always love. The mature ones always have such great wisdom to share with the younger ones. "Sisters, do you pray to be deeply loved, respected, desired, hungered for and adored? Do you wish for a man to respect you like a queen, and value you as a precious gift from God. Amen?" I said boldly.

"Yes, Amen!" came the loud cheers from the audience.

"Guess what sisters, our brothers pray for the exact same thing from you. If a woman wants her man to treat her with respect, she has to *give* him something to respect."

The light of reality switched on in the room. "Furthermore sisters, disrespecting him by faking headaches, or not keeping yourself clean and sweet, are no excuse unless you are genuinely sick or you feel abused. If this is the case, the former (being ill) is of course a matter of discretion and prayer. The latter (abuse) requires counseling or serious intervention. For the purposes of this seminar, I am not referring to either case, but targeting it more towards you healthy women who desire to be part of a significant couple."

The women nodded their heads in agreement and the more mature ones nudged each other and said, "Uh-huh, she's right."

"So, how do we attract and keep a good man and yet not lose who we are in the process?" I asked rhetorically. Several hundred pairs of eyes stared at me with excitement.

"We can begin the process by dressing immaculately and respectfully. Sadly today sisters, many women even go into God's house wearing jeans, T-shirts, extremely short skirts with low cut tops and basically attired for a day out at *Sea World*, rather to praise our father and partake in the holy ceremony. This does not attract a man of God. He wants to see a refined woman who understands that she is in God's house."

They cheered in agreement. I told them that I had stood and watched a woman verbally cuss out her husband for gawping at one of these women. Yet no man is blind, and if his woman is unable, unwilling or unkempt, he is not going to have respect or desire for her either.

"Let me be clear sisters," I continued. "It is not about the purchase price of an outfit that is significant. Rather, a woman who presents herself to God and to the public in clean, modest, respectful, attractive and decent apparel will attract the kind of man that will always honor and respect her. Men are visual beings, and let us not fool ourselves that this is an inaccurate statement or observation. It is not only a biological fact, but a spiritual reference too. One only has to read the Song of Solomon, also known as *The Song of Songs* in the Word, to note how inward and outward beauty is prized in a woman and in the Church."

I asked one of the women to come and read from the *Song of Solomon*. You could have heard a pin drop in the room.

"Behold, thou art fair, my love; behold, thou art fair; thou hast doves' eyes within thy locks: thy hair is as a flock of goats that appear from mount Gilead. Thy teeth are like a flock of sheep that are even shorn, which came up from the washing. Whereof every one bears twins and none is barren among them. Thy lips are like a thread of scarlet, and thy speech is comely: thy temples are like a piece of a pomegranate within thy locks. Thy neck is like the tower of David builded for an armory, whereon there hang a thousand bucklers, all shields of mighty men. Thy two breasts are like two young roes that are twins, which feed among the lilies. Until the daybreak and the shadows flee away, I will get me to the mountain of myrrh, and to the hill of frankincense. Thou art all fair, my love; there is no spot in thee."

I waited a minute to let the words sink in, before continuing with my advice.

"I know hundreds of gentlemen from many different cultures. There is not much difference, sisters, in their ways, hopes, needs, dreams, desires, tastes and rights. Equally, I know hundreds of girls, young women and elders. As a woman myself, I know what I desire in a future husband, and I know what I can bring to the table based on the way my parents raised me with their forty-eight years of a happy marriage under their belt."

I had their attention.

"We all want to be proud of our mate. I would hope that we would all want to go to our Father in such a way that it shows him great reverence, respect and decency. We heard from the verses read which qualities are prized. Can anybody tell me which significant words stood out?"

The women began to shout out words that they had heard and understood from the passage. These words included clean, luscious, strong, elegant and appealing.

"Excellent," I praised them. "Let's dig deeper sisters and see how we can show our man respect."

"Please open your Bibles to the book of *Titus* 2: 1-5 'But as for you, teach what accords with sound doctrine. Older men are to be sober-minded, dignified, self-controlled, sound in faith, in love, and in steadfastness. Older women likewise are to be reverent in behavior, not slanderers or slaves to much wine. They are to teach what is good, and so train the young women to love their husbands and children, to be self-controlled, pure, working at home, kind, and submissive to their own husbands, that the word of God may not be reviled.'

Sisters, decent men value a woman who has her life in order. Who wants to be with anybody who cusses, complains and slops around with a sense of entitlement, or worse still, a complete lacking is self-confidence? A man wants his home to be a peaceful place from which to leave and return to each day. There is nothing much worse for a man than to come home, or go out socially with a woman who cannot hold her liquor, or her tongue. No man is going to remain in a relationship, or be faithful to a woman, who constantly denies him intimate comfort and pleasure as a form of emotional manipulation. No man will remain with a woman who criticizes and belittles him on every single point and who gossips and slanders. No man desires to be with a woman who dresses inappropriately, either provocatively in public, or sloppily at home or who over extends the family budget with impulsive and unnecessary purchases. Nobody wishes to be with a person who has no time management skills or who criticizes friends and family. No decent man will tolerate a woman who constantly puts others and things before him, his needs and the welfare of the family, relationship and home."

The women all stood up and cheered in agreement. I wanted the point to hit home very strongly, so I asked them to sit down. Once seated, I repeated the last few words of advice loudly and very, very slowly. They stood again and cheered with recognition that what I was trying to instill within them was correct. I motioned for them to sit again.

"In order for a man to give respect to his woman sisters, she must give him the respect he deserves. In order for that to happen, he has to have something to respect in you. Men want a woman who is open to them physically, emotionally, spiritually and sexually. A true man of God will encourage his woman to fulfill her calling to God, and he will support her ministry, growth, health, nourishment, confidence and sense of womanhood with strength, loyalty, love, kindness and devotion. For a couple to respect each other, they must behave in a dignified and respectful way. To know that your opinion matters and that you are wholeheartedly trusted, gives you the confidence to live as Christ instructed."

The audience cheered even more loudly.

"Sisters," I continued, "Almighty God, plus a happy man, plus a happy woman equal a solid, stable and growing marriage and family. A solid family, plus a God fearing community equals a country that can survive anything that external forces may inflict."

Many of the women began to sing and dance. After a while, they were calmer and reseated.

"Treat yourselves and each other with respect, and remind yourselves often of what brought you together. Give the highest priority to the tenderness, gentleness and kindness that your relationship deserves. When frustration, difficulties and fear assail your relationship, as they threaten all relationships at one time or another, remember to focus on what is right between you, not only the part which seems wrong. In this way, you can ride out the storms when clouds hide the face of the sun in your lives, remembering that even if you lose sight of it for a moment, the sun is still there. And if each of you takes responsibility for the quality of your life together, it will be marked by abundance and delight, and blessed by our heavenly father eternally."

The singing and dancing continued for several minutes and everybody was praising the Lord.

Conclusion

It is human nature for some to profess or imagine that another person is either the problem or the solution to their own inadequacies.

It *is* spiritually appropriate to pray for the gift of a loving companion. However, self-preparation is also a crucial step in the process. We must be emotionally, physically, spiritually, financially and sexually whole before we can ever hope to bring a stranger into our life. We must learn to be still, calm and composed.

We all have expectations- many unrealistic. It is natural to feel disappointment when we discover something about a person, which reveals his or her story was a complete fabrication – that they are married when they had said they were single for instance. However, instead of taking that disappointment out on a prospective new mate, whether it is a man or a woman, we must develop dignity, integrity and a healthy realization that we are all separate human beings and cannot be tarred with the same brush.

There is great strength in composure. Learning to contain ones anger, and then to diffuse it with loving thoughts, gives you an inner power and strength that few can claim in their own lives and beings. This strength is very attractive to the opposite sex, especially the more mature in age. There is an appropriate time to be bold. There is the opportune moment to argue ones case. There is wisdom in ignoring false accusations and lies. Thus, it is a strong person who can radiate humility and who perfectly selects the temperament and action best suited for each occurrence. Inward peace is clear to see on the outside. Strength is not something you necessarily show to others verbally or physically and gentleness (which is never weak) is an appealing trait.

The best advice to offer you is to encourage sincere prayer in your search for the perfect companion. What qualities do you want in your future husband or wife? What attributes do you have to give them?

Consider where you meet this person and remember that it is a *reflection* of who they are. If it is in a club, a strip joint, a bar, a rowdy party or a place that is filthy and loud, please do not complain when they betray, lie and continue in that style after you have hooked up. You may feel that once you are together, that lifestyle is no longer necessary. However, I think you will more likely find that the established habit will continue whether you like it or not. If you do, so be it. If you do not, prepare to have your heart broken. If a married person chases after you, please do not be shocked when they betray you at some point in the future. I assure you, they will treat you in the exact same way because the flaw is not with their partner and nor will it be with you. If you want a lazy unkempt partner, go to where they hang out. If you want to be mistreated, go to where women are degraded.

However, if you want a decent, loyal, loving, caring husband or wife, look within your church or community where decent people attend respectable events. The litmus test of all examinations is this: watch how a perspective mate treats children, old people and animals and listen to how they talk about an ex-spouse, significant other and their family members. This will show you exactly how he or she will treat you after the honeymoon period is over.

Yes, we all know about the hidden texts and phone calls with whispered voices in the middle of the night; but I have always found that if a person is short tempered, harsh, indifferent or creepily obsessed, I know to walk away very, very fast!

Lesson 19: "Goodbye Mum!"

I will never forget waking up that morning in September 1998, and feeling as though, the dream that I had just experienced was in fact a reality. I knew that something very bad was about to happen to my mother. Now that I was back on my feet and recovering well, mum decided to move to the south of England to live within a few minutes' walk from my sister and her grandchildren. The relocation had gone smoothly and she was living in a modest home in a town that she had always loved and where we had spent many summers sailing at the Isle of Weight or Lymington. Whilst walking one afternoon, mum collided with a teenager on his skateboard, which resulted in her nose being broken. After looking at the photographs, she sent to me via snail mail, I was shocked to notice that she resembled a boxer after several rounds in the ring. I was so worried about her.

I woke from this dream knowing that I had to drive to her home immediately. It did not even occur to me to call ahead of time, for the dream had been so vivid. God had told me that this gift of vision would be one of the many ways he would communicate with me on earth and like Joseph or Jacob, my dreams and visions were so obvious that I never had to sit wondering what the symbols meant - I knew.

The drive took me close to six hours and when I walked into the kitchen mum was standing over the sink vomiting blood. I cannot recall my mother ever being seriously ill in her life. She was the kind of dignified person who never complained about anything. Her personality was typically British which meant bravely soldiering on to the end. She was gravely ill now and could not even look up for a moment to ask me why I was standing there in her home.

When she had finished heaving, I put a coat around her and took her immediately to the hospital. They examined her and requested us to come back the next day for tests. I can be a very tough cookie and you must never cross me when it comes to my family or friends. I simply do not take "No," for an answer. It is not my nature to shrug my shoulder and accept a mediocre response. Furthermore, I am a very protective and tenacious woman who has the intelligence to match you on most levels of education. I am strong and although *immensely* compassionate and loving, I will not stand by and watch a loved one suffer or my Lord mocked.

I stuck my heels firmly in the ground and insisted they do the tests right there and then. I refused to listen to their pathetic excuses and reminded them who my family was. It is amazing how name-dropping can help sometimes. I rarely use my connections, but if I have to – I do and I make no apologies for fighting for what I know to be true or for what I need.

Within an hour, the tests came back with the prognosis of esophageal cancer. I will never forget that moment. My sister stood crying and I tried to hide my sense of shock and sadness. Immediately, my two concerns were how mum was feeling and what the best strategy would be to beat this disease. Mum was completely calm. We asked the usual questions about treatment options and we requested the doctors to be candid. I insisted on a second opinion. Although I sensed that the prognosis would be identical to the first one, I still wanted to ensure that *we* were fully aware of the nature of the beast.

Now I say "We," because illness is a team effort and cancer, as with all potentially terminal diseases, requires the family to be on the same page. We spent the next few days researching, talking and praying. I told mum that at the end of the day, this was her illness and the decision as to what treatment she wanted, was up to her. I promised her that we would give her one hundred percent of ourselves and whatever she needed, she would have it immediately. The following week, after days of agonizing discussions with private specialists and administrators, mum announced that she did not want to go through the free national health service (which is grossly inadequate) and had chosen palliative care. She had asked the specialists what the treatments would cost and when they gave her the estimate, which was obscenely expensive, she turned to me as said that she could not afford it.

I was completely unprepared for mum's decision to die. I assured her that I had the necessary funds. I told her that she had nothing to worry about in terms of the cost for treatment. I gently reminded her that she was to choose the treatment she felt she could handle in order for us to get this cancer into remission. Mum was in her seventies and could not comprehend the thought of radiation, surgery and chemotherapy she nervously admitted.

"I'm not like you Christine," she said. "You can cope with pain. I cannot." I explained to her that without it, unless there was a miracle, she would die. Again, she looked at the specialists and said she was choosing palliative care with the understanding that this option would lead to her eventual death.

"How long do I have Doctor?" she quietly asked.

"I would say about three months," was the doctor's reply. I all but collapsed. My dream had prepared me for a serious problem, but I never imagined it meant that mum was about to die. My mother asked the doctor to explain what was going to happen on a practical level and he explained the medical care that she would receive. Unexpectedly, he dropped the price of this care on her lap again with an emphasis that if she chose not to accept the pain relief, it would be cheaper.

I was outraged. It was an unprofessional and cruel announcement that was not acceptable to me and I immediately stood up and literally pulled the doctor outside by his arm. I firmly told him that I would be paying all the bills. I reiterated that his job was to ensure her comfort and that I would settle the financial aspect. I insisted on being updated regularly and that no procedure would be done without my knowledge and understanding of the side effects to each drug given. The doctor began to tell me how much the treatment could escalate and inferred that I might not have the significant funds available. I pointed out that the financial aspect was between the administration department and me, and that I would sell all my assets if necessary.

Mum often asked about her account. I lied to her. I admit it and I make no apologies to anybody. I did what I had to do and sold whatever was required - End of story.

Mum actually lived for ten months, and it was one of the most precious ten months of my life. We went from being mother and daughter to very close, dear friends. I moved in with her to share in that experience and I did my best to help nurse her twenty-four hours a day. As the cancer tumor grew in size, she was no longer able to eat, but did enjoy watching every single cookery show known to man on TV. Towards the end, she slept a great deal and I used to rest my head on her lap as she dozed. I did not sleep in a bed the entire time I was with her. She was afraid that the cancer was going to be painful and so I would sit with my hands upon her chest area. She did not experience any pain until a few days before her death.

Most days I was able to care for her at home. However, at one point, she needed to go to hospital for a few days to implant a stent to help her swallow fluids. When I visited the next morning after surgery, I found her shivering with cold and neglect. I was so angry that I checked her out, took her home and arranged for private care.

We knew that she would need specialized care towards the end and my sister and I did the rounds of the hospices. We found a truly wonderful one and mum began to go there a couple of days each week. It was good for her as this meant that she was mixing with others who were sharing in her experience themselves and they laughed and had fun. Towards the end, I drove her to see friends, as she wanted to say "Goodbye," to them. It was very emotional to be honest with you and I was so proud of her bravery and willingness to accept the situation with dignity. Her friends clearly felt awkward at first, but mum told them not to be sad and reassured them that they would reunite in heaven. Many of them were relieved to know that I was caring for her and I did my best to remain calm and cheerful and disguise my sadness and fear.

A few days before her death she asked me to sit down and plan her funeral together. I remained as focused as possible for I knew that this was very important to her. Mum's faith was everything and as I had always felt so guilty over the way my father had died and how out of control his funeral had been, I wanted this to be perfect. She had specific music, hymns and messages that she wanted played and conveyed and we drew up an itemized list. Once completed, she asked me to take her to the ocean. From there she wanted to go shopping. God bless her, she could hardly walk, and I asked her specifically what shops she wanted to go into.

"I wish to buy my burial clothes Christine and I need you to help me do that," she said. I was in awe of her bravery!

I stopped in the hospice to borrow a wheelchair. I was able to carry her around the home, but I needed something more reliable to maneuver her around the shops. My mother was a courageous, poised and dignified woman to the last. She chose a beautiful cream lacy blouse with a burgundy paisley skirt, brown stockings, cream gloves and brown shoes that enhanced the entire ensemble. We went into another store where she chose two purses; one was brown and the other was gold. She confessed with amusement that she had always wanted a golden purse. Her intent was to enjoy it to her last breath, at which time she wanted me to accept it as a gift from her.

Sitting in the car smiling at her purchases, she turned to me, took my hand and whispered, "I'm ready now."

Mum became very ill at the hospice the following morning, so they decided to keep her in observation for a few days. When I visited her, she said to me, "You said that if I wanted a last wish I could have it."

I nodded my head and tenderly said, "Mum, you can have absolutely anything. I will get it!"

She looked me straight in the eye and said, "I want to hold a new born lamb please."

I was stunned as that was not something that I had anticipated, although I knew the symbolic meaning of Jesus being the shepherd, with us being his sheep. Mum had always spoken of that image which comforted her. The hospice policy did not even allow for pet dogs, least of all a sheep. I gave her the thumbs up and left.

Sitting in the car outside, I prayed that I could fulfill this last wish. With a farm in mind, I drove to talk to the farmer. Mum had wanted a lamb, and a lamb she was going to have. I explained to the elderly farmer that my mother was dying and that her last wish was to hold a lamb. I asked him if he would very kindly lend me one of his for a couple of hours and I promised to return it in one piece. He looked very skeptical and hesitant. It is amazing what the sight of a bunch of crisp green notes can do to change a person's mind.

As my father used to say, "Everything has a price. You just have to keep presenting money until the limit is agreed."

I picked a lamb and proceeded to take it back to the hospice. I ran inside, opened the window, ran back to the car and climbed through the window with the said creature under my arm. Mum giggled aloud.

The lamb was not happy. In fact, it was so unhappy that it began squirm and *bleat* – loudly. I could hear somebody coming. I threw a blanket over the lamb's body and when the door opened, I went into one the best animal impressions you have ever heard in your life. I was so convincing, you would have almost sworn that a real life sheep was sitting on mum's lap. I winked at mum and bleated. She told the doctor that I had always been a comedian and quite adept at impersonations. Shaking his head and laughing, he left.

I removed the blanket and the lamb blinked his eyes and shook his head. "*Shhh,*" I said pointing my finger at it.

I asked mum why having this lamb to hold today was so important and she began to recite the twenty-third Psalm. Once she had tearfully recited her favorite verses she looked at me and said, "Christine, I am a sheep of the good Shepherd. He knows me by name and I am his. I am going to live with him very soon. I wanted to hold a lamb and prepare myself. I love Jesus!"

"I understand mum," I assured her. "I love him too and I know he will welcome you home and you will live with him in his house forever."

I opened the window, climbed out clutching the lamb under my arm and returned to the farm. I told him that he had made my mother very happy and that I was so grateful for his trust in me. He told me that he had thought about what I had said and proceeded to ask me many questions about the Christian faith. Suffice to say, within an hour, he had given his life to Christ. Amen.

Mum seemed significantly energized after holding the lamb. I was unaware that this can often happen towards the end when a patient appears to go into a state of renewed energy. This state of significant renewal is temporary though in a terminally ill patient.

I was the European financial director for a Native American Indian corporation based on the Navajo Nation in Arizona, USA at the time. My responsibilities included attending international meetings with heads of state, scientists and corporate investors. I was responsible for securing multi-million dollars to construct institutions and programs within the 585 federally recognized Native American Indian nations. I also attended tribal councils and assisted in mediation between Indian and non-Indian authorities. I briefed my chairperson on mum's condition.

One morning, I received an urgent call from him to fly to New Mexico in the United States, to mediate in a serious tribal issue. My company insisted I fly immediately and as my sister did not feel able to care for mum in my absence, I had to trust in a recommended nursing home to care for her over the next four days. That was my biggest mistake, which I deeply regret. I flew to America when I should have stayed with mum.

In-between tribal meetings I called the nursing home to hear that mum's health had begun to deteriorate. I told my boss that I was immediately flying back to England. Although he understood the urgency of my situation, he pointed out that I had a responsibility to the positive outcome of the situation at work. I was outraged at his insensitivity and refused to give this dispute priority over my mother or son. I pointed out that they had negotiated perfectly well without me in the past and that nothing was more important to me than my family.

The ten-hour flight back to London seemed particularly laborious and with each passing hour, I felt great sadness. When I arrived at Heathrow airport there was an over the speaker announcement for me. I found my way to the customer service booth who handed me the message. It asked me to call my employer urgently. I was almost relieved to hear it was not a fatal message about mum. I duly telephoned them. They insisted that I needed to get back to America on the next flight. My principal reminded me of my professional responsibilities and added that being sentimental and emotional was a sign of weakness. To say I was angry would be a gross understatement and what I said is unrepeatable in polite company. They had the gall to make me choose between the long-term benefits of my job over the short-term life of my mother. When the conversation ended, I had duly resigned. One of my clients had come to the airport to meet me and drive me to the nursing home.

I will never forget walking into her room that Thursday morning on June 24, 1999. Mum was slumped to the side of a decrepit chair and sitting in her urine stained clothes. She was cold to the touch and so weak that she was unable to look at me. It is rare for me to get very angry, but seeing this sight infuriated me. I wanted to transfer her to the hospice immediately. They had always cared for her in a kind and professional manner. However, mum was too weak to be moved in any significant way. My sister had not been particularly active in mum's care as she had her family to care for. I called her to the hospital and said we had to make decisions together as a family.

The first thing I needed to do was to get her into bed and into a comfortable position. After gently picking her up in my arms and carrying her to the bed, I tenderly placed her between the sheets. She looked at me with such gratitude. I lovingly washed her and changed her clothes and although the nursing staff fought me all the way, they soon came to realize that I was very serious when I said, "I'll pay you whatever you need for Mum to stay here, but only I will care for her. Beyond the legal things that you have to do with your tests, if I need your help, I will ask you."

I called friends and family to visit, as I knew these were the last few hours of her life. Mum looked at me with tears in her eyes and whispered, "Please don't leave me to die alone." I looked into her beautiful blue eyes, cupped her face with my soft hands and said, "Mum, I love you. I promise that I will not leave you for a second. I will sit here and hold you to the end!"

I did not eat, drink or sleep. I refused to be distracted and I did not want to have to go to the bathroom and leave her alone. I had faithfully promised to stay with her and that was what I intended to do. I had read many reports of loved ones dying after they had left the room briefly. I was not about to betray her request and show that kind of weakness.

On Friday, the pastor came and mum and I took communion with him. It meant a great deal to her. My son was now ten years old and during the entire decline of mum's health, I was careful to ensure that he understood what was happening to his grandmother. After what had happened to me all those years previously with my grandmother's death, I was not about to let the same thing happen to him. Mum and Geoff had always shared a strong and loving bond. Considering his tender age, Geoff was so brave. I took his little hand and calmly explained that this was the last time he was going to see his granny alive. We had already talked about death and heaven, so he somewhat understood. I asked him to come up to her, hold her hand, look into her eyes and thank her for everything she had done for him in his life. I encouraged him to tell her that he loved her. I reassured him that she was completely aware of him, but with being so weak, her ability to respond was limited.

He sat next to her and did just that and more. I was so proud of him. After a while, he kissed her and said, "Granny, I know you will see Jesus soon. Will you say hello to him from me?" Such is the innocence of a child. My son asked me if we could take a picture together so that he would always have it. Mum did her best to smile God bless her.

The last two verbal things she said to me just before slipping into unconsciousness was, "Forgive me. Thank you."

"There is nothing to forgive or thank me for mum," I replied.

"I'm sorry," and she was gone. Her breathing pattern transformed from a series of rapid gasping breaths, which were fewer in duration, to a raspy tone from her throat that audibly rattled for a few hours. I had never watched anybody die. One minute I thought she had passed away and then she would take a breath.

At six o'clock on Monday evening, the doctor announced her end was imminent as she was unresponsive to all the tests. In this deep state of unconsciousness, she would soon succumb to death. I sat holding her in my arms whilst my sister stood at the end of the bed. The room was almost silent and we had closed the curtains.

Mum began to stir and gently awaken. I thought I had to be dreaming, but I realized this was a fact. She turned that frail body slowly around and looked right in my eyes. Her expression was of pure love and I could clearly see, inwardly feel and sense that she was saying, "I love you."

"Oh mum," I whispered in response. "I love you too. Thank you for all you have done for me. Now go and be with dad and God in heaven."

I kissed her forehead and held her as tight as I dare. Her frail body slightly pulled away from my arms, turned over and repositioned itself on the left side. She inhaled one last breath of air, sighed and exhaled slowly for the very last time.

Peacefulness lingered in the room for a few minutes. It reminded me of the day I had held my newborn son at my breast, observing his breathing and sensing the life coursing through his tiny veins. Life and death fills you with the same sense of awe. I prayed for my mother's safe passage to heaven knowing that it would be even more beautiful than she could ever have imagined.

It was hard to leave her in order for the staff to complete their duties and when we came back into the room, it did not look like mum lying there. Later, as I walked into her home knowing she would never return there, I felt completely disjointed and sad. Every morning for the next few days, I visited her at the funeral home. I know they found it unconventional for a loved one to visit so often, but I did not care. Respecting her body was of paramount importance to me. Perhaps it was my way of dealing with this huge loss in my life. Looking at her body was like staring at a mannequin. I had never seen a dead body before and as is my way, I wanted to observe it and meditate upon the process.

We began the laborious task of cleaning up and selling the home and contents. These days were one long blur of people coming and going. I was also in a situation of dealing with my own pending marriage in America, which I had put off due to my mother's sudden illness. It was all coming to a head and I felt stressed with all the decisions that required immediate answers. I had not slept properly in months and my mind was racing. I struggled over what to say to my son with regard to moving to America and there was little time for me to pray, meditate or consider my future.

Hundreds attended the memorial service in the south of England. I was so proud of my son for despite his tender age, he insisted on greeting each mourner with a shake of the hand and a cheerful "Welcome!" as they paraded in and out of the church. He even walked by my side behind the coffin. After the service, we followed the hearse up to the north of England, which took several hours. The funeral was the following morning in the idyllic graveyard at St. Mary's Church. Mum's coffin was to be above my father's in the family plot. As foolish as this is going to sound, I had never seen inside a grave before and I admit that I was somewhat afraid, as dad had been in the ground for sixteen years. I was not sure if we would see my father's skeleton and rather than ask others what to expect, I stood hesitantly by the gravesite. Much to my relief, there was to be a layer of dirt between the coffins.

Since her death, I had not shed a tear. Many of my close friends were there to support me and pay their respects to my mother and family, including Gareth and my mentor and best friend Jeff Boxen. Another very dear and close friend, Rod Tyson, held me up. Without them, there is no way I would have had the strength to deal with seeing my Mum's coffin lowered into the ground. I cannot describe that moment to you – It was horrific. You may have gone through this yourself, thus you will know what I am talking about when I say it feels frighteningly final.

There were gravediggers standing nearby like vultures. They had removed their shirts and were whistling. My sister and other family members left the gravesite and Jeff Boxen and I stood there silently observing the tragic scene. The gravediggers asked us how long we were going to be, as they needed to fill in the grave. As they came closer, I insisted that they put on their shirts, stop whistling and have some semblance of decency and decorum. They mumbled profanities that made Jeff gasp with anger. I grabbed their shovels and refused to allow them near.

"If you refuse to do this sacred ceremony with respect, then go!" I shouted. "I will bury my mother myself!" I added. They shrugged their shoulders apparently and walked off to smoke a cigarette.

After an hour or so, the grave was almost full. Jeff encouraged me to stop punishing myself in this way, for my hands were bleeding and my clothes were torn. He gently persuaded me to allow the men who had now dressed themselves, to finish the job. They had apparently been observing this scene and Jeff later told me that they had gone from being angry to remorseful. The pastor of the church had come down to comfort me and together with Jeff, dealt with the cries and wails from the deepest depths of my soul. To this day, I cannot tell you how I got from the graveyard to my home in the south of England. I honestly do not remember.

That was the last time that I ever saw my family. As the grave of my parents was finally secure, the English chapter of my book was complete. Every year, on the anniversary of mum's death, my friends Jeff Boxen and Rod Tyson visited my parent's grave and placed flowers upon it before taking and sending me pictures of them paying their respects.

Prior to my mother's death, I had found the gravesite of my beloved grandmother. It had been a difficult search and her burial place was nestled between two marked graves. Tragically, there was no stone marking her identity, which I thought was odd. I asked my mother if I could please arrange for a dignified headstone, but she vehemently refused. When I pressed for a logical reason she said, "My mother was at home the day you were abused. Now let it go!" I was speechless for mum never expressed anger and had never discussed that incident with me until that moment. I sighed - everything it seemed in my childhood was either a mystery or a secret.

With Jeff's death in early 2014, I lost another part of my life that had so much meaning and value. This last anniversary in 2014 meant no pictures from him at my parent's resting place.

Rather than focusing too much attention on their grave, I have consciously told myself that their essence is alive in one of the rooms in God's mansion.

Conclusion

I shared this personal story with you as openly as I possibly could, in order for you to think about your own lives and that of your precious family. We cannot avoid death – it is a part of life.

It is a subject that people feel uncomfortable discussing and yet if you can be honest, you can find great comfort in these days. There are many who face the sadness of a loved one dying suddenly. There was no opportunity for them to say "Thank you, I love you and goodbye." For these grieving people, there is a void. Time does not heal their wounds, especially if their loved one was murdered or committed suicide with no letter or explanation as to why they felt the need to end what is a sacred gift – the present of life on earth.

My wisdom in this matter includes encouraging you to please make a last *Will* or *Testament* and be compassionate in it. It is deeply damaging when people use this legal document to hurt their loved ones with deliberate omissions and shocking secrets. We are not animals; we are human beings. Thus, there is no reason to cause unnecessary burdens, which emotionally and financially destroy others. It is just as damaging to leave a family with no written instructions. This simply serves to cause months and sometimes years of probate and other legal proceedings that can result in a family losing their home. Even if you believe that you have nothing of value to leave the world, at least write that in a *Will* as this will ensure a much smoother transition for loved ones after you have gone.

You do not have to go through death alone and I urge you to accept the help of hospice. If you have read my lesson on death, then you will know that your Guardian Angel will be with you and he or she will accompany you to heaven.

You are God's child and I promise you that he will welcome you home if you have embraced him. Take comfort in that and God bless you.

Lesson 20: "Off we go!"

God had shown me at the gates of heaven that I would move to North America to fulfill the work that I had been created to do. It sounds simple enough I guess. Yet until one comes face to face with that destiny, one does not really comprehend the required monumental changes and plans that precede such a *gigantic* relocation. For years, I had wondered how this was ever going to be possible. I was still so ill after the illness. God had shown me that I would be living and studying with Native American Indians at first, but if you were to be told that, would you even know how that was possible? I certainly did not. God moves in mysterious ways....

During recovery from the meningitis, my rehabilitation team had sent me on courses to learn computer skills. I was surfing the net one day, when I found myself looking at chat rooms. Ironically, I had never been into one before, and I have never been into one since. There was one room in particular that caught my interest. It had the group title of *Native Americans*.

Within a few weeks, I was talking to an Osage Sioux attorney, who was the Chairman of a major humanitarian project. He patiently answered all my stereotype style questions, which included exposing my sheer ignorance of his people. When we think of Native American Indians in Europe, we romantically imagine that they still live in the ways of pre nineteen hundred. The movies *Last of the Mohicans* and *Dances with Wolves,* give us the romantic impression of how these amazing tribal people lived for centuries. I was no different from the vast majority of people who honestly thought their ways remained intact. As I began to read the history of the battles of *Little Big Horn* and *Wounded Knee,* I found plenty of Native Americans to answer my questions, including my new Osage Sioux friend and his family.

Over time, our conversations led to serious discussions about this company and its projects. My connections in the financial world in

England were beneficial. This Company represented all 585 federally recognized sovereign nations by funding tourism awareness, health, science, agriculture, housing and a myriad of other essential programs, to which many of the tribal leaders had inadequate access. I received an invitation to meet with the organization at their headquarters. I declined at that point in time because my walking was still wobbly, and although the seizures had all but disappeared, I did not feel strong enough to fly to a foreign country yet.

Over the course of the next twelve months, we had daily discussions about the projects and I began to reach out to people that I knew who I felt might wish to help the tribal people. Eventually in 1997, I felt well enough to travel to America to meet with the directors of this organization. I spent the next three weeks touring various sovereign nations including the Hopi, White Mountain Apache, Cherokee, Hualapai, Ak-Chin, Zuni, and the Navajo. To say that this was a fascinating experience would be a gross understatement. I found everybody to be most generous and kind, but I can say with all honesty, that I was not prepared for some of the things I discovered; including the alcohol and drug addiction problems, domestic violence and poverty. I was unaccustomed to seeing such things and it was heart wrenching.

I had never faced witchcraft either and I nervously laughed when warned before one particular meeting not to leave even a strand of my hair in a particular village. My host met that laugh with an angry look and advised me that if I ignored him, my carelessness could lead to my death. I could see that he was not jesting and part of me wondered what I had agreed to join.

I was as respectful as it is possible to be and I saw this tour as one of those rare opportunities in life that few get to experience. I stayed with native elders who were over a hundred years old. I slept under the stars with them, in the stunningly beautiful Grand Canyon and Monument Valley in Arizona. I attended daily briefings where we discussed the 585 nations with tribal leaders and benefactors. I left America as their European financial director.

As promised, Jeff Boxen had sent me on many training courses throughout Europe. I developed a good sense for selling and business. With his mentoring, I had grown a vast network of entrepreneurs who often worked with me on franchising ventures around the world. I was accustomed to western style business but completely "Wet behind the ears," as they say, in tribal knowledge, customs and culture.

During one final meeting where we sat for many hours waiting for it to begin, I leaned over to my new employer and asked him when the meeting was to commence. Nobody had arrived except us. He pointed out to me that this was my first lesson in, "Indian time." He told me that the meeting would begin sometime between sunrise and sunset within this full moon cycle. I laughed! I honestly thought he was joking. This was like a scene out of the movies. He was serious and sternly reminded me to take his lead and not to ever think that life here was like the ways of the white man in England. I inquired as to how many people were attending the meeting and was met with a, "Whoever comes – comes."

This was my first major lesson in Indian business and tribal politics. I quickly learned to keep all comments to myself. They had told me to keep my return date open and I was beginning to understand the wisdom in that advice. One learns in Indian country to let things flow. It would be a hard habit to break as meetings back home started punctually. In fact, it was drummed into me that it was far better to be an hour early, than to be a minute late in England. I was unaccustomed to sitting around waiting for people to arrive, but I wanted to be respectful and open-minded, as I felt so honored to be part of these historical discussions.

I worked diligently and learned advanced business practices including tribal law, negotiation and public policy. For several years, I commuted between London, England and the United States on a frequent basis, attending meetings and securing significant funding for the myriad of projects under my jurisdiction.

During one of these tribal meetings, I met a powerful chief and medicine man from the Hopi Nation, (the oldest tribe in the United States). With every subsequent meeting, our relationship deepened and he felt very strongly that our union was a fulfillment of prophecy and that we should be husband and wife. My employer and future husband had major differences (a gross understatement) based upon personal and tribal issues. It became very uncomfortable. This is part of my life is private as I respect the nations too much to disclose anything of what I saw and experienced. There are far too many people willing to betray the trust of these dignified people by sharing things that are sacred and private. I am not one of those traitors. I learned their lessons well and gratefully received many blessings.

When my future husband approached my family for my hand in marriage, they all agreed with the exception of my mother who was very worried at first. Several years before, I had been romantically involved with a man who, despite my disabilities, wanted to marry me. I thought I knew him and I was confident he loved me very much. I discovered on our wedding day at the altar that he had another woman to whom he is now married. The public humiliation had been difficult to recover from and my mother was hesitant to see another man mistreat me. Eventually, my fiancé had won my mother's heart and she was excited to know that I was going to stand with a *great leader* and help his people to fulfill all the well-known historical promises and prophecies of their tribe throughout the world.

The most important person that I had to consider when making the decision to move to America was my son. Since my illness and our divorce, Geoff's father and I shared legal custody. He lived primarily with his father, but we saw each other often. It is one thing to make that agonizing choice when one is disabled and living in the same country, it is an entirely different story when one is considering relocating. I knew that God wanted me to do this and I prayed that he would guide my steps and protect the relationship I had with my child.

With the news that mum was dying of cancer, I told my fiancé that there was absolutely no way that I could or would relocate at this time. Thankfully, he was incredibly supportive. My mother loved him very much. He would send her daily words of encouragement and he promised her, my son and family that he would protect and love me with his life.

A few days after we had buried mum, I faced the agonizing moment of kissing my son, "Goodbye." It was horrendous. Thank God for planes, phones, computers and mail. Over the years, we have maintained an awesome relationship and have spent wonderful vacations together back home and here in America.

In hindsight, rather than marrying so soon after mum's death, I should have waited a year to give myself time to mourn. When I reflect upon this time, I wonder why I agreed to such a monumental event at a time when I was distraught. It was foolish of me. However, I loved my husband very much. He was an inspirational leader, who I deeply admired and he felt that our marriage would give me stability. Sadly, it was brief which only served to make me feel even less secure and more alone. There were too many problems, including another woman who attacked me and left me for dead. I became deathly ill and my family and me were attacked with witchcraft which rendered us all physically, emotionally and spiritually weak. When I was finally able to leave the Nation, I left far worse off in many ways and wandered around dazed, injured and desperate for somebody to show me mercy. I was too ashamed to return to England and frankly, given the way I looked, I knew that to return would have created a major diplomatic incident. I was also aware that God wanted me to remain in the United States of America.

Just before I left the Reservation, I had spent time in prayer. Native American medicine men had taught me how to enter into a deep meditative state and to go into the wilderness to seek wisdom and visions in the confines of nature. God had instructed me to study other faiths and ways, but had warned me that if this took me off my path, he would send me signs or move me. He removed me from the Nation abruptly. The night before I left, I was sitting on one of the mesas meditating. My Guardian Angel appeared to me, surrounded by a bright light. By his side was the dog that I had been helping to heal. He told me that it was time for me to leave and that the sadness and injuries would be healed. Furthermore, he assured me that thousands of people all over the world would now benefit from the next phase in my walk with God. He encouraged me to have faith and to pack my sacks with essential items.

I had come there with crates of belongings shipped from overseas and I left the Nation with a few black trash sacks of clothes. Frankly, I did not know where I was going as I took a truck and drove away. A few weeks previously, we had been visiting spiritual people in Sedona, Arizona. A woman there had given me her card and told me that if I ever needed help, I was to call her. Therefore, I did. I spent the next twelve months living and teaching at her seminary as well as studying for my doctorate in theology.

Conclusion

When one walks in the light of Christ, one must be prepared to travel where he guides. It takes *great* courage to have this level of faith and to walk in places that you can clearly feel are dark and foreboding. One must have the faith to know that if God leads you to a problem, he will lead you through it. Sometimes we cannot see the lessons ahead of us, nor can we possibly know what trials will meet us along the way. As one of God's sheep, we must be vigilant and awake. The wolf (Satan) is very hungry, and until he realizes that you are one of the shepherd's own, he will circle you and plan to grab and eat you at the earliest opportunity. Even when saved, you must remain focused on Jesus, for the wolf is ready to pounce. Our great Shepherd (whose voice we know and trust) stands there to protect his own.

As I have matured in years, I have seen this repeatedly. Few, particularly in the western world, will ever face the kind of things that I have. I say, "Thank God," for that. One might suppose that they are safe within the compounds of their four walled homes and free from the dangers of accidents, thieves and characters of ill repute. To a certain degree that might be true. However, life requires us to participate actively within it. The practical aspects of life involve shopping and work. Even a hermit has to eat!

Every day we read about cars, and even planes crashing into peoples' houses unexpectedly. Tornados, earthquakes, flash floods, avalanches, forest fires, hurricanes and tropical storms that destroy entire neighborhoods, hit with little notice. Then there are those who commit acts of burglary, rape, terrorism and murder; who stalk their victims' like a prowling hungry, snarling wolf. Who can see that evil coming? The answer is obvious - nobody.

So what should we do when a perceived opportunity appears? We must pray of course and use great wisdom and discernment. One must meditate upon whether it is God leading you to this or Satan. God *will* protect you if you are one of his sheep and he will not let you fall without being by your side.

In short, we must learn to walk by faith!

Lesson 21: Miracles happen!

I have said this many times throughout my life – God moves in mysterious ways! You can see on my original British passport that I was wearing bi-lateral hearing aids. The meningitis had caused profound hearing loss and without these amazing devices, I could not hear anything at all. The hospitals had performed a myriad of examinations including CT and MRI scans, auditory brain stem response to test nerve pathways in my brain to measure how well the nerve was helping me to hear and to track how fast sound travelled along this nerve.

I met with the audiologist. It was very disconcerting to sit wearing headphones waiting to click the device, which indicated when I could hear a sound. At one point, I wrote a note to the technician to ask her when the test was going to begin, to which she informed me that it had begun some ten minutes previously. My doctors had decided that I was a perfect candidate for a cochlea implant procedure. I was to have surgery later that year.

Whilst working with the Native Americans, I had studied with a few renowned medicine men who were devout Christians. Spiritual leaders from around the world, including a powerful Lama from Tibet, travelled to seek the wisdom of these great men. They had grown to respect me and often referred their people to come to learn meditation and to receive vision and wisdom from me. One of the elders came forward one evening and offered their services to help me. He said that the elders had met in council and had agreed that I was a special gift from almighty God and could benefit from a service of healing.

He and I spent several days in preparation, whilst others gathered things together for the healing ceremony. These days involved fasting of food and water, sitting in complete silence and prayer under the extreme heat of the sun, limited sleep and the partaking of certain herbs to cleanse my body of toxins.

I am not at liberty to discuss that sacred service where we asked almighty God to heal me. Suffice to say, four days later, the vast majority of my hearing had returned, the tinnitus had disappeared and I was no longer suffering with the dizziness, seizures or sickness. I walked out of that ceremony feeling strong and rejuvenated. It quite simply changed my life forever!

The Elders who helped me know who they are, and they know how grateful I will always be to them. They were a conduit for God to move through them to me. Their willingness to help me, and my faith to trust in them, gave me the opportunity to continue my journey through life, renewed and restored.

Conclusion

From the first word in Genesis, to the last word in Revelation, we learn about the miraculous powers of God on earth. Furthermore, Jesus Christ himself gave authority to his disciples and followers to pray in his name when they needed to perform acts that were beyond the average person's idea of, "Possible."

In John 5:1-15 you will read about a man who had been ill for thirty-eight years. He had lain beside a pool (known for its miraculous healing power) called Bethesda. Like others, this man trusted that the water contained something that would heal him of his condition if he could simply crawl into it. Without assistance though, he was unable to drag his body to the water when a person stirred it. Jesus asked him if he wanted healing and the man replied that he did want wellness but added that he was incapable of helping himself. Jesus told him to stand up as a healed man, take his bed, and go home. The man then found himself in trouble with the Jewish leaders. Since it was the Sabbath day, their traditional laws said that it was unlawful for him to carry his bed that day. The man said that he was doing as the man with obviously more power and authority told him. Jesus slipped away before the Jewish leaders could find him. However, later Jesus found the man in the Temple and gave him spiritual healing for his sins too.

In the Gospel of Marc, you will read about a deaf man brought to Jesus when he was with a great crowd. We do not know how long this man had been deaf or what had caused his disability. Jesus took the man aside and communicated with him. He indicated to the man that he understood the condition by touching his ears, spitting and touching his tongue. After looking up to heaven, which may have been a visual indication of who he was and where his power came from, Jesus said "Ephphatha," which is the Aramaic word meaning to open. Jesus opened this man's ears and freed his tongue and the Bible says the man spoke plainly. Beyond the miracle of restoring this man's hearing, I think it is important to emphasize that this change in the man's ability to communicate was significant. We do not know if this man had ever been able hear the language he was now speaking. Either way, his restored hearing and speech was a miracle.

Lesson 22: Knowledge

Faith is a personal adherence and submission of man to God who reveals himself through Jesus and the Holy Spirit. It involves acceptance of the intellect and desire to this self-realization. Faith is a supernatural gift from God and in order to believe, a person needs the interior help of the Holy Spirit. Believing is both a human act, (conscious and free) and a parochial act that unites us with God (Father) and the church (Mother). Furthermore, we believe everything of the world; including all things handed down from one generation to the next (including divinely written words) come from him to guide us. This faith is necessary if we are to continue to reside within his glorious mansion after death.

This faith draws us ever closer to God. Without faith in God, the essential values of life would surely perish. Fear of the unknown was unquestionably one of several factors in the origin of belief in religion. Another was the concern of bad fortune, pain and death. Human beings have always attempted to control such evils by defensive magic, which I never believed existed until I had lived amongst tribal people. However, an instinctive faith in life tempered man's awe of natural forces with the idea that protection, help, and even fear came through supplication, barter, or sacrifice.

I have spent decades studying this subject and learning tolerance and understanding towards why some believe certain things. My father told me more times that I can recount now, that if I wanted to be successful in life, I had to make the concerted effort to know what people believed in, practiced and utilized to motivate themselves every day. He felt strongly that one simply could not be successful in the business world if one was clueless to the spiritual makeup of that country. He would tell me that people would undoubtedly challenge my Christian faith as I matured and that I had better know my belief system inside out and upside down. He insisted that I study hard to be a good apologist and added that one must truly know the other's religion in order to have a credible answer that they could verify. My father insisted I study the religions of the world.

Therefore, my five decades on earth, have combined business and spirituality. I have studied theology and comparative religion to post-doctoral degree level with a keen interest in linguistics, science, psychology and philosophy. I have lived a disciplined life, and studied within many schools, seminaries and monasteries where rabbis, sensei, professors, old masters and elders have taught me from the Talmud, Torah, Kabbala, Bible and Dharma. I have learned philosophy, counseling, meditation, martial arts and reiki where I have humbly earned the titles of Grand Master and Rōshi.

After all these many years of dedicated training, God called me to be a Roman Catholic. As I pray with my rosary each day, I have finally found the perfect way for me to bring all the disciplines together to help me reflect upon the mysteries of our Lord.

Sadly, I have found that some people find my theological journey somewhat disconcerting. It seems acceptable to read of other religions for examination purposes, but taboo to actually live and learn within the communities. I believe that in this day of global travel, diverse communities and a workplace teaming with exciting energy and advancements by colleagues from diverse cultures, we should try to understand each other. Furthermore, I believe the walls of ignorance can disappear when we take the time to learn about our neighbors. We all want and need the same things from life and we are all part of the family of God.

To reassure the more conservative Christians; I did not actively engage in polytheism, nor did I ever turn from God or Lord Jesus for a second. Was I aware of practices that were uncomfortable to me? Yes. When I felt compromised, I graciously walked away. Whilst sitting in temples and monasteries, I simply imagined that I was in God's house and I turned my eyes and attention away from any idols within. I did not, (nor would I) pay homage to anything other than God, through our Savior.

My faith in God is one hundred percent solid. In fact, in anything, my faith is stronger now more than ever because I have enjoyed a unique relationship with him. I adore God and one only has to meet me to see how precious our Savior is to me. When you have been to the gates of heaven, I can assure you that you do not look at life in the same way as other people. Even with the best intention, some have vision, which is either cloudy or narrow. Others profess their faith through fear and ego. I have a humble and contrite heart that recognizes that every living thing is God's creation and I am bold to profess that Jesus Christ is my Lord.

Every human being I have met without exception wondered about why we are here and, where do we go after we have died. Furthermore, to one degree or another, most people think about the mind and soul and contemplate their role in the adventure we call, "Life."

Men, women and children spend much time contemplating the body, to the point of outward and inward obsession with clothing it, painting and piercing it to attract a mate, nourishing it, exercising it, prolonging its life span and making it an efficient vehicle for the years we are here on earth. We stare in mirrors and stand on scales willing our bodies to be heavier, lighter or slimmer and our muscles to be chiseled and strong. Some pray to be darker skinned whilst others apply ointments to be fair. Whereas some surgeries remove excess skin or digits, others implant lifesaving organs to extend the life of the patient on the surgical table. We all agree that caring for our bodies is as essential as putting oil, water and gas in the car. Both the car and body are vehicles, which we depend upon to take us from destination point to another.

It is not until the vast majority of us begin to lose our memory or face our (or a loved one's) imminent death, that we contemplate the two invisible components that make us human beings. I am referring to the mind and to the soul.

What does the Bible teach us about our mind? We learn not to *conform* to this world. Rather we should *transform* by the renewal of our mind and test to discern the will of God. He will always demonstrate what is good, acceptable and perfect. We are not encouraged to accept what others tell us like a bunch of lemmings. On the contrary, we are to push through dogma and hearsay, and develop our own relationship with God, based on what we discover to be the truth about him. Do we come to this realization instantly? No! We are encouraged to think about the goodness of life. We should dwell upon the greater things and release our attachment to negativity at all times, for otherwise, they grab a hold on us and we cannot see the glory of the Lord.

We are to keep our mind on him. By being in constant concentration on God, we achieve a state of peace, which others are naturally attracted to. A peaceful person instills a sense of respect and trust in others. One might easily notice a tyrant or a drama queen, who rants and raves and demands immediate attention. Goodness knows we fear terrorists and try to subdue dictators. We fear them, but we do not respect them. People confuse fear and respect. They are not the same. Leaders who have proven qualities that we can depend upon to guide us in all circumstances earn respect. They are calm, dignified, stable and mature. Fear may well command attention. Yet, all throughout history, dictators have always found their demise and oftentimes through the bravery of a mutiny of men.

The Bible teaches us to have perfect peace. When you have learned to live in a state of mind that is humble and still, you are able to tap into the powerful resources of the source, which is God. Through prayer and meditation, you will find that state of peace. This peace from God, which surpasses all understanding, will guard your heart and your mind in Christ Jesus. This peace is not detectable in the brain even though machines can document the effects of that calmness. This peace manifests through the invisible presence of the Holy Spirit. We are assured that whatever is true, whatever is honorable, whatever is just, whatever is pure, whatever is lovely, whatever is commendable, if there is any excellence, if there is anything worthy of praise, to think about these blessings. In other words, you have to engage your mind on all the positive things around you, in order to appreciate your gifts. The result of this thinking with an appreciative mindset, gives you a feeling of peace and gratitude.

Sadly, I have met many people throughout my life who said, "I don't have time for God," or "I do not have time to pray. Besides, God never gives me what I ask for, so what is the point of speaking into thin air?" Others have said to me, "When I die, I die and that's the end of me. I'm far too busy trying to make more money than worrying about when I might croak." Sadly, I have even met people who said, "I can't bare this life. The more I think about war and death, the more I worry. I find myself thinking about why I'm thinking and the more I think about why I'm thinking, the more I think I'm going crazy! I wish I was dead."

Yet, even more disturbing are the people high with drugs who have completely become mindless or unaware. They feel nothing normal. They are oblivious to the world around. Their only thought is when there next fix will be and how they will afford to buy the drug of choice.

Thinking is important, but over-thinking can be a disease or a compulsion. Life is about balance. Through years of study and meditation in monastic retreat, I have had a great deal of time to reflect upon my mind and faith. When God created us, he gave us the ability to love and know him in a unique way. Of all his creatures, only humankind has this profound ability. All creatures can think, but only the human has the capacity to think about God (Creator) and appreciate what he blesses him or her with each day.

Many say to me, "I don't understand what the mind is." Let me break it down simply for you. We equate the mind with thinking and that thinking is associated with the brain. It gives us a starting point or frame of logical reference. The brain is a container and the mind is the object or thing within it, much like a cosmetic case with a lipstick inside or a wallet containing cash. There are some phrases we often use including, "Unlocking the door to the mind." We all believe that the mind holds the key to knowledge. It is as if the mind is the book, the brain is the library room and the head is the building we walk into, to find the book that will educate.

I always find it interesting that we perceive the mind to be, "Locked away." It is as if the knowledge within it is, "Secret," and only those with the special key or combination code can enter to learn the mysteries. In some respects, this is true. If you have ever tried to remember the name of an actor or a city for instance when playing in a quiz game, it can almost feel like the answer is on the tip of your tongue. Sometimes you can recall the correct answer, and other times you cannot. Hours may pass when other things occupy your thoughts and concentration, when unexpectedly; you suddenly recall the name of that actor or place.

Why does that happen you might ask? When God created us, he gave us a complex mind. This multifaceted capability enables us to think in the present, past and future in order to store, think communicate and imagine. The mind gathers information through books, computers, trial and error and mentoring. This information gives us exciting skills to lead safe and productive lives in society.

Our mind has the potential to imagine. Leonardo da Vinci knew it, Walt Disney knew it, Mozart knew it, Thomas Edison knew it, and so did every great inventor you can name.

Conclusion

Today, our children have more technology than anybody in the past and it is crucial that we encourage them to take full advantage of these gifts of knowledge. Let us cease to make negative, evil, destructive and harmful products, including these horrific and violent games on computers, IPads and handheld devices that only increase the violence in our communities. Instead, let us continue to help them to visualize a world of possibilities with programs that encourage healthy thought. God gave us a mind to create and distribute life-changing tools for health and development. Let us give our children the key to open the door to their mind through education and let us teach them how to expand their intellectual capacity.

As we realize the need for exercising our limbs and joints for optimal health, I additionally believe that exercising the mind is equally important. A crucial way to do this is to read and engage in puzzles that use all hemispheres of the brain. Meditation is also a crucial practice in strengthening the capabilities of this powerful creation within us.

The brain has to be stimulated in order for the mind to upload (remember essential information) software. We recognize that a car needs a key in the ignition to ignite the mechanisms to fire up and accelerate. A car needs a body, wheels, brakes, an engine, water, gas and oil fed into in to it, or it will quickly fail to serve. The survival of the natural world also requires a powerful capacity to think and recall. The essential survival skills pass through the hierarchy like a transmitter. Each new member learns the migration paths, ancient burial grounds, spawning rivers and superior feeding grounds and incredibly, these crucial journeys are invisible. Animals, birds and insects do not have human maps. Rather, they must store information and adapt when necessary.

From birth to death, human beings have the capacity to learn new ideas and skills every day. The disabling factor to a human mind is the belief that it is limited to location and ancestral ineptness. "You will never amount to anything, because you are like your father!" are destructive words that cause the mind to malfunction. "You can be anything you put your mind to!" are inspiring words that ignite the mind to expand beyond comprehension.

When did you last pick up a pen with your left hand (if right handed,) and write in a journal about your day?

When was the last time you went to a bookstore and picked up a book from a different section?

Please read something completely opposite to your normal genre over the next few weeks. It can be fun to close your eyes, and walk down an aisle. After a moment or two, pick a book that you cannot see. Open your eyes and open your mind. Take it home and read it from cover to cover. This is how you expand your knowledge and learn new and exciting things about our world.

When was the last time you listened to a style of music that was completely different to anything you had heard before?

A mind opening exercise is to listen to music with your eyes shut. Once you have settled yourself, begin the process of identifying every instrument. If necessary, play the music repeatedly. This stimulates your mind to different sounds and you might notice where in your body you feel the tones. An instrument like a double base for instance, may have a deep tone and be felt at the bottom of your back. In comparison, a violin produces a higher tone. If you wear headphones, you might feel the higher tone of the harp or violin on your forehead.

When was the last time you sat outside in nature - blindfolded?

Sensing the extremes of temperature, textures, sounds, smells and tastes can be illuminating. When one is unable to see, it is fascinating to open ones being to sensing clouds covering the sun, insects buzzing from flower to flower and even the perception of knowing that a creature is watching you can be exceptionally enlightening.

In monastic retreat, I spent days in complete darkness. I can assure you, your inner hearing and vision becomes magnified as you relax. I find today that when I meditate with my rosary that I am not only thinking about the life of our Lord, but I am also relaxed and peaceful. With each bead that passes through my fingers, the scene I am reflecting upon has deeper meaning and fills me with a sense of humble reverence.

Lesson 23: Trust in God

I began meditation training as a teenager and it has slowly developed over the last fifty years. My teachers from India, Tibet, Japan, China and America, all understood that I was a Christian. They would say it was fascinating to train a person who saw life through the eyes of Jesus. They respected me when I would excuse myself from certain classes that I felt were not in line with my belief system and they affirmed that God had obviously sent me to them to strengthen them. I have gone from staring into space to holding my rosary and contemplating the mysteries of Christ's life.

It was not until I had been to the gates of heaven that God anointed me in a very powerful way. Some of you may know that I hosted two live nightly syndicated radio programs in Phoenix, Arizona. I answered our listeners' questions using intuition. This began after an appearance on a talk show back in the year 2000 where I had been so accurate with my insightful assessment, that the producers had offered me my own radio shows. Rapidly, these radio programs became a huge success and hundreds of thousands of listeners followed us for a year. I wanted to help people and yet, deep down, I knew that I was wrong to convey the future to them. I fooled myself into thinking this was what God wanted me to do. In hindsight, perhaps it was not.

Many wondered why I stopped doing that work and in particular, why I had stopped appearing on other radio and TV shows, touring and giving spiritual lectures. My producers did not want me to talk about God, but to keep the ratings up by giving the audience what they wanted (predictions). I fought with the managers and hosts of shows, who despite my request, continued to promote me as some new age psychic. I felt like a performing orca. I wanted to talk about the love of God and the miracles of Christ, but nobody in the waters I was swimming in, were interested.

The only time when I felt that my gift was beneficial was when I worked alongside law enforcement agencies, who asked me to assist them with major criminal investigations. At first, I was happy to be engaged in this work, especially when we were able to find missing children before they were killed and discarded bodies. The imprisonment of dangerous criminals and the peace of mind to families gave me a feeling of accomplishment. However, this work was very demanding and exhausting and it meant that my world revolved around a dark energy, which I was tired of trying to shake off each month.

In addition, several Tibetan masters wisely counseled me that by telling people of things that were going to happen in their lives, I was in fact doing them a major disservice and that by allowing dark energy to occupy my being, I was opening myself up to physical, spiritual and emotional harm. They unanimously agreed that I would be seen as a respected Christian teacher of God, thus to allow these fools to cheapen the astonishing gifts of the Holy Spirit, that I clearly possessed, was beneath me. I walked away from that work and new age world and I will never return to it.

Despite being against the will of God, some might ask, "Why is it wrong to want to know about (or talk to people about) our future?" Firstly, unless God is specifically giving you a vision, when we focus our attention on what has occurred in the past, or what is to come in the future, we rob ourselves, (and others) of the crucial lessons and beauty of the present. The devil loves to mislead us and if he can get you reliant upon another individual to guide you, he will. If he can lead you away from trusting in God's goodness, he will. If he can fill you with fear, envy, greed and need, he will. He may even tell you to ignore what I am saying and this would be very applicable to either a person who works with divination or another who seeks the advice of a psychic for instance. I assure you that the vast majority of people in this profession are wonderful individuals with beautiful hearts. The devil particularly loves to use them, for what better than to take a loving and compassionate son or daughter of God and manipulate them for his disgusting deceit. When a compassionate person finds that his or her gift is bringing comfort on a daily basis, they feel as though they are using their gift for the good. Thus, I do not condemn those who are making a living from divination, but worry about them and those they serve.

In these last days, I assure you that the devil is not just prowling around in the wings anymore, but rather, openly and blatantly snatching as many sheep as he can get his grubby mitts on. Now more than ever, we have to guard against his lies and wise up to his methods of soul gathering. These tactics include over indulgence of unhealthy food, sex and the illusion of the perfect body and the compulsion to shop until we drop. These evil plans include the need to control and to invent the technology to destroy. He wants the media frenzy and desire for slanderous gossip to burn with you and he subtly encourages you to study in the pursuit of information gathering so you can learn what we were never supposed to know because God knew that this would be the ruin of humanity.

The less we come to God, the easier it is for the devil to snatch us away. Remaining focused on God as a sheep safely grazing in his pasture, protects you from being unnecessarily injured.

Life is a mystery and we cannot define or explain certain events, traits or signs. Learning how to manage extraordinary (supernatural) gifts requires a *stable* mind, a *balanced* personality and a firm grasp on reality, science and *biblical wisdom*. God is very specific about this and it is black and white.

I have thought about this subject a great deal and I have had to pray and meditate upon what is acceptable to God. I have seen things my entire life that defy logical explanation. God has bestowed the ability upon me to occasionally see and interpret in ways similar to Joseph and Nehemiah in the Old Testament. I know that the Holy Spirit works through me today. I am his faithful servant, thus I simply go to where he leads me. I stand there and pray for his guidance and I speak to allow his words to teach and guide. Subsequently, I cannot ever take credit for anything that happens in my life. It is never I. It is always him. If there is a blunder, the fault is mine. If I make a mistake, it is surely, because my ego has sneaked in and taken over. God faithfully directs my life. His staff nudges me to where there is a need to offer his comfort and courage.

Let me give you an example. We had just moved to Wyoming and did not know our way around. It was a dark, stormy day and the wind was blowing fiercely. A familiar feeling from God came over me. I knew that I had to go to a place called Casper, but I had no clue where that was. I asked my friend and he shrugged his shoulders. I told him that I had to go there immediately. He pointed out the atrocious weather conditions and seeing that this was irrelevant to me, he knew nothing he could say would deter me. I assured him that he did not have to accompany me, to which he laughed and shook his head. We searched the route and drove some three hours. No sooner had we arrived than I felt the urge to leave. My friend looked at me with a combination of anger and frustration. However, he knew not to argue with me and we began the long drive home.

By now, the snow was falling heavily and visibility was poor. When deciding whether to take the country road or the freeway, God instilled the back road into my psyche. My friend did not want to drive on that stretch of road, so I took the wheel. The road was slippery, dark and remote. Even with the windscreen wipers on full blast, the snow was causing major visibility problems. We did not pass or see a single vehicle in both directions and my friend angrily and sarcastically verbalized that observation.

A powerful feeling of the Holy Spirit surged through my body and I knew something massively important was about to occur. Sure enough, out of nowhere, this truck overtook us at great speed. It swerved from side to side and as the tires lost their grip, the truck hit the embankment, flipped in the air and landed in a deep ditch. My friend shrieked as I gradually and safely slowed down and stopped. I calmly, yet firmly instructed him to remain by the side of the road and call for emergency assistance. He had forgotten to bring his cell phone, so I told him to stand there and flag the next vehicle. He pointed out that we had not seen a single truck in miles and I reassured him that God would send somebody to help. I reiterated that he was not to leave the vehicle, regardless of what he might see.

I climbed down the embankment to the mangled truck. It lay upside down and the windows were all broken. I managed to position myself in such a way that I could open the door slightly at first. Inside was a young woman covered in blood, but I noted she was conscious. She was still dazed and unsure of what had just happened. Repeatedly she mumbled something about Billings, Montana.

"I have to get to Billings," she wailed. "Last week I was late. He hit me."

"Don't move," I gently said to her.

My friend yelled down and told me that a truck had stopped. He said they had a cell phone and had alerted the emergency services of our location. He reassured me that help was on its way.

"Listen to me sweetheart," I said as I turned my attention back to the woman. "You are very fortunate that we were here or goodness knows what would have happened to you. What is your name?" I asked.

"Jen," she replied. I asked her if she was in any pain and I checked her pulse and breathing at the same time. She told me that her legs were trapped and hurting. It was dark in there and as I felt around, I noticed that the steering wheel was lodging her to such an extent that she could not move.

"Jen," I continued. "Please listen to me. My name is Christine and God sent me to help you. Try to stay calm as help is on its way."

As I was talking to her, she gasped. "Angel!" I looked around me but could not see one, although I could sense many were there that day. "It's huge!" she cried. I began to smell fuel. My gut sensed something very bad was about to potentially occur and I began to pray to God for his divine intervention. I could not move Jen, so I tried to offer her comfort by touching her arm, which was clearly broken with a compound fracture.

"What's that smell?" Jen mumbled. "Am I going to die?"

"Listen to me sweetheart. I am here with you and God is here with us. Whatever happens I promise you that I will not leave you," I tried to reassure her. I knew God was protecting us with his holy light and grace. I figured that the worst-case scenario would be the truck catching fire. There was no way for me to cut her loose. Thus, I concluded I would have to just stay and die with her. I was not (am not) afraid of dying, but I was afraid of how we would both cope with burning to death.

"Abba," I prayed. "I know you brought me here and I know you're with me. Father, if I am to die with Jen, please spare us from suffering and please bring us home swiftly. Give me the courage to remain here with her and please ensure nobody else crashes tonight on these treacherous roads. Lord, bring us help. In Jesus name, I pray. Amen."

"I'm a Catholic," Jen mumbled. This was excellent information, as I needed to bring some semblance of spiritual peace to this horrific situation. I began to say the rosary with her and with each repetition, the smell of gasoline was becoming more repugnant. The engine was still hot and I knew that the vehicle could ignite at any moment.

"I'm going to die!" Jen cried.

"Jen," I sternly said. "I know help is coming and I promise you I will not leave you. Whatever happens, we will face it together. I know God is with us." The next few minutes were very stressful as you can imagine.

Thankfully, within a few minutes, I could hear the sirens in the distance. I was escorted up by the paramedics, interviewed by the police and had the blessed fortune to see Jen cut out of the wreck and brought safely into the ambulance. The rest of that story would be inappropriate of me to recall. Praise and adulation should not go to me, but to God who intervened that day and showed that he is in control and extends his merciful favor to those who look upon him to guide them in whatever way he chooses to communicate. My friend took one look at his driver (me), who by now was shivering with the cold and smiled with pride. There was no need for either one of us to speak. God had called us and we had faithfully obeyed.

Months previously, I had been sitting in a coffee shop when the Holy Spirit came upon me to drive home on a particular freeway in Phoenix. I questioned that feeling, because it would take me in the opposite direction of where I would normally go. I prayed for God's guidance. The feeling became stronger and I knew it was God. As I was driving, I saw a crash site ahead, which forced me to stop. There was absolute carnage from the accident. A man came running up to my window and shouted, "Help me!"

I ran passed the cars strewn along the road, to an elderly man who lay in the middle of the road with blood trickling from of his ears and oozing from his head and face. I always carry latex gloves with me and as I placed them on my hands, I asked the man (who had come to my car) what had happened and I instructed a witness to call 911.

"We don't know what to do!" this man shouted at me.

"I'm not a doctor either," I told him.

"Help him!" another yelled at me. I repeated that I was not a medical professional.

"You're holy, it's obvious you can help him," a woman chimed in. I looked quizzically at her and wondered what had made her make such an observation and just assumed that God was shining and giving us all His confidence. I knelt before the injured man and prayed. He was unable to speak or move and I was not even certain if he could hear me. Nevertheless, I told him who I was and that God had sent me to help him. People began to say to one another, "She is an Angel."

Before I got the chance to tell them that I was just a humble human being, a man grabbed me and said, "Listen to me!" He was a doctor (thank God) and together we prepped the injured man for an airlift to the intensive care unit at a hospital several miles away. We later learned the injured man had been crossing the highway, suffered a stroke and had subsequently fallen in front of a gasoline truck, which had been pulling out of a side street. I flew in the helicopter to the hospital holding the man's head. Later that night, I lay in bed thanking God for being with the elderly man and I prayed that he either would heal or die peacefully. I later learned that he had recovered and his family sent me a beautiful letter.

I could go on and on, story after story.

Conclusion

Thus, to conclude, I do not allow myself to imagine the future with a fanciful desire to manipulate the course of events. I do not attempt to visualize other human beings who have the gift of free will and whose destiny may not have anything to do with the course of my life. Yes, I make plans for things like conferences and gatherings of friends and family. I am a very logical, yet creative person. However, those practical plans have fluidity to them. I almost expect God to alter the event, day, time, location and subject matter at any moment. For today, I warmly share my teachings, prayer, friendship and comforting love with every being I meet and I look only to God for my needs.

Human beings have a tendency to either obsess or walk through their lives oblivious to the needs of those around them each day. They either wallow around in the past or worry about future events that may or may not affect them negatively. Adults in particular, fail to keep focused on current situations. Their lack of concentration affects productivity at work and stifles their ability to engage within their family structure.

People find comfort in reliving and recounting the stories of days gone by when their lives had meaning and purpose. This can be sweet when an elderly person recounts his or her days in the war, or how they met the love of their life. We need our elders to talk about the past, for by doing so; we are able to document essential stories, customs, traditions and cultures; including languages, dances, music and geographical monuments and other important nuggets of wisdom. However, there is a huge difference between recounting such events and knowledge and gloomily wallowing around to the point that we are incapable of recovering from a negative behavior pattern, or event. The latter example stunts our growth and recovery.

Projecting into the future can be equally foolish (and dangerous) for a myriad of reasons. Nobody is able to see accurately what is going to happen in his or her life and nobody, (including me) knows the exact moment of death. Far too many people waste precious breath in their quest to learn how to manipulate their future and their money is squandered away on gems, cards and other divination tools to help them glimpse unknown events, which do not pay their bills or help the needy. God foresaw this and prohibited it.

Superstition, idolatry, divination and magic are not of God. I have struggled with this for many years and I have had to recognize it within myself. I grew up in a culture bathed in superstition and I was temporarily married into a tribal culture. I have had to learn to trust God. The main reason most people seek those who profess to see the future, is because their current situation is not ideal and they want to know when (or if) it is going to improve. People worry about many things in life including the companionship of a loving partner, a fulfilling career or relocation.

God assures that he *is* aware of our needs and he promises us that when he takes us to a situation, he brings us through it. Thus, we do not need to rely on anything (or anybody other than him) to ease our suffering. Today, when I sense something, I spend significant time in prayer with God asking for his guidance.

Sadly, many people are oblivious to others around them, which not only limit their opportunities, but also have the negative impact of shutting out the (real) world. Seeking others to dabble around may seem harmless enough, but again, there are more charlatans than genuine messengers sent by God. The former will gladly help you part with your money on your quest for answers and the latter will come to realize that the best way to help you is to listen and encourage you to pray to the God.

As one of my respected teachers, Lama Surya Das always says, "Be in now-ness and be in stillness. Nothing more to do than enjoy the view." I would add to this by saying, "Let your attention rest upon God and trust in him to provide your every need. Amen."

When we sit quietly, we can hear God speak to us. Be still and know that he is with you. If we run about like chickens with our heads chopped off, how are we ever going to feel at peace today? Let the past go and if that takes writing it down in the form of a book, then begin writing. If you have people who hurt you, spend time in prayer and ask God to help you to forgive them. If you have hurt others and can connect with them, then write or call them to apologize. The crucial thing to remember is not to drag up old issues to expose old wounds. Simply open your heart and love.

Let the future unfold in its perfect time. Yes, set a few goals but allow those objectives to materialize through God and in God's perfect timing, order and circumstance. He wants us to ask him and he wants to know our concerns and needs. Prayer is free and an ever constant presence and gift. You do not need to go to others for validation or to learn how to force a positive result. God will provide for you as readily as he does for every creature, bird, being and ecological occurrence.

I promise you God will give you everything you need for today and that is all you need to know to survive, to thrive and to be the perfect child He created you to be.

Lesson 24: Meditation and Prayer

Meditation should be a *very* important part of your life. Perhaps you have never given it much thought until now. In which case, let us look at what meditation is and what it is not.

For people like me who are Catholics, the daily practice of prayer with a rosary, (whilst contemplating the mysteries of Christ) or the reflecting upon a passage from scripture is comforting. Others (including myself) listen to beautiful music or simply sit in peaceful silence after prayer and it is a wonderful way to draw ever closer to our father God.

My students often ask me, "Did Jesus meditate?" Meditation would have been no stranger to Jesus of Nazareth and the Bible talks about it several times in the Old Testament. There were Buddhist missionaries in Palestine during the time of Jesus, so he would have been familiar with their practices as well.

If we look deeply at the teachings of Jesus contained in the Sermon on the Mount, (Matthew 6: 5-8) I believe we find evidence that Jesus did in fact meditate, and instructed his disciples to do likewise. In his teaching on *Prayer*, Jesus taught: "And when you pray, do not be like the hypocrites, for they love to pray standing in the synagogues and on the street corners to be seen by men. I tell you, they have received their reward in full. But when you pray, go into your room and close the door and pray to your Father who is unseen. Then Your Father, who sees what is done in secret, will reward you. And when you pray do not keep on babbling like pagans, for they think they will be heard for their many words. Do not be like them, for your Father knows what you need before you ask."

Jesus teaches his followers to pray in solitude, using as few words as possible. Brief, seems to be what Jesus teaches concerning prayer. Yet many times in the Gospel accounts, Jesus is described often as spending an entire night in prayer before making a major ministerial move. We learn that Jesus rose from sleep hours before his other disciples so he could go into a quiet place to pray. Jesus went into the desert for forty days and forty nights to fast and pray. If Jesus believed in keeping spoken prayers short, what would he be doing for hours or even days on end? I believe he was spending time listening to God and being with God. In short, Jesus meditated.

Meditation is above all a quest. When I lived and studied with my Native American Indian teachers, they would often refer to our hours of training as, "Spirit quests." The mind seeks to understand the why and how of life, in order to adhere and respond to what Lord God is asking. It can be very challenging to maintain the great discipline of attentiveness and I will often advise my students not to sit staring into space, but rather to study sacred Scriptures, especially the Gospels. It is helpful to meditate on what we read as it leads us to contemplate our own lives. Thus, we begin to open up the, *book of life*. We pass from thinking to reality. Through humbleness we are able to open our hearts and seek God's will for our life, by praying, "Not my will, but thy will be done."

Our ultimate wish is to enter into the kingdom of heaven upon death. We see this blissful reunion with the Trinity as the cessation of all suffering. Anguish and pain is a battle all human beings struggle to defeat. Our suffering comes from our perceptions and oftentimes, our perceptions are false and based upon ignorance. We have wrong perceptions about others and ourselves, which cause fear, and violence, hatred and segregation. Before we can ever hope to be at peace, we have to remove these wrong perceptions, which in turn remove our suffering. This peace gives us love for all life in return.

There are countless books, videos and wise teachers to lead you through the art of meditation. It is not as simple as sitting down, reading a book, closing your eyes and diving into this practice. Nor can you say that you are going to switch off for ten minutes and relax. If you have ever tried to meditate without the guidance of a wise and learned teacher, you will have quickly discovered a few things that made the process quite impossible initially. Firstly, the mind is like a wild mustang that refuses to allow any man to use his techniques to tame it for his own needs, or a mischievous monkey that prefers to swing from tree to tree than to sit and quietly eat a peeled banana.

Thoughts start occurring like, "Did I turn off the oven?" or "How long will it take for me to relax?" and "Am I doing this right?" or "What was that sound I just heard?" The mind quite literally plays tricks on us at first. Even with an experienced practitioner, these thoughts pop up quite regularly. The only difference between a newbie and an advanced meditator is that the more advanced person does not fight the thought, but relaxes and allows it to float by like a cloud in the sky.

The next obvious issue is one of comfort. Everybody asks the same question, "What is the right position to meditate?" Obviously, some people simply cannot sit on the floor cross-legged for health reasons. Others feel complete stillness by sitting on a chair and there are many who prefer to lie down. My only advice to the last position is that if you are lying down, you are very likely to fall asleep. Sleeping is not meditating; it is napping. I have developed my own style developed in monastic retreat. To this day it is still painful for me to sit in the manner my masters' trained me. However, I use this pain to strengthen my mind and to discipline myself to rise above that uncomfortableness. This is not yoga, but my way of ensuring that I do not fall asleep.

Meditation has been an investment of time and effort and I am grateful to all of my teachers. I do teach others how to meditate and it is a compulsory part of the day for my students. Unfortunately, in the Christian world, there are not many practitioners such as myself. There is a strange philosophy that meditation is at best unnecessary and at worse, somewhat evil. Some immature ministers have a tendency to encourage everybody to pray and yet have no solution to the question of how to pray in a calm manner that enables God to communicate effectively with his sheep. The problem is not God, but man. Human beings cannot sit still to listen. My students have learned how to be effective prayers and effective listeners who know to turn to the teachings of Jesus Christ to cultivate a passion for compassion.

In my humble opinion, prayer without knowing how to meditate is limited. If we were to have a one-way garbled conversation with ourselves, we would be classified as being, "Borderline insane." If we want to strengthen our faith and lead fuller, more satisfying lives, we must learn to be still and listen to God's guidance after prayer. Conversation is a two way street.

Have you ever tried listening to somebody when surrounded by traffic noise, loud music or other deafening sounds? It is impossible to concentrate fully and if nothing else, it can be potentially dangerous if we cannot hear warning signals.

Meditation gives us the ability to calm our mind and to sit quietly, even in a busy office, train station, airport or club. When one is able to look around and notice the rushing about of others activity - and not be affected by it at all - it immediately gives one the clarity and peace which others cannot imagine. Meditation, when practiced daily, gives you strength. I am referring to personality and spiritual strength rather than physical, although the latter also enhances our beings as a major benefit. Being composed and calm is a truly powerful gift. Where those who are distressed, angry, stressed or hyper-excited are incapable of making rational decisions, a calm levelheaded person is able to think their way out of difficulty whilst emanating a sense of serenity.

Permit me to break this down simply. When we pray, we speak to God either outwardly or inwardly. We must then sit quietly and permit God to speak to us in whatever form he chooses. This might include an image or a feeling of serenity for instance. As we wait for him to speak, we simply breathe evenly and calmly. This calmness is meditation. Reflection or thinking is active. It requires you to process information and recall events. Thinking and reflection is therefore not meditation in my opinion because you are not relaxed when you are delving around in the library of your mind. Meditation is a simple process of emptying your mind of all thoughts by peacefully breathing in and out.

This is how I meditate. After I have read a piece of scripture, I think about it for a while. I may even make some notes in that reflection or pray. I then sit comfortably, close my eyes, breathe in through my nostrils and exhale through my mouth thus allowing my entire being to relax and meditate. Whilst in meditation mode, I am not thinking about anything.

I might notice a sound, but it does not disturb me. I have no need to eat, drink, sleep or move in this position. I simply allow the love of God to envelop me like a mist of beautiful morning dew. I am neither hot nor cold. I am just still.

When I think about Jesus Christ, I try to imagine what it must have been like for him on the night of his betrayal, as he sat praying and meditating in the garden of Gethsemane. We learn from Scripture that he was so disturbed that he sweats drops of his own blood. This was no ordinary man. He was God's son and a very accomplished meditation practitioner. Contemplate this for a moment. Imagine if you knew that within hours you were going to be scourged, mocked and crucified. Consider what it would feel like to know that you were about to suffer the jury's punishment for the sins of every single person that ever lived or who will come after your death. Yes, that is the pain of tens of millions of men, women and children. The horror of being betrayed, scourged, crucified, spat upon and agonizingly ostracized from God by the very same people who waved palm branches and cried with joy only a few days previously, was shown to Jesus in the garden.

It is unimaginable and terrifying to think about and yet, he had to contemplate it. Jesus had no choice for it was his destiny; such was and is his love for us all. The only way that he could possibly have coped with this horrendous murder is I am certain, in part, due to his strength of prayer, love (for his father and us), courage and meditation practice, which gave him that stillness and trust in God, which he told us all to have.

Meditation energizes our mind and body and allows us to be alert, awake and aware. You might recall how frustrated Jesus was with his chosen disciples. Rather than being watchful and mindful when he was in the garden, they continually fell asleep. They could not keep watch for one brief hour. They were not meditating but napping.

Would you be able to stay alert if God asked you to accompany him today?

Conclusion

Meditation is an investment in life.I am a huge advocate for teaching children this technique early on. Far easier to grow up knowing how to be still than it is to wait until one is struggling later in life to decide to begin. Having said that though, you are never too old to learn this essential practice and I have helped many hospice patients to prepare for their last breath, by teaching them how to rest and relax their mind.

Our Lord taught us, "But when you pray, go into your room and close the door and pray to your Father who is unseen." That room he is referring to is not only a physical place within our houses, but also a part of our inner selves including our mind, heart and soul. God hears those inner conversations and responds with clear direction and favor.

I have one note of caution. Many so-called experts claim to be qualified instructors. At worst, even an inept teacher can give you the basics of technique. However, meditation is a discipline that one can compare by saying it is the difference between jogging to your mailbox at the end of the drive and running a twenty-five mile marathon. The former does not need months or years of nutritional guidance or physical fitness for the average person. The latter requires dedication that most people are simply unable or unwilling to invest the effort required to succeed. Thus, whom you choose to teach you this essential practice is a very important decision.

You will have learned from this chapter that every single person needs to be able to meditate. If one cannot see the benefit of this practice in their personal or professional life today, then contemplate the day you are sick or afraid. How do you plan to cope with the pain or loss? How will you settle your mind when circumstances are beyond your control? We *will* all die one day and I can assure you with my hospice ministry that those who had never taken the time or trouble to learn how to rest their mind, suffered far worse at the end. Alternatively, those who had practiced meditation and prayer in combination breathed calmly and suffered less pain. This calmness does not come from the outside. Rather, this peace is cultivated from within. Given the choice of serenity or anxiousness, I would hope you would choose to be still.

Finally, cultivating contemplative prayer is very important. It is during this time each day that we come together with our Lord. We simply concentrate on loving him. Meditation is not necessarily something that we can do every day, but finding the time to be alone with him, is vitally important. Furthermore, I dare to suggest that spending time with the Lord is more essential than anything else is. This is not a practice of thinking, but feeling.

When one joins with the Lord, one feels unimaginable love and compassion. We hand ourselves over to him and bathe in his all-encompassing love and mercy. There is no pretense in his presence. He knows us because he formed us. Here, alone with God we pray as his child, of the forgiven sinner who welcomes the love by which he or she is loved and who wishes to respond to it by loving even more. This love comes from the Holy Spirit, which is a gift of grace by God to the humble hearted. I like to call this, "Communion." We gaze upon his glory, we listen to his Word in silence and we participate in the mystery of Christ when we recall the celebration of the Eucharist.

Whereas some practitioners and teachers insist that they think and feel nothing in their meditation practice, as a practicing Catholic Christian, I think and deeply feel love towards God, which is far from, "Nothing." In fact, contemplative prayer and meditation is the most beautiful part of my day and it enables me to open my heart to everybody I meet. To those who ask, "How often should we pray?" I tell them, "Without ceasing."

Lesson 25: Introductions

After completing an extended monastic retreat towards the end of 2007, I left my full-time religious studies and returned to the business world where I began a five-year Chamber of Commerce career. I rose from a humble business manager to president and chief executive officer within that period and proudly served my county, state and international departments, in addition to being a United Nations representative.

As you know, I was born and raised in England, which is famous for its etiquette. Thus, it was natural for me to make introductions and I implemented some strategies that had not been successful for others in the past. I wholeheartedly threw myself into this work and helped thousands of small, medium and large companies along the way.

The thought of public speaking to most people is a nerve-wracking concept. Yet, whether we like it or not, when we wish to grow our companies, we must be able to describe our services to others. I conducted a series of training sessions and specialized forums, which focused on guiding executives in the art of customer service and specifically in effective methods of introducing their products and services to potential investors and clients.

If you are in the business world, you will ultimately attend networking events including breakfasts, luncheons and after hours. You will be able to attest to the fact that these events can be informative and occasionally beneficial in terms of meeting potential customers. However, they can also be a mass of faces, which you will never get to meet or work with on a professional level. Everybody there is trying to promote their organization as well, and the organizers have a common tendency to herd you all into a room, present you with a name badge and encourage you to, "Go and meet everybody!" That is like saying to a baby, "Just stand up and walk!" It sounds simple. However, unless a person is naturally gregarious, it is not easy at all. In fact, for some men and women, walking up to a complete stranger, or worse still a group of complete strangers, is as terrifying as it was back in their school days where they had to make friends in the playground.

The natural tendency is scan the room to find a familiar face that you will gravitate towards and spend the vast majority of the time. On one level, it is pleasant to meet up with friends. Unfortunately, that is not how you are going to grow your network or to your company!

The events we organized were completely different to the norm, which should not surprise you given what you know about me so far. I would gather everybody's details days before the event. I studied every single person before his or her arrival. I knew who they were, where they were from, what they sold, what they needed and all the ins and outs of what made that company, product and person tick. In other words, I had profiled them down to the finest detail. I would sit with their cards laid out in front of me and plan how I was going to bring those that could be of benefit to each other, together. On the day of the event, I would let everybody wander around the room.

After a while, I would walk up to a person, take them by the hand and lead them to another whom I had already decided would be a good match. I would introduce them by saying for example, "Mark, I'd like to introduce you to Jan. Jan, Mark is with ABC, based in Texas. His company manufactures digital products and I thought you two could do some great work together. Mark, Jan is with the BBD, which is a non-profit organization in Washington. They focus on producing audio books for the blind. I thought with all your connections in duplication and marketing you two could have a meaningful relationship and cross-exchange of connections." I would stay with the couple for a minute or so before heading off to bring others together in a similar way. After an hour, one could stand and marvel at the excitement in the room and the benefit of this intimate strategy is obvious.

The roundtable training sessions took that important strategy to another exciting level. Twenty-five rotating executives met with me in the boardroom once a month. These respected classes became widely known and entrepreneurs would travel long distances to attend them. Women flew in from as far as California and one man even flew in from Canada for this two-hour session in New Jersey.

Occasionally, we would have two or three people who were in the same line of work. Rather than seeing this as a drawback or competition, I helped them to explore their areas of specialty that would undoubtedly reveal differences. We examined the philanthropic endeavors each was passionate about which led to the group offering to help each other's endeavors.

During the first few minutes of each class, I would ask each participant to stand and introduce him or herself to the group. I would also rise and give them a special name that we would forever use to describe or introduce them. Most human beings have poor memories and find it difficult to match another's face with their name. Thus, my dynamic approach to name identification was highly beneficial

Let me give you an example of this unique technique. My name is Christine and I am a humanitarian, evangelist, recording artist, keynote speaker, filmmaker, author and entrepreneur. At that time, you could have added that I worked at the Chamber of Commerce. This is a great deal of information and I doubt most of you would remember half of it. However, if I were to have said to you that I am "Christine Connects," you would be intrigued as these two words are easy to remember and describe perfectly who I am and what I do for a living. I like to use alliterations as it makes it even easier to remember. My name is Christine. I bring people together through my huge pipeline of clients, sponsors and benefactors. To this day, many people refer to me as "Christine Connects." It is my trademark, you might say. Let me give you another example. I had a client whose company specialized in document shredding. His name was Steve. I named him, "Shredding Steve." From that day forwards, when people saw him, they would say, "It's Shredding Steve!" and they knew that when they needed paper or electronic files destroying, the man to call was their new trusted friend, Steve. We had, "Mike Mechanic," "Floral Fiona," "Chris Cab," "Lawyer Len," "Simon Speaks," and "Arty Allen," to name a few. I am sure you can guess what they all did for a living.

I highly recommend you implement this name identification strategy today. Every company has to have a mission statement and a vision of where they intend to take the company over the next few years. Few are able to describe their services in two words. If you can find a perfect name, nobody will ever forget you!

Many organizations ask me to be their keynote speaker at breakfasts, dinners and award ceremonies. I like to utilize these opportunities in such a way that everybody leaves having learned something new. Personally, I abhor award dinners and events where the speaker drones on with a mundane, monotonous tone, which is boring, tiring, and a complete waste of our time. I like my presentations to be unique, of course.

When a new Chamber member joined my book of business, I insisted on them giving me one hundred business cards, plus fliers and brochures. After a few months, I had 450 members under my jurisdiction. I had personally brought them all in, which meant hours of conversations over the phone and meetings outside of work, in order for me to grasp every tiny detail about them. My colleagues thought I was crazy at first, but after seeing how successful my approach was, they tried to implement it themselves. With each new member, I began to strategize as to whom, within my network, I could introduce them to which would ultimately result in a business deal. I took those hundred business cards with me everywhere I went twenty-four hours a day, seven days a week for the entire year. In the beginning, I was able to put them in a brief case. After a while though, I had outgrown that and had to transfer those cards to a medium sized suitcase. After a year, I had transitioned to a huge suitcase that required help to get it in and out of my car.

I would go to meetings and expositions, stack those cards on the table, and begin to talk about our members. I recall at one major event, a man came up to my table and said, "Are you the Chamber of Commerce?" I nodded that we were. "Why don't you have any fliers or posters on the Chamber?" He asked. I told him that all these business cards in front of him were the Chamber, because the Chamber *is* its members. He explained to me what his company did and so I began to talk to him about members he could engage. Looking skeptical, he said that he found this somewhat ridiculous, for none of the other Chambers' worked in this way.

I challenged him to pick any card and call them. He did just that. When he came back to me he was grinning from ear to ear as he relayed how the member had raved about how much business they had got from me taking them everywhere I went. He was so impressed that he immediately joined and went on to be a huge advocate of our organization, and a very dear friend.

When I went to give keynote speeches, my suitcase would come with me. I would stand on the stage and begin with a story to relax everybody. I injected my introduction with a bit of humor to wake the audience up from their carbohydrate inertia. I would then say something like, "I bet you are all wondering why I am standing here with a suitcase next to me?" The audience would nod their heads and a few would giggle nervously. I continued to talk without discussing what was in the case. After a few minutes I would say, "I bet you are all wondering if this British woman is also a ventriloquist huh?" Everybody would begin to laugh loudly and nudge each other in agreement. Still I said nothing about the case or its contents. A few minutes would pass and then I asked the host to bring a large table up to the podium. Very slowly, I would open up my case and begin to put the stacks of cards on the table. You could have heard a pin drop every time I did this. I would tell the audience that this was the Chamber of Commerce and this was my profiling strategy. I explained that I knew every single company down to the minutest detail. With this information, I assured them that I knew I could help everybody be successful as long as they continued to maintain the relationships formed.

One evening, a man boldly challenged me in front of an audience of a thousand men and women at an awards dinner. He stood up and mocked this display by saying nobody could possibly recall such widespread information from over 450 companies. I invited him to come onto the podium and tell me what his organization did. The audience was aghast that this man dared to insult me, but I motioned them to settle down and listen.

I love objections because it gives me the opportunity to demonstrate how knowing ones product thoroughly, one is able to show a customer how this product or service can truly benefit them. You should never shy from a, "No," or an "It won't help me!" When you are selling a product, you are also selling yourself. You must know your subject inside and out and you must demonstrate how this item will help the other to be more successful and happy with its features, advantages and benefits. An objection is merely an expression of misunderstanding and confusion. Show a person interest and concern, and you have a customer and referrals for life.

I asked the man at the dinner a few key questions. Once I understood exactly who he was, I began to scan the 450 piles of cards and identify whom he needed to be talking to in terms of a long-term business partnership. I had discovered with my questions that he was in real estate, specializing in industrial transactions. I picked out companies who were architects, attorneys, land developers, excavators, property developers and soil analysis experts to name a few. I gave him contact names within each organization, including the receptionists who would probably answer the phones.

He was intrigued but challenged me again. "Why have you given me a soil analysis expert?" he questioned with a sarcastic tone in his voice. Again, the audience audibly gasped at his obvious rudeness. I pointed out to him, that if he was selling a piece of property on uninspected land with possible undisclosed toxic waste, the purchaser could sue years later. Furthermore, I pointed out to him that if one of his clients decided to construct a new building on land he was selling, it would need thorough analysis for the exact same issues including poisons, chemical imbalance and even skeletal remains. I concluded with emphasizing the importance of having many tools in your bag.

His face was a picture of awe and respect. From that day to this, Len and I are very close friends. The audience stood up and clapped for over ten minutes. There was nothing more that I needed to add to my presentation because everybody understood the importance of connections.

Conclusion

Remember: all relationships matter. Few of us marry a person that we know nothing about. We meet by chance or by introduction; and then we date. We learn as much as we can about that other man or woman during that discovery period and we figure out if he or she is a good match. If that person is not right for us, we might decide to introduce them to one of our close friends who would be more compatible.

Business is also a relationship. We do business with people we know, trust and like. We only do business with people we detest, when we have no other option available than to engage with them or their company. Life is a dance. You can choose to do the waltz, the tango, the cha-cha cha or boogie on down disco style. Some of you might like to hip-hop and others might prefer to just stand and wiggle their hips from side to side. Whatever floats your boat! Unless you are, Rip Van Winkle or comatose in another way, you have to interact with other people. Learning to take an interest in them, their companies, products, services and needs is paramount. Developing strong working relationships is crucial for your success.

Here are a few tips for extraordinary success. Firstly, select two words to describe who you are and what you do. Trust me; you will thank me for this one day.

Secondly, instead of going to networking meetings conducted like a sheep grazing experiment, find somewhere that is energetic.

Thirdly, choose an organization where the leader has a firm grasp on who is in the room and additionally knows how to introduce you to appropriate clients.

Fourthly, walking into a dark room might be romantic and sexy with a companion, but it is a useless atmosphere when you are trying to conduct business.

Fifthly, remember to take a sincere interest in what others do and need. People will remember you for your manners, attention and sincere interest towards them.

Lastly, be smartly dressed, breath fresh and wearing a warm smile.

If you stand with a frown on your face and your body language closed, nobody will want to come close to you.

Build up your Rolodex with people that you have a strong working relationship. Take time to familiarize yourself with his or her company including who answers the phones and processes your orders. Everybody is important and this investment of time will pay off handsomely.

August 4, 2009

To Whom It May Concern:

This letter is in support of Christine Overton and her involvement in supporting senior citizens, nursing home residents and those receiving palliative care for which she may be applying or showing interest. Christine has faithfully served in our Abider Services program at Pioneer Manor since its inception nearly a year ago. The program provides presence during the final days or hours of a person's life to assure that the individual does not face death alone.

Christine has the gentle spirit and sense of respect and dignity that we require to serve our residents/patients and the kind personality necessary to represent our organization to these clients and their families at such a demanding time during the end stages of life. Her gentle demeanor and caring discipline more than qualifies her to provide such service. Her pleasant manner and deportment makes it an absolute delight to be in her presence. She is a good conversationalist and shows prudence in her choice of words when dealing with either colleagues or clients.

I personally extend my recommendation for Christine to serve in other communities and institutions in a similar manner. She is highly respected by her peers, often going above and beyond her required obligation, filling in the gap and sacrificing her personal time in order meet the need, with pleasantry, grace and finesse. We will miss her, indeed.

Sincerely,

Rev. Bob W. Rudichar
Chaplain Services Coordinator
Campbell County CISM Team Coordinator
Campbell County Memorial Hospital
(307)688-1540
rudichabw@ccmh.net

P.O. Box 3011
Gillette, WY 82717-3011
307.688.1000
www.ccmh.net

Lesson 26: Hospice

During my years of living in Wyoming, I had the profound honor of being part of the Hospice Ministry team. A dynamic pastor of the local church managed this *Abider* project in Campbell County. I trained to sit with patients in their last twenty-four hours of life, so they did not die alone. We also offered a peaceful presence and support to families of the dying, and to the nurses and doctors within the unit.

Having cared for my mother those ten months leading up to her death, I felt well equipped to help others in their final days. Frankly, the thought of somebody dying alone saddens me. Even if the man or woman is not consciously aware that anybody is with them, I do believe that everybody still deserves the comfort of having their hand held and prayers said for them up to the last breath. Their families were always so grateful for our support and it was humbling to be part of the ministry.

As I sat with patients, I reflected upon three pieces of scripture including Psalm 94:19 which says, "When the cares of my heart are many, your consolations cheer my soul."

I always felt strengthened when I recalled the words from Isaiah 41:10, 13 "Fear not, for I am with you; be not dismayed, for I am your God; I will strengthen you, I will help you, I will uphold you with my righteous right hand. For I, the Lord your God, hold your right hand; it is I who say to you, 'Fear not, I am the one who helps you.'"

I would often read 2 Corinthians 1:3-4 to family members because the words always comforted them. "Blessed be the God and Father of our Lord Jesus Christ, the Father of mercies and God of all comfort, who comforts us in all our affliction, so that we may be able to comfort those who are in any affliction, with the comfort with which we ourselves are comforted by God."

Most patients facing death are understandably afraid. Even those who are devout in their faith, still revert to being little children who need mercy and kindness as they prepare to go home to heaven. Having a positive, kind and gentle person by their side, gives them and their loved ones a sense of peace and strength. Our job was to be the hand of Christ, holding them and instilling a sense of genuine comfort. I cannot emphasize that enough. A dying soul needs a tender touch.

I recall one patient whom everybody had expected to die days before, and yet she hung on to life, restless and disturbed. I sat by her bed taking a discreet sip of water. The room was completely silent, and the shades were drawn. This woman opened her eyes and gestured to me that she, too, wanted a drink. I waited for a moment to see if she would fall asleep again, but she did not. I sanitized my hands before leaving the room and told the nursing staff that this woman was asking for some water.

By law, we performed no medical procedures, and I was required to report changes or needs to nursing staff. On this particular day, the staff nurse on duty was certain that it was highly unlikely that this patient could even swallow. However, the nurse respected me and agreed to provide a drink. A few minutes later, the dying woman had consumed an entire bottle of water. As she was dozing off, she abruptly opened her eyes and looked at me. "Help me," she whispered. I thought I had misheard but she repeated her request. I softly asked her what she needed help with, but she could not answer and I assumed the morphine was causing delirium. After several minutes, she looked at me anxiously and said, "Help me." She then repeated a man's name several times. I stepped out of the room and asked the nurses whom this person was that she kept repeating. They told me that it was her son, who lived in another state. They said that he was in a difficult position as his wife was also dying, and he could not be in two places at the same time.

"Has he had the opportunity to perhaps speak to her over the phone?" I enquired.

Everybody looked at me and shook their heads. "No," they said. "We hadn't even thought of that idea."

I am one of those "Think outside of the box," kinds of personalities. I simply refuse to admit defeat. I examine a situation to discover the solution rather than conclude there is no alternative but to surrender. "Please can we call her son and give my idea a shot?" I asked.

"Absolutely," they replied. "That is such a great solution," they all agreed. We took a phone into the room, called her son, put the phone on speaker and gave them a few minutes of privacy. I prayed this would bring them both peaceful closures. After a while, we quietly returned to our patient's room. Her anxious expression was gone. In its place was complete calmness. Whatever her son had said to her, it had filled her with obvious tranquility. I gently held her hand and recited the twenty-third Psalm. She looked at me and smiled. Eventually, she closed her eyes, took one last breath and began her journey to heaven. It was beautiful, peaceful and very loving. Her daughter-in-law also made that journey later that day, and even though one would expect her son to be beside himself with grief at the loss of the two most important women in his life, he was happy. Despite not being able to visit his mother and wife due to them being in two separate states, he had been able to utilize telecommunication to offer comfort. He felt peaceful and we felt gratitude.

I had a dear friend whose final words left us with an amazing insight. As he was dying, I sat with his wife and brothers. He opened his eyes and quietly said, "Christine, it's snowing! It is so beautiful!"

"What is he talking about?" his wife asked me.

I explained that often morphine made some patients delirious whilst others professed to see visions. I advised her to be calm.

"Christine, it's hot and cold with the snow!" Ed repeated several times. I comforted him the only way I knew how which included holding his hand and wiping his brow. After a few hours, he died a very peaceful death.

Several days later, I attended the scattering of his ashes in the dry, hot desert canyons of Arizona. It was mid-August and the sun was particularly hot that day. What occurred next is something that will remain etched in my memory forever. It began to snow above us and we shivered with the cold. As his ashes were released into the sky, it was so beautiful and everybody gasped aloud, "It's snowing Christine, it's snowing! It's so beautiful!"

Had my friend Ed seen his future ascension as he lay dying that night? We all thought so. We imagined that he was looking down from heaven that ash scattering day with a huge smile on his face. He was right on his deathbed when he said, "It is so beautiful!" It *was* beautiful!

Conclusion

Being with another human being at the end of their life is a tremendous honor, and a responsibility that I have always found enormously humbling. It requires you to sit in stillness. It urges you to do nothing more than to hold a space of love, mercy, gentleness and peace. It encourages you to hold their hand as a gift of compassionate tenderness, whilst praying with unconditional loving kindness.

You might care to talk to the hospital chaplain and enquire as to whether the hospital has a program such as the one I am trained. If it does and you feel as though you would be suitable candidate, you should let him or her know that you are available and willing to serve. If your community does not have such a service, you might care to suggest organizing one.

Lesson 27: Nature

A baby observes and learns about life from its parents. Without their care and wisdom, an innocent child will surely die. God may give them their form and life breath, but it is the surrounding adults who have the authority, and the responsibility to ensure that their child has food, water, good health and covering for his or her precious body. This natural instinct to protect and nurture, determines whether the baby will survive or die.

We can also see this across the natural world, with the exception of those species that enter the world alone and fly, swim or crawl quickly for their survival. If you have ever observed turtles for example, the moment they break out of their shells, they hurriedly scamper to the ocean for protection. Butterflies that have broken out of the chrysalis, hang for a short time for the wings to strengthen and then they fly. Naturally, predators are on standby, and many of those turtles or butterflies become dinner for the hungry scavengers and unsuccessfully make it to the waters or skies beyond. I find it wonderful that God provides everything that each creature requires.

In my travels around the world, I have noticed that every culture has a system in place to care for the children within its community. All life is sacred and every surrounding life form, including the vegetation and creatures, has a vital role to play in the continuation of the planet, as we know it. Who taught us to care in such a way? At one point in time, man had to learn how to survive. So who was the teacher that instructed man on how to live and thrive in such a diverse world as Earth? One might argue that it is instinct that drives us all, including nature, but who planted that instinct within us and within the very cellular makeup of trees and creatures, insects and fish? It is of course our creator God.

He creates us through conception. The woman's egg and the man's seed join and the miraculous mystery of life begin. In the case of human beings, we carry our children for nine months, although many born earlier have the ability to survive and grow. All life gives birth and all life requires the sun, water, air and food. All life requires protection from outside elements and the cooperation of each other to provide for its survival. All life ceases to be when God decides upon its final breath. There has never been a single person who knew exactly when that moment would be and it is part of the mystery of our mighty Creator and King.

I have always had a very close affinity with nature. As a child, I would sit for hours observing creatures going about their day-to-day existence. I would not only see things, but I would look and observe animals and insects down to the minutest of details. I not only heard the sounds of birds, animals and insects, but I consciously listened to the tiniest of movements that few even notice, like the rustle of a leaf being disturbed by a creature beneath it.

I was with some of my students one day and we were meditating outside. I had told them to pick a place where they all felt happy to sit for several hours and I was instructing them on the ability to notice even the faintest of sounds when one is composed. They asked me for an example. I told them that several feet away, tucked underneath the front door to this building was a butterfly in a spider's web. I knew they must have been looking at each other with an expression of skepticism, so I suggested they all go and see. They returned dumb founded as they had seen a butterfly caught and yet they could not comprehend how I had heard it from such a long distance away. Seeing the insect struggling raised a dilemma for them. They wanted to set it free and could not deal with the thought of leaving it so vulnerable. One of them went and released it and they laughed as it flew around and landed in front of us – all red, yellow and beautiful. Out of nowhere, a magpie swooped down and snatched the butterfly for its snack and they all gasped in horror. I still had my eyes closed, but was aware of the turn in events. I explained to them that nature is intricately balanced, everything has its place and everything is food for each other. I told them that it is not our right to play God and force nature to comply with our wishes and whims. They sat and contemplated that for the rest of the day.

Over the years, I have had formal training in animal behavior from wise and learned teachers who taught me multiple techniques to calm and heal creatures (through prayer and meditation) from physical and mental abuse. I cannot fathom how anybody can consciously mistreat or neglect any life form, unless they are one of the unfortunate ones plagued with a mental affliction. Even then, it is incomprehensible to me that outsiders do not notice animal neglect and report it to authorities. How can a person stand by and watch an animal suffer? How can somebody deliberately starve, beat and chain an animal to a post or lock it in a confining cage? What goes through the mind of such an individual who has no regard for one of God's beloved creatures?

We learn in the book of Proverbs that, "Whoever is righteous has regard for the life of his beast, but the mercy of the wicked is cruel."

Some might argue that animals and other creatures are below us in the hierarchy of life. They say they are nothing in comparison to human beings, thus we have the right to lord over them and they must learn the lesson of submission. To me, there is an almost sinister aspect to that sense of entitlement. In the first book of the Bible and the Torah, God gives very precise details about creatures. "Let us make man in our image, after our likeness. And let them have dominion over the fish of the sea and over the birds of the heavens and over the livestock and over all the earth and over every creeping thing that creeps on the earth."

God created man in his own image and He blessed the man and woman. He told them to, "Be fruitful and multiply and fill the earth and subdue it and have dominion over the fish of the sea and over the birds of the heavens and over every living thing that moves on the earth."

The words "Dominion over," in that last paragraph offers no justifiable reasons for cruelty or neglect. This use of authority is not an excuse for abusive behavior of fish, birds, animals or creeping creatures upon and around the bed of this earth. Indeed, these words translate to mean that we are the managers who must keep some semblance of respectful order down here on earth. God has given us the ability to know right from wrong and to be responsible for our actions. We are therefore supposed to treat each other with respect. An employee may fear his boss who demands he work longer hours or lie to a customer about the safety of a product. He might submit to any demand placed upon him. However, this submission is not from respect and ultimately the employee will resign from the company or lash out with violence against the employer. The manager who respects his workers and knows each one by name will undoubtedly reap the rewards of his kindness. His staff is loyal, dedicated and hard working. His company's reputation in society will be one of fairness.

The animal kingdom requires respectful behavior. Let us observe a horse. In days gone by, its life and job was to take its owner from place to place, or before cars and tractors came into being; he would pull and gallop with all his might to aid in the tilling of the ground, or in the delivering of a message. He would ride with his master into battle, and act as a sturdy platform when leading an injured soldier home. Was the horse born tame and poised for work? The obvious answer of course is, "No, it had to learn and be broken in as an effective partner." However, here is the key; broken in does not mean beating to submission to break him; like the human torture of waterboarding. Breaking in is a systematic routine that involves much time, patience and care. In general, a horse's loyalty greatly depends upon the type of training or breaking in that it receives. Horses that are broken in to follow their leader out of respect are much more enjoyable and beneficial than those that follow out of fear.

As with all human relationships, we must gain trust and respect before creatures will work with and for us. There has to be a connection and bond between man and horse for instance. If a horse is afraid of his master or does not fully trust him, the relationship will not reach its full potential. This trust and respect is cultivated through patience and kindness. The master talks to him and grooms him, which forms a bond. Even before attempting to mount the animal, groundbreaking has to occur. A lunge line attaches to the horse's halter and he follows commands as he moves in a large circle around its trainer. Just as we teach a dog to sit, stand, come, down and stay, a master teaches his horse to, halt, walk and back.

The animal walks beside his master. He respects the space of its leader. Horses are strong minded and his master knows to be gentle when introducing the riding equipment. In the beginning, the animal may be afraid or timid with the unfamiliar sights and sounds of the riding tack. The horse must become accustomed to having a bit in its mouth. The bit is placed in the horse's mouth for short intervals of time and worked up to longer periods. The horse must also become familiar with the weight and sound of a saddle on its back. As its master prepares to mount him, he has only ever seen him below or at eye level. It requires gentleness to mount the horses back. Initially, the master lies across the saddle and lowers his weight gently so as not to spook him. Slowly and gently, the master's left foot is placed into the stirrup and then his right leg is swung over the back of the horse with care not to kick it. He has to stay low, hold tight onto the saddle and begin to walk gently. This leads to verbal commands and a faster transition from walking to trot. The horse and his master become one ball of energy.

Imagine if the owner of the horse is abusive. Instead of gentleness, he whips the animal in the attempt to make him docile and treats him with anger. He starves the creature to submission. He refuses to care for his feet by the neglecting his shoes and tightening his harness to the point that it imbeds itself into the flesh of the beast. He pulls and yells at him and forces the poor creature to submit to his authority. Do you think that horse will live long?

It is the same with every single creature on this planet, including human beings. A parent has dominion over its child. The mother and father have the authority and the instruction to teach that baby how to use the toilet when it is old enough. The baby must learn to crawl safely and to walk upright with care. It must learn commands and vital information of what is safe to touch and eat. Until old enough to fend for ourselves, God has implanted an instinct within us. In order to survive in harmony, every creature, (including human beings) has to transfer data to the next generation. The DNA information combined with the invisible migration paths are necessary lessons to ensure that extinction does not affect a particular species. A chain is only as strong as its weakest link.

Furthermore, every single aspect of creation (including plants and water) nourish, sustain and protect the other life forms. To destroy one species is potentially similar to knocking down a supporting wall – the domino affect causes drastic damage in the long-term plan of the planet. Where there is life, there is hope.

God requires us to understand that he gave us birds to lay eggs for us to eat and discarded feathers to line our coats and pillows for warmth and comfort. He created some of these birds with the strength and intellect to carry important messages to foreign lands on our behalf. Certain animals, including dogs, have an almost instinctive wish to bond closely with and help guide its human masters. They can detect illness, be trained to be the eyes and ears of a blind or deaf person and even work alongside emergency workers in the detection of bombs, or lost humans. They have courage, tenacity and loyalty. As independent and aloof as cats tend to be, even they have learned to sit beside their masters with peace. Sheep give us meat and wool. Cows give us life-sustaining milk. Pigs give us of their bodies and deer do the same. We cull the sick and injured with care and responsibility. We cut back on those beasts that threaten our livestock, and we protect our animals from death and disease.

Some wonder why we have lions, tigers, polar bears and monkeys. They say, surely these creatures were created for more than mere entertainment. What is an orca or whale meant to gift us? Is a zoo, circus, safari park or animal park useful, educational or is it selfish entertainment? Why do we need animal shelters and sanctuaries? Should we be eating everything that has life, including lobsters, crabs and other sea life forms? Should we snatch a calf from his mother, hold him in a tiny pen in preparation for slaughter? Is our desire for a more tender dinner tonight humane? Do we really need to pump our creatures with preservatives and force them to behave in ways that God did not create within their DNA? I will be discussing these very important subjects and more, in my next book.

For now, kindly think about all creatures that exist by your side, under your feet and above your head in the sky. The book of Job in the Bible teaches us to, "Ask the beasts, and they will teach you; the birds of the heavens, and they will tell you; or the bushes of the earth, and they will teach you; and the fish of the sea will declare to you. Who among all these does not know that the hand of the Lord has done this? In his hand is the life of every living thing and the breath of all mankind."

In Psalm 50, God tell us, "For every beast of the forest is mine, the cattle on a thousand hills. I know all the birds of the hills, and all that moves in the field is mine. If I were hungry, I would not tell you, for the world and its fullness are mine." In other words, every life form belongs to God. We are to recognize each of their strengths and weaknesses and task them with appropriate jobs. Jesus tells us to, "Look at the birds of the air: they neither sow nor reap nor gather into barns, and yet your heavenly Father feeds them. Are you not of more value than they?" God reassures us that he cares about every single creature. He has created everything in such a way that we have exactly what we need for food, water, clothing and protection.

We make clothes either to cover ourselves for warmth and ceremonial occasions or to disguise ourselves when hunting. God has done the exact same thing for his creatures in the form of camouflage. I am sure you could name all kinds of green creatures including lizards, birds and fish. However, did you know that a sloth is the only green mammal on the planet? It eats leaves that require several days to process and its laid-back approach to life renders it vulnerable to predators. Thus, God has given it a significant green layer atop its brown fur. Creation has a combination of materials, coloration or illumination for concealment, either by making animals or objects hard to see or by disguising them as something else. Some creatures have motion dazzle, which confuses the observer with a conspicuous pattern, making the object visible but harder to locate.

Beavers have physical features including a broad paddled tail and sharp teeth to chew through a tree trunk and to build dams, canals and lodges. They have an alarm signal: when startled or frightened, a swimming beaver will rapidly dive while forcefully slapping the water with its broad tail, audible over great distances above and below water. This serves as a warning to beavers in the area. Once a beaver has sounded the alarm, nearby beavers will dive and may not reemerge for some time. Beavers are slow on land, but are good swimmers, and can stay under water for as long as fifteen minutes.

When God created life, he used exact precision. All these millions of years later, we are still discovering hidden species and inventing equipment to help us understand how, when and why nature performs in certain rhythms and mannerism. When God made the earth, he filled it with water, vegetation, rocks and creatures. He formed humankind in his own image and commanded them to tend to his creation. All procreating creatures were male and female. Humankind had authority to name every aspect of creation and to put procedures into place to protect them. He was to care for, not abuse or destroy God's creation.

Conclusion

God has given us the gift of life with free will. He has provided us with guidelines, promises and specific commandments. When one adheres to his laws, one is able to enjoy a fruitful and meaningful existence with other human beings and creatures. God has given man a woman to accompany him on earth and he has created astonishing creatures to live alongside him as protectors, companions, food and inspiration.

Man's role is to be responsible for the earth and to cultivate it without greed. Man is to show kindness, mercy and mature responsibility to and for all creatures and life forms on earth.

The apostle Luke asks us to, "Consider the ravens: they neither sow nor reap, they have neither storehouse nor barn, and yet God feeds them. Of how much more value are you than the birds!"

All life is born. Eventually, in one way or another, all life dies. Certain parts of us grow when needed for a particular event. A placenta for instance protects an embryo until it is ready to be born. We are told in Ecclesiastes 12:7 "And the dust returns to the earth as it was, and the spirit returns to God who gave it."

God gave man intellect. Man has used this intellect to invent many devices to help him know the time and communicate more effectively with other beings. In his quest to advance and discover new planets and methods of cheating death, he has developed weapons to destroy others, tools to bulldoze and redesign, and machines to preserve those he deems precious. Today, humankind has in effect thrown a boomerang. Every device he has created to destroy, comes back to destroy him.

Over time, man has forgotten the ability to rest. There was once a time when man bonded and knew the gift of a close-knit community. Today he has ostracized himself from the one thing that matters the most - family. Seldom does he sit and contemplate the true meaning of life. Rarely does he notice the creatures struggling to survive unless they are directly involved in his ability to live.

In Jeremiah, we are reminded that, "Even the stork in the heavens knows her times, and the turtledove, swallow, and crane keep the time of their coming, but my people know not the rules of the Lord."

When I was with God at the gates of heaven, he told me to remind people that they must learn to respect all the feathered, furred and finned. We must preserve our waters against over fishing and we must cease to use it as a dumping ground for waste. We must protect our skies from pollution and our land from toxic waste. Our forests are rapidly disappearing and its inhabitants are becoming homeless and threatened, thus if our future generations are to have a world that is safe and habitable, we must all take a proactive stance in preserving it. It is not the job for one or two, but the responsibility of everyone.

Who is the manager that God put in charge of creation? I am and you are! We have a joint responsibility to manage our world and to fulfill his command.

Are you living responsibly?

Lesson 28: Leadership

We established in previous chapters that leadership is a crucial ingredient to life. Are we born leaders or do we have to foster the necessary qualities over time? We can look back through time and note those extraordinary men and women who demonstrated exceptional courage and strength as they stared into the face of tyranny. These bold and charismatic leaders inspired the confidence in others to stand up for justice, and to stare down those who threatened to annihilate the infrastructure of a peaceful, God-fearing community.

When we think about leaders and consider whom we admire and wish to emulate, military and political heroes' spring to mind like George Washington, Harry Truman, General David Petraeus, General Norman Schwarzkopf, Chief Sitting Bull, General Douglas MacArthur, General George S. Patton, Lieutenant Colonel Oliver North and Napoleon Bonaparte. We recall the radical, forward thinking political and civil leaders including Abraham Lincoln, Winston Churchill, and Martin Luther King Jr., Mikhail Gorbachev, Thomas Jefferson, Ronald Reagan, Nelson Mandela and Margaret Thatcher, to name a few. We recall the religious leaders and martyrs including our Lord Jesus Christ, St. Joan of Arc, Moses, St. John the Baptist, St. Peter, George Fox, John Wesley, St. John Paul II, St. Mother Theresa, Buddha, Lao-tzu, Confucius, Bishop Fulton Sheen and Gandhi-ji. We are able to learn from our living spiritual teachers including Rev. Dr. Billy and Franklyn Graham, H.H. the Dalai Lama, Bishop T.D. Jakes, Archbishop Rowan Williams, Sri Sri Ravi Shankar-ji and Pope Francis.

We marvel at the inspirational innovators of inventions including Leonardo Da Vinci, Edwin Land, George Westinghouse, Thomas Edison, Alexander Graham Bell, Nikola Tesla and Archimedes of Syracuse. One could keep adding to this list and in no time at all, one could fill an entire book with all the amazing men and women who have touched our lives with their pure genius and compassion. I cannot omit one of the most outstanding leaders of my time, her Royal Highness Princess Diana who was the epitome of a world leader who quite simply exemplified loving service to all humanity. She was our *Queen of hearts.*

Throughout history, thousands of men and women have influenced humankind and stood out above the crowd. Many of these individuals have inspired positive innovation that catapulted us from sickness to health, from earth to the moon, from static to mobile and from caves to skyscrapers.

There are others however, who dedicated their lives to systematically undoing all that was good and righteous in our world; men who played God and chose to destroy with complete selfish disregard for the value of human life. These murderers include: Adolf Hitler, Joseph Stalin, Vlad the Impaler, Osama bin Laden, Fidel Castro, Pol Pot, Idi Amin, Mao Zedong, Ivan the Terrible, Genghis Khan and Saddam Hussein. As evil as these men were, they too had personalities that were capable of leading others to implement their destructive strategies. They were able to inflict unimaginable suffering and pain. Their dishonesty covered up all signs of their blatant murder as they defended their leaders with an almost shocking sense of loyalty and narcissism.

With guidance, practice and maturity, we can all inspire leading ideas and changes within our home, community, organization and beyond. However, there is a huge difference between being an ordinary leader, and being a great leader. An average person can certainly manage a successful department or company and may even hold a political seat on the town council. However, a great leader has something extra special. Greatness is a rare jewel. It is the difference between a student and his master. It is the difference between genius and unschooled. That *greatness* is unique and when this powerful individual is in your presence, you have an overwhelming feeling of awe and respect for them. Right to your core, you keenly sense that this person has the confidence, passion, dignity, tenacity, compassion, and experience to take you from mediocre to the personification of excellence in record time.

Great leaders steer our armed services and countries. They have a wise and effective plan. They know the strategy needed to succeed and they pick the most capable men and women to implement their orders. With bravery, training and arms, the followers stand up when they hear the battle cry, "*Forward*!" When the great leader announces that this is the day and the moment, the followers feel both euphoria and trepidation, but they trust in their leader to guide them to victory.

My late father was a former military officer. In his opinion, ignorance was not bliss, as the famous saying quoted. He believed that ignorance was dangerous. He would often tell me that foolish people voted with little knowledge or thought and that when they put their check mark on the ballot, few even knew the name of the candidate they were supporting, least of all what that individual represented. He insisted on my public policy education from a very early age. My school did not teach me much about politics, so he would expect me to learn at home with him in debating and discussion. To my father, there was no room for failure or excuses in life. He was strong, fearless and deeply respected by everybody who knew him. He instilled within me an unquenchable thirst for knowledge and an open-minded interest in everything from religion to law. He was a very adept poker player. One simply could not figure out what he was thinking most of the time. He had that famous *poker* face, which hid any indications of bad cards in his hand. I was fascinated why nobody ever dare challenge him over anything in life, and his level head and sense of decency were traits I admired above all else. He was a rare man.

I met another man several years later who reminded me of my father. Amir was the county commissioner. He was not only a great leader who influenced my life on an equal level to my father and Jeff Boxen; he was also the absolute love of my life. I met him one Friday afternoon whilst working for the county Chamber of Commerce. He felt an urge to come inside, just as I was on my way out to a meeting. We literally collided and from that moment on, my life was never the same again.

We stood staring at one another in complete silence for a few minutes. Yes, it was like a dream. When steered towards my office, we continued to look in to each other's eyes without words, as we sat on either side of my desk. We held each other's hands and smiled, with no sound exchanged for over an hour. It was quite simply magical. I knew nothing about him at all. He was in essence a complete stranger to me. I fell instantly in love with him, and had he proposed marriage, I would have accepted without hesitation. I am aware that this sounds absurd, but my heart knew that he was the man for me.

The love we shared will always fill my heart and soul with a knowing that I received an extraordinary blessing. Amir was close to sixty-eight years old when we met. An age difference of some twenty-six years meant nothing to me, but it caused outrage amongst the women of the town, who went out of their way to protest our union in a particularly nasty and selfish way. People can be so cruel and close-minded. What does age, color of skin, height, culture or positon mean when two people are in love? Yes, we can debate this from a myriad of points of view. However, lovers, regardless of their appearance will always find a way to be together.

Tragically, Amir had an accident whilst in Florida four years later, which rendered him severely disabled and unable to function normally again. I all but lost it at the hospital, as I sat holding his hand. How can you possibly express such grief and sadness to those who have not felt the same depth of love? He was and always will be a precious love gift from God.

Amir had a well-defined black and white philosophy when it came to politics, finance and business. He had struggled through life in India, with a father who nursed a drug addiction. At the age of eighteen, he escaped that miserable life and came to the country of his dreams – America. With only a few bucks in his pocket, he had paid for an education in the United States by washing dishes. He became a teacher, and then a bank president. From there he advanced into real estate and went on to be the first minority commissioner in Wyoming. He was very proud to be an Indian and equally proud to be an American. We combined our love for India, America and England with everything we did together. Each night after dinner, Amir would go and hose down the patio to cool it and as we sat enjoying the cool night air, he would tell me stories of India and the miracles of Jesus Christ.

He had the dedicated hard work ethic of an Indian man and devoted himself to those less fortunate. He formed a foundation and awarded his entire salary to those who needed a grant for their education. He worked tirelessly to build and operate shelters for boys and girls with drug addiction and family problems. Regardless of his age, if something needed doing, digging, constructing, destroying, managing or making – Amir was there to lead, with sleeves rolled up and that magnetic personality that drew people to him with passion and purpose. He was respectful and dignified. He was a true man of the people who went out of his way to remember all the ins and outs of their personal and professional lives, including remembering to send cards of congratulations on anniversaries.

As a bank president, he situated his desk by the door, so that every time a customer entered to do a transaction, they saw Amir first. He insisted that every employee called the customer by name. When this did not happen, the employee went home with no pay. He would spend hours studying countless books and notes from meetings. He would go through every single budget issue, and if he disagreed with anything, he had no hesitation in making his feelings known respectfully, but firmly. On one occasion, he adamantly refused to attend a commission meeting, and no amount of begging him or me, would convince him to budge from his feelings of disapproval at wastage or corruption. He was (is) a dignified man of strict principal and extremely private and protective of our relationship. He thought about his words very carefully before he spoke. It was this ability to remain stone silent, which said far more than any words could ever portray.

We would spend most evenings together, and every weekend. Amir took the time and effort to know me inside out and his gifts were exactly what I needed to be peaceful, nurtured and content. These times were so precious and an amazing learning opportunity for me. He could be very stern sometimes, and although his bluntness was alarming at first, I quickly understood that he was preparing me for the next step in my life. I knew this was the opportunity to shadow a very great leader. He was a resilient man who asked for no favors, but generously gave of himself to anybody who came to him for help. His philosophy was, "I don't like handouts. I like hand ups!"

His favorite song of all time was *The Gambler* written by Don Schlitz and recorded by American country music artist, Kenny Rogers. He would tell me repeatedly to listen, learn and implement the strategy of a poker winner. I always laugh when I hear it, for my father, Jeff Boxen and Amir's great leadership influence on my life, is clearly the message contained within the bed of this song.

Conclusion

So what should we be looking for when choosing a leader to follow? Certainly they must be a good planner; exceptionally skilled at mission strategy, as it is not just about money and technology, but lives at stake. They must be a quick thinker, as leaders often face situations that may be a matter of life and death. They must be able to find quick and safe solutions to problems. They must possess great people skills and be an effective communicator. They must be patient and an active listener. They must be approachable and must be able to reach out to others. Their temperament must be cool even in the tightest of situations.

A great leader must always lead by example and exemplify strength of character with values and ethics. They must be determined, disciplined, and intelligent and have an inquisitive mind that absorbs information quickly. In addition to this, a general in the military or a president of an organization must be capable of furnishing equipment and supplies. They must be resourceful, active, careful, hardy and quick-witted. They must be a combination of gentle and brutal. They must be capable of both caution and surprise.

They must be skillful in defense and attack and have the capacity to know what the enemy or a competitor is planning next. They must be honest with sincerity, integrity and candor as this inspires trust. Their actions must stem from reason and moral principle rather than childlike desires or feelings. They must be forward-looking and able to set goals with a clear vision for the future. Last, but by no means least, a great leader must seek out diversity.

Lesson 29: Relocation

I awoke one morning at the beginning of June with a definite feeling that I would not be in Wyoming in September. In fact, I was a hundred percent certain that I would never return to Wyoming.

I sat with a feeling of profound sadness and even nervousness in my heart. I loved being there. Admittedly, the cold temperatures were challenging, but I had grown to love the open skies and the sounds of the cougars and bears. I enjoyed camping in Yellowstone National Park with the buffalo and wolves and helping to exercise horses as a cowgirl. I had wonderful, caring close friends, plus a fantastic job with the Chamber of Commerce with a president I deeply respected and admired. My hospice ministry was fulfilling and I had graduated from leadership institute and the citizen's police academy, which was an inspirational experience. I languished in the love of Amir and I could not imagine ever leaving him or this beautiful state.

Many of the older women had made our relationship very difficult and one or two had boldly even gone to his chambers to convey their disgust. Some of the men were not too happy either and they could not understand why I was with a man old enough to be my father when they were young enough to be a suitable husband. After one particularly nasty confrontation, we sat trying to decide how to deal with the negativity of this relentless and bizarre public interference. At one point Amir had suggested we stop seeing each other to let things quieten down from the criticism. It was a dreadful time that caused us both much sadness.

After his seventieth birthday, Amir decided that he was being utterly selfish by loving me to the point that I was (in his opinion) "Stuck," in a small town who did not appreciate my gifts and talents. He firmly believed that God did not send me back to earth in 1989, to sit in Wyoming making telephone calls for a Chamber of Commerce. He said watching me in my office was like watching an animal in a cage, and he wanted me to have the courage to leave. I thought he meant that he would be coming with me, but I was wrong. He told me that he had been there for over thirty-five years, and still had two years to go before fulfilling his obligation as the county commissioner. He knew he was to stay there and he knew there was a husband (not him) in my future elsewhere. We argued about this for several days. I wanted to know if I had done something to offend or upset him, but he laughed when I suggested that it was something that I had done wrong. In his opinion, I was as close to perfection as any human being could possibly be. I also knew that he had profound dreams, visions and wisdom. He firmly told me that he knew my future husband would appear within six years, but in order for that union to occur, I had to leave this small town and allow God to direct my life.

I prayed and meditated about our conversation for a few weeks. Therefore, when I awoke with that all too familiar knowing within me that this was a very clear instruction from God; I was extremely upset, to put it mildly. I called Amir. He wisely suggested I take the day off work and spend it in prayer and meditation alone with God. After an hour or so, I had the absolute knowing that I was to leave and went in to work to resign. You could have knocked my president over with a feather. Everybody knew how much I was in love with Amir, and the notion that I would ever leave him, was unfathomable. Julie (my president) did not inform the Board of Directors of my decision as she felt I would change my mind and stay.

As the weeks passed, I could see September on my calendar quickly approaching. I literally had no clue where God was leading me. I would just sense within me during the day, and hear in my dreams at night, "Trust me my child. Have faith." I did have faith. One cannot go to the gates of heaven and return, as I had done, if one did not trust, and know to obey. God told me to leave England and my family, which was a mighty sacrifice. Now I was to leave a man I deeply loved and to go to an unknown destination, with no clear purpose in mind. God was not asking me to think about relocation, he was commanding me to trust that he would lead me to the next chapter in my life. He gave me a vision of being in my truck, which contained only a few essential belongings. I was to drive to the southern border of the state and I was to be there on the last day of August. He did not share with me where I was going to relocate, which meant that I would know as the days progressed.

I packed up my truck with essential items, including personal things of value. The rest of my belongings, including furniture and pottery remained for the family that moved in afterwards. God had told me to travel light. Quite unexpectedly one night in the middle of August, I received a phone call from Jin, an old family friend, who had been our general doctor in England. I had not seen him since I was ten years old, when he had moved to America with his family. He had been my grandmother's physician I later discovered and my family had respected him highly; and was very sad to see him leave.

If you had asked me to name ten people who could have called me from the past, I would never have even put him on the list. Yet ironically, as soon as he spoke, I knew who it was. The obvious question most would ask is how he found me. I had been instrumental in helping a diabetic institute in Arizona years before. As a physician, and specialist in diabetes, he had just been there to lecture. Conversation led to discussing who had helped build the institute. They showed him a photograph of yours truly. Even though I am no longer that child, he recognized me and asked if anybody knew how to reach me. He got my phone number by calling various people who knew me, which led to him calling me that night. We chatted for hours. I told him all about my life to date and we discussed my imminent relocation.

Being a grounded, mature and extremely wise Asian Indian doctor, the thought of me driving off into the sunset defied understanding. "Where are you planning to go to?" he asked.

"I don't know yet. God hasn't told me."

"What are you planning to do?" he retorted.

"I have no clue. I guess go to the border of Wyoming and wait For God to tell me what to do. I trust God to lead me. He's never let me down before," I assured him.

"Don't you feel any fear at all?" Jin asked with a tone of apprehension and concern.

"No Jin, I don't. This is a hard move for me as I have ties here that I am not happy to cut, but I also know that I am on earth to serve God and I have a calling to fulfill. Earth is not my home. Heaven is where I will return one day. Whilst I am here, I have specific work to do and if you are going to be in my life Jin, you will have to learn to accept this fact," I said with a stern voice of caution.

"Why don't you ask God if you can come to New Jersey? You can stay with me for a few days. I would love to see you again. Do you know where New Jersey is? It's a very long drive; do you think you could manage it?" he said with a chuckle in his voice.

"I will pray about it for sure and yes, I know where New Jersey is. As for can I drive that distance, the answer is assuredly yes. I have driven all over America alone, and in fact, I enjoy seeing this country by road. Give me a few days please to meditate upon your kind offer," I replied politely.

Two weeks later, on the day before my departure, my colleagues had a farewell party. The office was full with people coming to wish me well. It was humbling and very emotional. Even some of the ones who had made my life very difficult over Amir, came with a few kind words, and even apologies. Many were in tears and nobody could believe I was actually on my way out of the state forever. I received touching letters from the governor and state senators and representatives, thanking me for my huge contribution. Amir stood next to me and thanked everybody for coming. He held my hand defiantly and stroked away the tears off my cheeks. I stood shaking most of the time and when I leant my head against his shoulder, I could not keep the tears inside. It was quite simply horrendous and very sad.

"Jaan," he quietly said. "You must not cry in public. Be strong and leave this place with dignity. Don't let these women see weakness."

"But this is heartbreaking babe," I cried.

"I know it is," he consoled. "But don't let these people think you are unsure. God is sending you onwards to do his work. Nobody here will understand that, but I do and I am proud of you. Love you babe."

Somehow, I managed to pose for pictures and everybody was very kind to me. Amir and I spent that last evening together. Neither of us said very much at all. We just sat on the couch as usual, with my head gently resting on his lap, the sacred ritual that had always given me a feeling of absolute peace and love. We prayed together and cried as we held each other tightly. My heart quite simply broke in pieces.

"Oh my Jaan," he whispered repeatedly. Lovers in the Punjabi and Hindi language use this sacred word "Jaan," to describe a love that is significantly profound that the lover would literally die for him or her. They say that this person has stolen your heart and will not give it back to you and, in all honesty, you do not want it back from them because you love them so dearly. This was the name he always called me. Even after his terrible accident years later, when he could barely communicate from the bleeding on his brain; as soon as he saw me he said, "Jaan; my beautiful Jaan!"

I woke early the next morning and after breakfast, I got into my truck. I only drove a few feet, and stopped. "Why are you doing this to me God?" I cried. "Please don't ask me to leave Amir!" I begged. I got out the truck and ran back to him. I just could not cope with this at all. He held me tightly for a few more minutes before saying, "Jaan, you are not ordinary like me or others. You are special. You are my angel. You have given me much more love and joy than anybody has in my life. You have taught me what true love is and you have shown me kindness and respect in ways I have never felt before. Babe, I will always be with you, and you will always be with me for eternity. However, you have to go, and you have to do God's work, for this is his command. I love you more than you will ever know, but you have to follow his plan. Now go and don't look back!" He kissed me passionately one last time, walked into his house and shut the door.

Somehow, (God alone knows how) I managed to drive to the southern border of Wyoming, where God gave me the command to drive to New Jersey. Most of that trip was a blur.

I pulled into a motel in Nebraska one night and quickly fell asleep. I awoke with a very definite image of the words, "NJCC." I did not have a clue what that meant. Those letters haunted me the entire day. I asked God to clarify them to me and he said, "New Jersey Chamber of

Commerce." I Googled this organization and called. The vice president took my call and explained that there were no employment opportunities. I continued driving. The next day the feeling was even stronger than the day before. I knew that I had to call the NJCC again. The head of marketing answered the phone this time, but he also confirmed that there were no jobs available.

The following day all I could think about was this Chamber. God said to me, "You will be working at the NJCC for two years, and it will begin the week you arrive!" You cannot be more precise than that I thought to myself. Therefore, I boldly picked up the phone and called again. This time I asked for an email address for the person in charge of sales and membership. I went onto the internet at a gas station and sent her my resume. Within an hour, she had called me back and we discussed my background and possible opportunities within her department. I made an appointment for an interview at the end of the week.

Arriving in New Jersey was a massive culture shock after the laid-back life of Wyoming. I felt like I was driving in the Grand Prix and was scared to death of crashing my truck. It took a few weeks to get used to the way everybody aggressively drove on the east coast. I stayed with Jin for a few days. He was so kind, caring, compassionate and gentle with me. Truly, God had put a very wonderful old friend back into my life. He helped me to settle there and supported me with great wisdom and strength.

Within a couple of days of arriving in New Jersey, I drove down to the state Chamber of Commerce, which was nearing its centenary celebration. Everybody was very surprised to hear the basics of my story and even the most skeptical of them had to agree that my credentials were superior. Despite having no employment vacancies, they created a position for me in the business development department, which was a tremendous honor, and a fantastic learning opportunity that I will neither regret, nor forget. Considering all the Chamber of Commerce offices in New Jersey, God had sent me to the most prestigious opposite the Governor's office and I felt quite overwhelmed.

The president, a dignified, powerful and highly influential woman, enquired as to where I was living. When I told her that I did not have a home, furniture or much of anything, except what was in my truck, she offered me a room in her huge mansion. I politely declined. I was still waiting for God to tell me where he wanted me to be and it did not feel that it was with her. She looked at me as if I was insane and I can still recall her expression as I shrugged my shoulder and smiled. Months later, she recalled the day I had arrived with an almost sense of awe and pride. Nobody had quite met anybody like me before and they all had to get used to complete strangers wandering in off the streets to meet me. These strangers included men who travelled from India to find a woman called, "Dr. Christine Overton."

As I drove up to the northern part of New Jersey and back to stay with Jin, I had a vision. God showed me swans and glass. Obviously, I had no idea what swans and glass meant, but knew this familiar feeling, which simply asked me to have faith and obey. After forty-five minutes of driving, I felt the urge to pull off the freeway and head down a beautiful winding forest road. I marveled at how idyllic everywhere was around me. In the distance, I saw an apartment complex, nestled within the trees, next to a babbling brook and whilst admiring its beauty, I imagined what a wonderful place this had to be to reside. As I approached the complex, I saw a huge sign that identified it. Can you guess what was on that sign? Yes, it had a picture of a glorious white swan. God has a great sense of humor and his visions are always accurate! I laughed aloud.

I drove in and parked my car in the only space available - *Future resident.* I went in to the office to enquire about the availability of homes to rent. The leasing agent informed me that they only had one apartment available, which had been free for quite a while. I asked why that was, and she said, "The balcony is not open like the others. A previous tenant enclosed it without permission and nobody wants it. It is yours if you clear our background check."

"When you say it's enclosed," I asked. "What exactly do you mean?"

Can you guess what she said? "Well," she replied. "It's enclosed with glass. With you being English, It's a bit like a conservatory I guess," I laughed so hard that she looked confused.

"I'll take it!" I excitedly exclaimed. "Please give me the forms to complete and oh please kindly outline what else I need to do in order to live here?"

"Would you like to see it?" she asked.

"That won't be necessary thank you. I am sure it's perfect for me!" I added.

"But don't you need to see it to know whether your furniture will fit?" she said with a confused tone in her voice.

"I don't have any furniture, so that won't be a problem." I replied.

Yes, she looked at me as if I were either insane or a criminal, but after an exemplary background check, the guarantee of income from a prestigious job, wonderful references plus cash, she was calm.

Within two days, I had moved in and I lived there very happily for four years.

Conclusion

For those of you who truly wish to follow God, and live a life of service to humanity, you must understand that your life is not going to be simple, or free from suffering and relocation. One only has to look at the Jewish people to see that.

For those of you who do have the courage to adhere to his word, the reward may not necessarily be evident here on earth. Faith requires us to be bold. Faith requires us to listen to his still small voice, which guides us safely to the Promised Land. He commands us to obey his call to love and care for all his sheep, with the exact same care that Jesus demonstrated throughout his own life. To say that one is truly a follower of Christ, one must be prepared to live as he lived, to pick up ones cross and walk with him unconditionally to their last breath.

In the Gospel of Luke 18, Jesus spoke to a young man who was very rich, but asked our Lord how he could lead an even more holy life in his sight. Jesus told him, "You still lack one thing. Sell everything you have and give to the poor, and you will have treasure in heaven. Then come, follow me." When he heard this, he became very sad, because he was a man of great wealth. Jesus looked at him and said, "How hard it is for the rich to enter the kingdom of God! Indeed, it is easier for a camel to go through the eye of a needle than for a rich man to enter the kingdom of God." Those who heard this asked, "Who then can be saved?" Jesus replied, "What is impossible with men is possible with God." Peter said to him, "We have left all we had to follow you!" "I tell you the truth," Jesus said to them. "No one who has left home or wife or brothers or parents or children for the sake of the kingdom of God will fail to receive many times as much in this age and, in the age to come, eternal life."

Some imagine those words and instructions only belong to the Biblical days of our ancestors, that in all reality, modern life expects us to conform to society's rules of convention and common sense. As easy as it would be to disregard rules, or to say that life today is not about picking up one's cross and following a historical character, those of us who are committed to Christ; or in my case have additionally been to the gates of heaven, cannot do anything to brush this reality aside. On the contrary, the only brushing off that I can legitimately do, is to pick up my shoes and brush off the sand and dirt from the bottom.

A true follower of Jesus Christ has to find the strength within him or herself to keep looking forwards to eternal life, and to resist the temptation of wallowing around in the past. Life on earth is short. Life in heaven is eternal. The question one has to ask oneself is am I prepared to serve God faithfully knowing that I may not see any substantial reward in my life on earth.

If you can keep your head up, even when your heart is breaking and continue to love all human beings and creatures, then I promise you that when you arrive in heaven, the angels sing loudly and the blessed Trinity say, "Welcome home my child!"

Lesson 30: India

One afternoon in November 2010, my phone rang at the Chamber of Commerce. The receptionist told me three men from India were in the boardroom asking to talk to me. I looked at my schedule puzzled. When I saw nobody was due to be meeting with me, I smiled. Having strangers wandering in to see me had become a very normal event in my life.

When I walked into the boardroom, I noticed that one of the men was blind. As I approached them, they became very emotional and to say they greeted with great enthusiasm would be a gross understatement. "Dr. Overton-ji, it is a great honor for us to meet you," they chorused. Before I even had a chance to respond they continued, "Dr., we are from the H.V. Desai eye hospital in Pune, India. We are here in America to solicit private funding for our organization. We perform free eye surgeries for the blind in India. People recommended that we look for you and we searched all over America praying that we would find you. We spoke to Mr. Vijay Dani Sir who said we could find you here. Please forgive us madam for visiting with no appointment. This is such an honor for us."

I am sure my face must have looked like a deer in headlights. It is one thing to have a stranger wander in off the streets of Trenton and I have even had a family fly from Washington State to Arizona for my help, after having a dream. I have opened the door to find Tibetan lamas and Native American Indian elders requesting me to follow them, after they had seen a vision. However, to have somebody fly from the other side of the world to find you is an entirely different matter. I asked the receptionist to bring us some tea as I began to evaluate the situation by asking many questions. My biggest concern was to discover if this organization was legitimate. In the past, groups had solicited my professional help to raise money or to be patron of their institutions. National and global committees and boards had invited me to take a seat and organizers of pageants and competitions had asked me to be their judge. Some of these were worth my time whilst others were disorganized and fiscally irresponsible.

When one works for an esteemed state Chamber of Commerce, one must behave impeccably and perform ones duties to a very high standard. It is a public profile office and as such, one has to tread carefully. One is not to involve oneself in anything that could cause scandal, gossip or negativity to that entity. One must be constantly aware of journalists or rumormongers, waiting to pounce on a sensational story. A year into my office, the board of directors had asked for my president's resignation.

Within a few months, more than a dozen of my colleagues had left through termination or resignation. There were lawsuits filed against senior staff members due to sexual harassment and an abusive working environment. Given the fact that the board of directors consisted of over sixty of the state's most prominent leaders, including a number of them who sat on the governor's committees, I knew to tread very carefully indeed.

After several hours, I was satisfied that these men, including Mr. Niranjan-ji Pandya were honest and decent, with a cause that excited me. I called a very dear friend of mine, Mr. H.R. Shah-ji who was the owner of TV Asia and a highly respected leader in the USA and India. The next morning I was on a TV show with these people from the H.V. Desai eye hospital. We discussed the procedures that they performed each day with a two hundred-bed capability including glaucoma surgery, cornea, medical retina, vitreo- retinal surgery, pediatric ophthalmology and cataract surgery. I thought it quite wonderful that we sat in this interview discussing blindness just before Diwali, which was (is) the festival of light in India. I loved the idea of helping people out of their darkness to light and I explained to my visitors that before I could honestly begin to raise money, I must visit and see the hospital for myself. They were very excited and invited me to go as soon as I could. I had known since 1989 that I would visit India and I figured this was the best way for me to serve God.

For two years, I had been extremely involved in the Asian Indian community. They had all been so kind to me and I was often a dignitary at their events. I marched in their parades and spoke on their podiums.

I worked with the deputy speaker of the house, Assemblyman Upendra Chivukula on many issues including healthcare, and appeared with him frequently at award ceremonies where we both received honors for our work in the community.

I served at the United Nations Headquarters in New York as a representative, where I attended meetings for trauma outreach prevention and sat on committees for genocide, elderly care and world spirituality issues. I had made very close friendships in the Indian communities of New Jersey and New York and spent the vast majority of my time in their company. A number of them sent their children to me to mentor including Thakor Bulsara-ji and Nisha. Thakor was a very dear friend of mine and would always serve as my primary bodyguard at events. I volunteered at health clinics for the Sikh community where our Lions club provided free eye and breast screening for the poor. As with all cultures, there was in fighting and I am certain that I made some foolish mistakes along the way with aligning myself to some who were politically unpopular. However, I admired and deeply respected the Indian community, not least because my ancestors were from there as well.

I was a regular guest at the Indian and Japanese consulates in Manhattan, New York. The consul generals and ambassadors were always very kind to me, and we shared a great working relationship. I worked with political leaders from all sides of the aisle and with mayors and other state officials. When the tsunami hit Japan in 2011, the Japanese Consul General in New York asked me to come and offer him my wisdom. I attended that meeting with former Mayor Jun Choi, an extraordinary world humanitarian leader Mr. Sitesh Mehtani-ji and Dr. Gita Patel whose grandfather had shared a prison cell with Mahatma Gandhi-ji. Together we sat quite numb by the horrific tragedy and discussed the nuclear problem that was rapidly escalating.

We decided to make a CD of prayers and to distribute much needed food. The Consul General and I planned to meet again regularly as the months followed. As much as I wanted to fly to Japan and distribute our products and food in person, my United Nations director wanted me to go to the Congo, Haiti or northern India.

It was now 2011. I was still recovering from the rectal surgeries, but two weeks after my last procedure, I called the directors from the H.V. Desai Eye hospital and arranged to fly over. With the change in administration, the resignations and disgraceful terminations of many of my wonderful colleagues, I felt I had no alternative than to also resign from the Chamber of Commerce. Sometimes in life you have to stand up for what you believe in, regardless of what that may mean to your career.

I was excited to fly to India and my first port of call was to Mumbai (also known as Bombay). A number of armed guards were waiting for me as I disembarked the plane. At first, I thought I was in some kind of trouble but they reassured me that they were the official welcome party for all international dignitaries and wanted to take me to my host in style. They respectfully escorted me passed the lines in military fashion, which set the tone for my entire few weeks in India. My political and religious connections back in North America had made sure that I would be safe, and Shri Niranjan-ji Pandya from the H.V. Desai eye hospital, who went on to win the distinguished Padma Shri medal of honor, went out of his way to make my trip beneficial and honorable.

I planned to stay with friends for a few days and then travel to Pune, a few hours south of there. It is impossible to describe the wonderful dichotomy of Mumbai. The aromas hit me as soon as I left the airport and consisted of sweet aromatic herbs, succulent food mixed with the stench of urine and feces. The constant noise, heavy traffic and mixture of wealth verses poverty were staggering. It was also heart wrenching to see the thousands of beggars on the streets, which came right up to my car window and pleaded with me for money. Many of these beggars were children with hands and feet amputated and eyes gouged out (some deliberately to make them more effective as beggars). I was shocked and deeply saddened to see this and I was not prepared whatsoever to experience that. My chauffer cautioned me not to give them money, as the traffic flow was slow.

Millions of people maneuvered around the streets in rickshaws, cars, on cycles and by foot. As you can probably imagine, day and night I heard the hustle and bustle of life including horns, singing, shouting, birds squawking, people praying, cows mooing, merchants selling and musical instruments playing non-stop. From every angle possible, life came above me, under me, around me and if we did not get out of the way, even over me without the blink of an eye. It was stressful at first, especially to a westerner unused to such extreme circumstances.

The heart wrenching poverty imprinted itself upon my soul. I had never felt more alive than when I was amongst the people in this magnificent country, where my ancestors had lived and died. I had met my godfather, Lord Louis Mountbatten several times before his death (execution by the IRA) in 1979. We were on vacation in Lymington when we heard the news and my father was devastated. My godfather had been the last viceroy to India and it was a very important part of his career and life. Thus, whilst there, I could not help but consider my biological roots, his significant work and Amir's life which definitely served to instill a sense of purpose and significance.

Transportation in Mumbai was hectic as you can imagine. Literally millions of people leapt on and off the moving trains and if one was not agile, one risked being killed in the rush and shoving pileup. The doors did not close properly and people did fall out of the carriages or off the sides and rooftops. Motor cycles had anything up to eight people riding them at the same time and what could not be held in front of them, was piled high on their head, regardless of the weight in the container. It was (is) truly a breathtaking city!

I can honestly say that every single person I met, with no exceptions from the lowliest to the rich, were immensely kind and welcoming. Every home I entered offered me a delicious cup of aromatic chai tea to drink and equally scrumptious curries and deserts. In the wealthier homes, even the servants seemed excited to meet me. I wore Punjabi clothes and tried my very best to speak basic Hindi wherever possible. I met the heads of the major TV station where we discussed a film project. I met with Bollywood celebrities, religious leaders and politicians who all entertained me at the most exclusive restaurants in the city. I felt so loved and appreciated.

I wanted very much to be amongst the ordinary folk too. I politely refused to have bodyguards with me for I did not want to draw unnecessary attention to myself. I would go out each day to the coast to meditate. After a few days, people began to gather around me. I would walk the streets and sit amongst the poor. I held children in my arms and held the hands of the dying and old. Not a day passed by without crowds of people around me as I sat and prayed with them. Even at the Cricket and Yacht Clubs where I stayed, people would come and ask me to bless them.

I flew to Bangalore to give an exclusive interview on their radio station network. Bengaluru or Bangalore is the third largest city in India and is the center of India's fifth-largest metropolitan area. The radio interviewed me for four hours. I was asked that if any wisdom came to me, to please share it with their listeners. When I had been at the TV station in Mumbai, I had received visions, which blew everybody's minds with the accuracy of what I had been able to see for them all. The show directors at the TV station had contacted the equivalent officials at the radio station in Bangalore, hence the invitation to take part in a first ever-exclusive talk show in India. Days before my arrival, the radio station had announced that I was coming as their chief guest. Tens of thousands of people sent in questions to ask me. Eight listeners came to the studio to meet me in person. The show was a huge success and the eight studio guests each received some semblance of wisdom from me and were happy with what they heard. I resisted sharing with them the visions I could see in their future, and instead concentrated on guiding them on a day-to-day basis.

The following week, Shri Vijay Dani-ji, who is a highly respected citizen of India and a major benefactor of the H.V. Desai eye hospital, came to visit me in Mumbai. I had been speaking to him for months and we had become good friends. After much discussion, I politely insisted on going to Pune via public transportation and not by chauffer driven or escorted cars. Vijay-ji insisted on accompanying me there, which was a welcome addition to the journey. Busses in India are not like the busses in the western world. Admittedly, they are not as crazy as their trains, but they do pose a challenge to us western folks. This was their hot climate season and naturally, one has the desire to drink a great deal of water. That in of itself is a challenge in India, as even bottled water is far from drinkable. I was suffering with the well-known problem of diarrhea, not to mention a couple of bouts of food poisoning. There would only be one stop along the way for a toilet break and I was somewhat nervous to be honest.

At the rest stop, I followed the other women to urinate in an outhouse. As I opened the door, I saw a mosquito-infested hole in the ground. I stared at it and then at the wall. There was no toilet paper. I pulled down my pants, crouched as low as I dare and performed my fastest ever pee ceremony to date. By the time the last drop had been trickled, my derrière was bitten so many times that I could hardly bare to move. Vijay-ji took one look at me and began to panic as my body was sweating with agony and swelling with the histamine. I reassured him that I would be just fine and that a British woman does not make an unnecessary fuss. I reminded him that I was in India to help the poor and that I would deal with my issues privately.

Eventually we arrived at the hospital. I have no adequate words to describe this amazingly wonderful institution. Frankly, it makes every western hospital I have ever seen, look grossly inadequate. I spent several days touring their facilities and visiting neighboring villages. I was so impressed that from a marketing person's perspective felt that this would be a great project to film. I was convinced that once shown in the western world, I would be able to help them raise significant awareness and funds. We began to make plans to begin the project within two weeks. Rotary International announced that they were presenting me with humanitarian awards within a few days. I decided to accept the award in Pune where I had already agreed to give a seminar to hundreds of executives. I returned to Mumbai and began to write the documentary script.

Two things became obvious. The mosquitos' network in Pune and Mumbai were communicating rapidly. Everywhere I went, they followed me in swarms. They would ignore everybody else, but feast on my body day and night. Although I had taken malaria pills prior to landing in India, these mosquitos had toxic venom. Within days, I was suffering with a malaria type illness. The welts on my body were huge and nothing eased the pain except during meditation. The bites became infected and I struggled to cope with the fever. You will notice in the film how sick I look. I clearly have a temperature and I struggled to play my part. Nevertheless, such is my personality that I will not accept defeat and I was determined to carry on despite the shivers and bouts of sickness.

My doctors in America were very concerned and insisted that I return home immediately. I told them that as soon as this film was completed and my responsibility fulfilled, I would then come back and not a day before. If the sickness, diarrhea and bites were not bad enough, I had a tooth that needed extracting. Once out, the gum became infected and I had no alternative than to book my flight home for the following week. Until then I had much to do including making the film, giving speeches and accepting the awards at the ceremony and I was determined to do that with dignity wearing a big smile on my face.

I boarded a train from Mumbai to Pune one morning at five o'clock. To use the word, "Boarded," is not very descriptive, so let me try again. I stood, squashed between thousands of people one morning with my suitcase and purse. As the train approached and only slowed down, I leapt on it. You could have yelled at me with a foghorn and I would not have heard you. Furthermore, there was so much noise, that no sound was comprehensible. It was a complete mass of chaos. I had booked a seat thank God and as I sat trying to catch my breath, I could see people climbing on to the roof and clinging to the sides. I was amazed to see them all smiling and it was inspirational.

I began to talk to a middle-aged man who was amused to observe me. He was amazed to hear my story and enthusiastic to tell everybody around us that I had come here alone to help the poor people of India. Everybody was clapping and touching my feet. Everywhere I went in India; people were shocked to hear of a single woman traveling there to help the poor and blind. Whereas I honestly thought nothing of it, (it is normal for me to globe trot with my humanitarian work) I guess it must have seemed strange to others. Nobody knew of my aristocratic background, which was exactly my intention.

Within an hour, the unthinkable happened. I needed to go to the toilet. My fellow passenger discouraged me from doing that and asked me to try to resist the urge. My body would not hear of it! "How long is it until we arrive in Pune, sir?" I asked. He told me two hours. Well that was not going to work for my bladder and up I stood. I cannot tell you that I walked like a sophisticated woman. On the contrary, I fell all over the place like a ship on a stormy sea, this way and that way, until I reached the lavatory door. I was now used to the holes in the ground! I opened the door to see the hole, which was home to a family of particularly hungry looking mosquitos. Oh how they loved to bite my juicy bottom!

When I eventually got back to my seat and settled, the man asked me if I was coping. I nodded that I was. I am not sure what he said to everybody, for many more came to touch my feet.

The next challenge involved how to get off the train at Pune without dying in the process. The man told me that the train did not come to a full stop, but rather kept moving, albeit slowly. My eyebrows raised, my jaw dropped and my stomach sank.

"You are teasing me of course Sir?" I asked. He shook his head from side to side. "Oh my God!" came out of my mouth several times.

Well there was only one thing to do and that was to jump! I would throw my case onto the platform and leap on to it, along with hundreds, if not thousands of others; and pray I survived to tell the tale. I knew that people died every day leaping off these trains and I did not wish to become the latest statistic!

Now in the process of planning this, I had forgotten that the hospital medical director, Colonel Deshpandi-ji would be there to greet me. As the train slowed down and the carriage door opened, I looked out into the sea of thousands of faces with absolute horror. Just as I was about to toss out my case and jump, I felt a hand grab me, although goodness knows how he knew where I was. Dear old Colonel-ji swept me up in his arms, threw my case to one of his workers and dragged me to the car outside, with no words exchanged.

Once in the car, he turned to look at me and said, "It is our great honor to see you again, Doctor. How are you, my dear?" How was I? That was an interesting question. Part of me was thinking, "Well, I've been up since two o'clock this morning and battled my way here on a crazy train. I have had a tooth extracted and I have a high fever. My body has a malaria type infection and the mosquito bites are all septic. I cannot keep much food down and I have horrible diarrhea. I keep being sick and quite honestly, forgive my language; I feel like shit!"

Instead, I chose to smile and cheerfully say, "Oh, I'm really looking forward to doing the film, Colonel-ji, and I'm so grateful that you came to meet me. Thank you so much, sir!" The latter seemed far more polite. We Brits believe in, "Stiff upper lips!"

The film crew was already at the hospital when I arrived and we sat down to plan the day. I asked Col. Deshpande-ji if I could go into the villages and streets blindfolded. I wanted to understand the challenges of the blind there and could not think of a better way to sense it than this. He agreed (somewhat cautiously) and accompanied the film crew and myself for a few hours. If I had thought that India was hectic and scary when I could see it, it was frighteningly chaotic when blindfolded. Frankly, crossing the road would have been utterly impossible without help. Walking around the farming areas without another to guide would also have been futile and very dangerous. Everybody was so kind to me and fascinated with my experiment.

I quickly realized that being blind in India was a terrible affliction. It was far worse than in the western world where we at least have white canes, guide dogs and a systematic structure for traffic flow. It became obvious that if a family had a blind member, either that person had to sit on the side, (as a burden) or another person had to be their eyes guiding them around all day. By giving a person the gift of eyesight, I understood that you were freeing up two people to work in the fields or towns.

Eyesight is a precious gift that most of us take for granted. It is not until you cannot see one day, that you completely understand what permanent darkness means. In India, people die every day and because of lack of education, widespread publicity or religious stigma, many of them do not donate their corneas. The hospital was aware of this and had a very proactive approach to education.

After a few hours, we returned to the hospital to meet the patients who had undergone cornea surgery that morning. When I had arrived earlier that day, I felt blessed to meet these patients. They could not see me and I could not see them either. We greeted each other verbally as I went around to pay my respects to every man, woman and child. During their surgery, I had recorded several hours of footage with doctors, surgeons, patients, families and the management team; including the famous and highly respected Shri Niranjan-ji Pandya, who had been one of the extraordinary men who visited me in America. Shri Niranjan Pandya-ji had lost his eyesight after a cricket ball had hit him on his head. This accident had detached his retinas and over a short period, he became blind for life. His parents had a good position in society and helped him to complete his education. As the years passed and he graduated college, Shri Pandya-ji threw himself into building a powerful organization, hospitals and research facilities in the name of preventable blindness. He is an extraordinary man, with a dynamic personality.

When the patients had recovered, they were fitted with a pair of dark glasses to wear for a few days to protect their eyes from the sun. After the removal of bandages, some were able to see for the first time ever and others for the first time in many years. It was very, very, very emotional. We all met and for the first time they were able to see the person behind the voice. I did not want them to see me until they had seen and thanked the staff and Shri Pandya-ji. I told them that it was these men and women they owed their sight. Yet, they insisted I join the celebration and all I could do was to fall on my knees and stroke their faces. Everybody cried when I touched the elders' feet and it was a day that I will never forget.

The following morning I sat with the editors as we cut and spliced the footage. We made a thirty-minute film in one day that was perfect enough to premier; such was the excellence of the film crew and the hospital staff. My interviews had gone smoothly in one take, making it easy to edit. I could not have been happier with how things panned out and everybody was amazed with the product. We played the film to the entire hospital staff, including senior surgeons, specialists and the chairperson who honored me with an award and said some very sweet things. We were now ready to take that film out into the world and gather significant funding.

The following day I gave a keynote speech to hundreds of executives at a hall in Pune, hosted by several Rotary clubs. I talked about the need to have vision in our professions and gave tips on strategy and networking. Everybody was very gracious and appreciative and I received my awards with humility.

Two days later, I was on a plane bound for New Jersey, USA. I spent those eighteen hours or so reflecting upon the last few weeks in India. I had made some remarkable friends and learned how astonishingly resilient life was over there. My respect for my Indian friends was greatly elevated and I prayed that God would permit me to return one day to serve under the new prime minister. I had received a very clear vision as to who the prime minster would be when I returned. It was the governor of Gujarat, Shri Narendra Modi -ji, whom I knew would be a powerful and enigmatic leader, (and he is).

Being a United Nations representative, I was able to show the film to an audience at the headquarters when I got back to North America. It was highly acclaimed with hundreds of compliments and promises of support for the hospital because of the compelling message contained within the project.

Conclusion

Sometimes it is good to deal with a problem directly and to go on an adventure to use your talents to help others in need. When one is able to see another culture in its raw and passionate state of being, and resist the temptation to live within one's own comfort level, one is able to appreciate how other people live.

As Mahatma Gandhi-ji so eloquently said, "A nation's culture resides in the hearts and in the soul of its people."

God bless Shri Modi-ji and God bless India!

Lesson 31: Motivation

A Message from the Chairman

Almost exactly one year ago, the Board of Directors of the Hanover Area Chamber of Commerce brought Dr. Christine Overton onboard as the President and CEO of our Chamber under a one-year contract. The Board tasked her with an almost impossible job: Take us from a local, New Jersey, geo-centric Chamber of Commerce to a far-reaching, wide-ranging international organization that seeks to foster business growth across international boundaries.

Twelve months later the results are self-evident. During the past year, Dr. Overton has moved the HACC ("reinvented" better describes what she did!) onto an international platform and we are now the United International Chamber of Commerce. As a direct result of Dr. Overton's strategic thinking, hard work and perseverance, we became an international organization in record time. It was not easy for her! In many instances, she had to persuade naysayers within our own organization. Nevertheless, thanks to her vision we are new, rebranded, growing and international. It would not ... it could not ... have happened without Dr. Overton's unwavering leadership for which we are most grateful.

As is our usual practice, we conduct a yearly strategic review of the organization's structure, prospects and plans for the future. Our review was especially critical this year because it coincided with the conclusion of Dr. Overton's contract. We reviewed where we stand and what we accomplished during the past twelve months during Dr. Overton's tenure. Dr. Overton did all we asked of her ... and much more. With the conclusion of her contract, we have restructured the leadership of the UICOC to try to plug the large void left by Dr. Overton's absence as our leader.

As for Dr. Christine Overton, who took us to this next level through her persistence, intelligence and visionary leadership, I am pleased to report that she will assume the position of President Emeritus within the UICOC. It is comforting to know that we will still be able to rely on her guidance, sound judgment and good cheer as "Christine Connects" as we move forward to expand the reach and programs of the United International Chamber of Commerce. Onward and upward!

Respectfully yours,
Steven F. Miller
Chairman of the Board

After my travels in India, I returned to America to face a new challenge as president and chief executive officer of a dwindling area Chamber of Commerce in New Jersey. It was failing, in part due to a highly successful county chamber some two miles up the road. Everybody expected us to fail and many of my peers tried to dissuade me from taking the job as they felt it would be professional suicide. Of course, people laughed at us in the beginning, but that served to fuel me with even more determination to succeed. I was conscious of the drawbacks and problems, which included a complete lack of funding. As I had never run from adversity in the past, or been afraid of a challenge, I thought, why not at least try.

I looked to my previous clients from the state Chamber; many of which had resigned when I left for India. I began to work on a daring strategic plan, which many mocked. I knew that in order for us to survive, we needed to make some radical decisions to knock down the walls surrounding us. This included restructuring the entire operation and thinking outside of the box. For years, I had watched how other chambers' functioned and I always found it incredibly distasteful to charge such exorbitant membership fees for inadequate services. I had seen senior executives pay themselves obscene salaries and I knew that members were not getting much bang for their buck.

In the economic climate of the last two decades, small businesses were genuinely suffering and they needed extra help to promote themselves.

The state Chamber of Commerce had insisted I ignore small businesses and instead concentrate on recruiting the bigger companies who had the money to invest in sponsorship. The dangling carrot was my commission structure, which paid more for bigger companies. It disgusted me frankly. Is money important? Of course, we all have to live. However, I did not line my pockets at the expense of those struggling to make ends meet and this was a major cause of disagreement between my superiors and me. Therefore, I dedicated my personal time to helping the smaller entrepreneurs. I would meet them between six and eight o'clock in the morning and between six and eleven o'clock each work day evening. I spent every weekend giving keynote speeches, attending events and giving training sessions to my members. Within a year, I was caring for close to five hundred companies and their staff. When I left the state Chamber, every single one of those members left at the same time. They refused to work with anybody else for they knew that they would not receive the help and guidance I had given them. They wanted to follow me.

I faced the presidency of my own Chamber knowing that in order to be successful and effective; I needed to bring peace and unity to the business community and authorities. I met with the mayor and council on several occasions in an attempt to bridge the gap between them and us. They graciously offered their council chambers for our meetings, which included breakfasts. We held other networking meetings at different members' restaurants and the chamber began to grow very quickly. Many joined because they loved the way I conducted meetings and training sessions. It was exciting to see and hear the buzz in the room. I brought in a very diverse set of directors who I knew well and trusted. I decided that the only way we were going to survive was to take the Chamber to an international level. I wanted us to collaborate with chambers not only around America, but also all over the world. I knew that we could link up with chambers in India, for instance, and I thought we could do some exciting exchange programs together in trade and commerce, which would be internationally effective.

I wanted to introduce a new way of working with companies that included making the chamber available to struggling organizations, which would mean they could join with no money exchanged. I felt strongly that if we could do major expositions around the country, then the bigger companies would want to sponsor these in exchange for the publicity and potential new customers. I felt this would sustain us. I also wanted to open the chamber up to young entrepreneurs, who at the age of fourteen, could begin to shadow the more experienced ones as interns, and learn business techniques by observation, practice, mentoring and role play.

Admittedly, a few within the Chamber did not want change. They liked this group being a local presence and were not comfortable with such a huge vision. As a leader, sometimes you have to see the bigger picture. You have to dare to change, and you have to have the courage to inspire and lead your people through unknown territory. The vast majority of members and directors were very excited, for they well knew, (first hand) my style of leadership and my passion was infectious and effective. They committed themselves to helping me make this happen and threw themselves wholeheartedly into the process.

I had one board member (who had been a client of mine) that travelled five hours round trip to attend meetings. Joe was a very dynamic man, who could vividly see the big picture and he offered his expertise in marketing to help take the vision from paper, to reality. I had a very passionate chairperson called Steve, who worked closely with the Pentagon, and I trusted him to advise me. I had quite a few military people on board too. These dynamic men from India had the necessary drive to push this plan ahead.

I undoubtedly learned more from the naysayers than the ones who believed in me. I had a treasurer that absolutely refused to give me updates and reports, for a reason nobody ever understood. During my job interview, he had battled with the directors and me, as he wanted to give away the dregs of the money to his charitable causes rather than invest it within the chamber. He would never attend meetings and it was extremely frustrating to try to run a company with no available funds. I tried every technique I could think of, and would even go to his office and try to converse with him. However, he treated me with utter disdain and it was very frustrating.

I had another director who went out of her way to split and create mutiny. She would make a controversial comment to one director sneakily in a side room, and then completely flip the exact same information and share it with a different person in another. Each time we sat down with the agenda in place and voting had begun, there was chaos in the boardroom. After a few months of negotiation and discussion, I had no choice but to force the issue of her leaving the chamber all together. I simply knew that there was no way to take us forward, when there was an obvious intent to pull us apart.

We were located in a ghost town it seemed. The entire plaza was at best asleep, with many of the stores empty or closing down. Even the council members laughed at me when I said we were going to put on a major event at Christmas. They knew the property owner and said there was no way he would cooperate with me. Retail is an important part of this country and the stores were struggling. I wanted to create a major Christmas weekend to entice shoppers to buy locally. Initially the proprietor was hesitant, but once he understood the plan, he was very enthusiastic. I explained to him that it was in his interest to work with the Chamber and the merchants because if they were successful, they would pay their rent to him. If they remained as they were, he could kiss his rent good-bye.

I met with the fire service to make sure we were in compliance, as I wanted to open up all the stores that were empty, and put vendors in them. I met with church leaders, council members, vendors and musicians. My board began to work on the promotional side, and by December, we put on a fantastic holiday event that I know the community will never forget. It was a major accomplishment for our team and even Santa and his elves came to the plaza on a vintage fire engine. We had arranged for the local women's battered shelter to have private time with him and they were so excited and grateful that their children who had seen hell that year, now had a fun time with Father Christmas. We also organized a private session with the handicapped children and Santa. The blind children were excited to hear the engine sirens and cuddle him and the deaf children were equally excited to see the big red engine and Santa's grotto. Singers sang, bands played and even the dogs were there to win a contest. Membership increased considerably and we won much respect in the community. I was very, very proud of our team.

The next phase in the plan was to change our Chamber name. If one sees the word "Area," one has a vision of a very small circumference. It is not conducive for credibility whatsoever in the business world. After several meetings, we had decided to call ourselves, "The United International Chamber of Commerce." That name alone said everything, and gave us the capacity to grow over time. Marketing and promotion is a key component to success. We all know that if you have a superior product, but nobody knows it exists, the project will quickly collapse because you will have failed to captivate consumers to purchase your wares over a competitor. However, if you have a purposeful strategy which is far-reaching and dynamic, people will purchase more products and your success is somewhat guaranteed if you repeat the process and adapt with changing trends.

We had put a dynamic plan together to launch the organization's new name at our first leadership summit. We knew that we needed a major dignitary and I wanted that individual to inspire and teach our participants in a unique way. I had access to hundreds of dignitaries and during my prayer time God told me to invite my former husband from the Hopi Nation as our keynote speaker. In attendance were military officers, bagpipers, senators, assembly members, mayors and other major dignitaries. It was successful and we launched the new Chamber with a growth of over four hundred percent in eight months.

At the end of my one-year contract, I handed the baton on to a capable former Indian military officer. I had successfully completed the task (which was to save the chamber). I was proud of what we had accomplished and I felt sure that it would do very well after I had moved on. Within a few weeks, he made the executive decision, (as was his right) to revert the organization back to an area Chamber. Sadly, the Chamber quickly dwindled and pretty much died when most of the membership and board of directors decided not to remain there with me gone from the helm. It was disappointing and disheartening to see all that hard work go down the drain, but we had experienced a great year.

Being their president was a fantastic learning experience for me and I am very happy that we implemented strategies. I know these ideas helped the economy and community significantly. Many partnerships formed and developed, which at the end of the day is exactly what a Chamber is supposed to do when it performs at its best. The motivation was to get everybody working together and to dare to reach out and try the impossible.

Conclusion

Sometimes in life, we come face to face with situations, which seem insurmountable. Tradition has a way of gluing things together positively, but it can have the negative effect of stagnation. People are comfortable with the familiar, and are nervous about change, especially if that means a very radical shift from the norm. There was a time when people mocked the ones who dared to say that man would go to the moon or that we would be able to communicate with each other across the world in seconds. Yet here we all are, chatting with people all over the globe via our cell phones and computers. Space travel is the norm today and we have discovered that the earth is round and not flat as many used to believe.

I am a firm believer in innovation, visualization, captivation, exploration, and motivation. One has to have a clear vision, with the drive to inspire others to invest their time, energy, money and influence, to make it work. Major change is scary; there is no doubt about that. A business that is failing, sits on a very precarious seesaw today. It is up one minute and down the next.

There was a time when the public purchased their items by meandering from store to store. It was a laid-back world then. The internet and big box stores who provide every major household device and luxury under one roof have replaced those days. Our lives appear to have hit the fast forward button. Everything today is fast paced and fast food convenience. Nobody wants to take the time to wander around shops anymore, unless it is Christmas or another major holiday. Even then, people are bargain hunting and will oftentimes know exactly where to shop for the best deals of the season.

If a company executive or proprietor wants to survive today, he must go to the public via selling his wares over the internet. If he sits waiting for traffic to come to him with his doors closed and a very drab exterior, the only activity is going to be the property owners throwing him out, or the banks foreclosing on their loans.

Marketing has become more important today than ever before. Tiny signs on the door do not work. Social media, TV, radio and electronic signs are the way forward, at least for the near future. The two main killers for business include those stores that are located off the freeway and hidden by trees and companies that are nestled in multi-level buildings. Unless one knows they are there via proactive marketing, I have no idea how they can possibly think they will attract customers and be successful.

Finally, every company executive and even every family member has to have a goal, dedication and the drive to motivate each other to succeed. One simply cannot sit and stare at a problem and magic it away with inertia. The only way to get out of a bad situation is to get up, strategize and execute the best feasible plan possible whilst thinking positively all the way.

Some believe that it is tragic when a goal fails to deliver a successful result. Personally, I believe it is far more tragic when you do not have a goal to begin with and just drift through life like dead wood.

Lesson 32: A Message

Few can humbly claim to have had the honor to host a Native American Indian chief in their home for a few days, and even fewer can say that this wise person, (from the oldest tribe) was once their husband. I had not seen him for over ten years and it was a truly amazing gift of prayer, forgiveness and reflection, not to mention an amazing opportunity to hear his advice and teaching.

I took him to my meditation place nearby, which was nestled deep within a forest, next to a beautiful little river, which was home to a myriad of birds and rodents. As we sat down to meditate, a huge golden eagle flew above us and we marveled at his cry of freedom. As we looked into the water, we saw an eagle feather floating beside us and as we picked it up, the eagle screeched again from the cloudless sky. It reminded me of the truly amazing journeys we had been on together, where I had learned so much about nature and the messages she was always so willing to share. We talked a great deal about the state of the world. We prayed (he is a Christian) for every creature and human being and discussed why it was vitally important to maintain a place of complete stillness and peace.

He reminded me of my Native American Indian Hopi ceremonial name, which is, *Loma Uh Nah Ya*. This means *Beautiful Heart* mother to all creation. I have always endeavored to live up to the honor of that name and responsibility with humbleness and courage. I am aware that many make flippant jokes about Indian names and I have met far too many new-age people who call themselves certain animal names thinking it gives them more credibility. Sadly, it does not. Not only is it insulting to the Native American's but if they realized how sacred a ceremonial name was, with a huge responsibility attached to it, they would not be so keen to adopt one. I rarely ever discuss my name and even now, I mention it with a very quiet voice, almost as softly as the names given me in Buddhist monastic retreat including, *Urgyen Yangchen Wangmo* and *Kagyu Sonnam Drolma* (which refer to power and healing abilities).

My former husband had spoken at our Chamber of Commerce summit where his words had profoundly touched the hearts of many who had come to hear him talk. It was a rare teaching, for this wise elder seldom spoke and never in public before. I knew that he would have insights that the western, and even eastern people had not heard before.

It has always been apparent to me that most human beings have lost touch with nature. Instead of taking the vital time to observe and learn, they have fallen into the trap of believing that they are above nature; that it is there for their sustenance, rather than co-creations who must work together, if planet earth is to remain alive. If I have learned nothing else from my former husband and nature, it is to have the utmost respect for all beings and to study each life form, in order to receive clarity within my own life. He taught me how to be in tune with the many messages from the trees and animals, birds and insects. I learned that those messages require humility and the willingness to have ones negative patterns exposed and reprogrammed.

He warned me that a natural disaster was about to strike the east coast of North America and that on a personal level I was about to face one of the biggest challenges of my life. I asked him to advise me on the best way to prepare for these events and asked him to pray that I would gain wisdom and understanding as to how I could help others once the storm had passed. His advice was to remain calm and vigilant. He wisely concluded that even the toughest lessons in life were a gift in growth and spiritual maturity; that I would not face anything that I could not recover from, as long as I continued to keep my eyes on God and not fall asleep with complacency. He encouraged me to meditate upon the eagle that was screeching above our heads and assured me that I would survive the terrible storms that were fast approaching.

We learn in the book of Isaiah that, "Gives power to the weak, and to those who have no might He increases strength. Even the youths shall faint and be weary, and the young men shall utterly fall. But those who wait on the Lord Shall renew their strength. They shall mount up with wings like eagles. They shall run and not be weary. They shall walk and not faint."

I spent the next few weeks relatively alone and in prayer, as I prepared for the approaching storms. I meditated a great deal upon the words from Isaiah and on what the eagle teaches us about life and death.

The eagle flies alone at high altitude. It avoids flying with other birds like the sparrow who cannot reach the same height even if it wanted to. Thus in life, we have to know when it is important to separate ourselves from others if we are to survive.

Eagles have strong vision and are able to focus on a target that is up to five kilometers away. When the eagle sites his prey, he specifically narrows his focus and does not deviate from its path until he has grabbed his prey. Thus, we must also learn to have vision and remain focused until we have succeeded in fulfilling what we have set out to accomplish.

Unlike vultures that eat dead animals, eagles only eat fresh prey. I concluded that it was very important for me to be vigilant about what my eyes and ears feasted upon and I stayed clear away from outdated news and negative TV programs.

I was somewhat nervous about the approaching storm, but I reflected upon the attitude of eagles who, when the clouds gather, get excited. Unlike all the other birds that hide in the leaves and branches of trees, eagles use the storm's wind to lift themselves above the clouds, thus giving them the opportunity to glide and rest their wings. I decided that once the storms were upon me I would relish their challenges and use them profitably, rather than hide away and pray for them to pass over me.

If this storm was to come from a relationship, I meditated upon what that would mean to me. I had long since decided that I would be far more careful when it came to intimacy and, like the eagle, to test before trust. When a female eagle meets a male mate and they want to mate, she flies down to earth with the male pursuing her and she picks a twig. She flies back into the air with the male pursuing her. Once she has reached an altitude high enough for her, she lets the twig fall to the ground and watches it as it falls. The male chases after the twig. The faster it falls, the faster he chases it. He has to catch it before it falls to the ground. He then brings it back to the female eagle. The female eagle grabs the twig, flies to an even higher altitude, and then drops the twig for the male to chase. This goes on for hours, with the height increasing until the female eagle feels sure that the male eagle has mastered the art of catching the twig, thus showing commitment. Then and only then, will she allow him to mate with her. I had long since determined that whether in private or in business, I had to test commitment of people intended for partnership.

Sudden change can be a very frightening event in our lives and few of us are prepared. The eagle teaches us an important lesson. The male and female eagle identifies a place very high on a cliff where no predators can reach. The male flies to earth and picks thorns and lays them on the crevice of the cliff, then flies to earth to collect several twig which he lays in the intended nest. He flies back to earth and picks soft grass to cover the thorns. When the first layering is complete, the process continues with layering grass upon thorns. The process is complete when he plucks his feathers and lays them on the nest. Once laid, both parents share in the responsibility of caring for the eggs.

Each eagle must pass an almost cruel, yet necessary test. Their mother throws them out of the nest repeatedly. Naturally, they are scared and jump back into the safety of their home. Each time the eagles are gone, their mother removes a soft layer, exposing the thorns. When the scared eaglets jump into their safe nest, the thorns injure them. When they bleed, the mother pushes them off the cliff into the air. As they shriek in fear, father eagle flies out and catches them on his back before they fall and brings them back to the cliff. This process continues until they learn to flap their wings and learn to fly.

When an eagle matures and grows old, his feathers become weak and cannot take him as fast as he should. When he feels weak and about to die, he retires to a place far away in the rocks. While there, he plunks out every feather on his body until he is completely bare. He stays in this hiding place until he has grown new feathers, then he can come out.

Conclusion

In a Native American myth we learn that Heron and Hummingbird were very good friends, even though one was tall, gangly, and awkward and one was small, sleek, and fast. They both loved to eat fish. The hummingbird preferred small fish like minnows and heron liked the large ones.

One day, Hummingbird said to his friend, "I am not sure there are enough fish in the world for both of our kind to eat. Why don't we have a race to see which of us should own the fish?" Heron thought that was a very good idea. They decided that they would race for four days. The finish line was an old dead tree next to a far-away river. Whichever of them sat on top of the tree first on the fourth day of the race would own all the fish in the world.

They started out the next morning. The hummingbird zipped along, flying around and around the heron, which was moving steadily forward, flapping his giant wings. Then the pretty flowers along the way would distract Hummingbird. He would flit from one to the other, tasting the nectar. When Hummingbird noticed that Heron was ahead of him, he hurried to catch up with him, zooming ahead as fast as he could, and leaving Heron far behind. Heron just kept flying steadily forward, flapping his giant wings. Hummingbird was tired from all his flitting. When it got dark, he decided to rest. He found a nice spot to perch and slept all night long. However, Heron just kept flying steadily forward all night long, flapping his giant wings.

When Hummingbird woke in the morning, Heron was far ahead. Hummingbird had to fly as fast as he could to catch up. He zoomed past the big, awkward Heron. Then Hummingbird noticed some pretty flowers nearby. He zip-zipped over to them and tasted their nectar. He was enjoying the pretty scenery and did not notice Heron flapping passed him with his great wings. Hummingbird finally remembered that he was racing with Heron, and flew as fast as he could to catch up with the big bird. Then he zipped along, flying around and around the Heron, who kept moving steadily forward, flapping his giant wings.

For two more days, the Hummingbird and the Heron raced toward the far-distant riverbank with the dead tree that was the finish line. Hummingbird had fun sipping nectar, flitting among the flowers, and resting at night. Heron stoically kept up a steady flap-flap-flapping of his giant wings, propelling himself forward through the air all day and all night.

Hummingbird woke from his sleep the morning of the fourth day, refreshed and invigorated. He flew zip-zip toward the riverbank with its dead tree. When it came into view, he saw Heron perched at the top of the tree! Heron had won the race by flying straight and steady through the night while Hummingbird slept.

Therefore, from that day forward, the Heron has owned all the fish in the rivers and lakes, and the Hummingbird has taken sips from the nectar of the many flowers that he enjoyed so much during the race.

Moral of the story

Life is about balance. There is an important lesson to learn from this amusing myth and other fables like the *tortoise and the hare* for instance. People compare life to a race. Whilst some sprint through it, others choose to live with a steady pace accompanied by an attitude of mature steadfastness.

There is a huge difference between walking *slowly* through life with a disciplined sense of awareness and wisdom than *plodding* through the years with a sense of undisciplined laziness, self-absorption and inertia.

The greatest lesson that I have learned is to grow old consciously and to understand when I need to sprint and when I need to slow down to conserve physical, mental and spiritual energy for the next phase.

Like the heron in our story, sometimes people can see our slowness as a weakness, and yet I have found that walking slowly has its advantages sometimes. I often say to people that I may not be as smart as they are, but I am not as dumb as I look. I am sure Heron said that to Hummingbird too. On the other hand, perhaps, he just sat looking at him with a wry smile and a knowing look of wisdom.

Let us reflect upon your own life and let us think about those eaglets for a moment. Are there any thorns hurting you today? In other word, when you try to repeat the same habits as yesterday, do you feel as though they are not as comfortable as they used to be? Perhaps it is time to grow up and put those things aside.

Do you think it is time for you to leave the nest? Alternatively, perhaps it is time to help your children gain the confidence to fly towards adulthood.

The female eagle tests the male to see if he is a good provider. Are you a strong and faithful companion? Are you a good provider?

Like the eagle who needs to be alone in order to recoup during old age. Do you need to take some time to be alone?

When the old eagle needs to rejuvenate, he pulls out his feathers until naked. As they grow back, he is strong again. What do you need to discard in order to grow stronger? Do you need to slow down? Do you need to reevaluate your values?

Finally, is it time for you to be quiet, to rest your mind from over-thinking and to begin to tune in to the natural world that is around you?

Even in the city, you can sit outside and observe ants and insects, birds and others creatures busily living their lives with a sense of natural preservation. With one swipe, you have the capacity to destroy just about any creature you will see. However, today, instead of annoyance, take a few minutes to admire that creature and observe why it is more alive than you in some respects are. Make a conscious effort to align yourself with everything around you, for by doing so; you will feel that essential connection that is so easy to forget we have with our fellow creatures of creation.

Lesson 33: Be prepared!

Living in England, one does not have to deal with hurricanes, tornados, volcanos or in fact, most of the natural challenges other countries face. There was an earth tremor though when I was pregnant with my son, back in 1988. I thought I was having a stroke when I felt it, but as I staggered to the window, I could see everybody else on the ground and realized what was happening. I was in California years later when a severe earthquake struck. I almost laughed to recall the one in England, which in hindsight seemed inconsequential in comparison. I had never heard of a vast forest fire and I certainly had never experienced subzero snow storms, until I arrived in Wyoming, USA. I thought England was hot in the summer until I lived in the desert of Arizona.

America reminded me of the story, *Goldilocks and the three bears.* When the air conditioning failed constantly in Phoenix, Arizona, I prayed that God would relocate me. It was so hot that we judged the temperature by how quickly a bar of chocolate would melt in the car. God moved me to Wyoming, (via Seattle, Washington for six months) where I had a glimpse into the weather penguins adore. Subzero temperatures where it even snows in June and where you virtually need dogs to mush, is an adventure. I learned to hunt with a rifle and bow, to butcher and preserve meat and to survive for weeks with no electricity, running water and heat. In addition, I learned to live in the wild by camping out at Yellowstone national park and I regularly rode horses on cattle farms. From there, as you know, I moved to New Jersey. New Jersey was a very similar climate to England and I felt very comfortable. In fact, I was thinking that life did not really get much better than this, when I awoke one morning to hear a major hurricane was on its way to our State. Hurricane Ivan blew off the chimney, which flooded my home. It was a wild and crazy event.

Now those of you, who know me well, know that I intensely dislike spiders. I do not care how big or how small they are. Even a small spider is too big! Many of you know that I have worked with tigers, bears and wolves. I have sat amongst wild alligators with no fear for my safety. For some reason, (I know is irrational) I cannot even look at a picture of a spider without feeling scared.

After a day of mopping up, (post hurricane Ivan) I went to bed. Correction - I went to my bedroom to go to sleep, but never actually made it to the bed. Above it was the biggest spider I had ever seen in my life. It was not a little black one; it was a very big, extremely hairy and dark brown creature of a spider. God alone knows how it had even got into my bedroom without me noticing it crawling. I was so scared, that I could not even scream. I shut the door and ran to my phone.

In the apartment below was my very close friend Joe. He had been so kind to me and had helped me lug furniture into my new apartment. He was also the maintenance person for the apartment management, so when folk moved out and left their furniture, he would always give me first refusal. He was a very special friend, strong, tall, handsome and brave. I needed a hero, so I called him.

"Joe there's a really big spider in my home," I cried. "Please come and get it out for me!"

"But Chrissy," he whispered. "I've got a lady here with me and we are about to...you know...get it on!"

"I'm so sorry to disturb you, but please help me Joe!" I wailed. I obviously sounded frantic, and he knew that I never asked for favors or help. I heard him running up the stairs, and I had the door already opened before he even reached it.

"This better be a *big* spider!" he said.

"I promise you it *is* big," I assured him.

"Where is it then?" he said with an almost sarcastic tone in his voice.

"It's in my bedroom Joe!" I replied. His eyebrows raised and he grinned. "Baby girl, if you wanted to make love to me, you didn't have to make up an excuse of a spider, you know. I would make love to you in a heartbeat baby," Joe chuckled with a gleam in his eyes.

"Joe, I'm being serious. It is in the bedroom. The spider is on my wall!"

Joe walked ambled the hallway and into the bedroom.

"Oh my God!" he yelled at the top of his lungs. He ran out of the room and stared at me in horror. "You said it was big. It's not big, it's (expletive) huge!"

"I told you," was my only reply.

"OK. Give me a big pan," he said with a very nervous tone in his voice. I went into the kitchen and gave him the biggest one I owned. He went back in and immediately came back out again. "Oh my God it doesn't even cover it!" He yelled. "OK, give me a bucket."

"You're so brave," I reassured him.

"How the (expletive) did this even get in here baby," he yelled from the crime scene.

"I don't know Joe," I shouted back. "I've been trying to clean up since the storm. I have water pouring down the darn chimney. Maybe it came down the chimney," I offered as a possible explanation.

Within seconds, Joe had come out of the room again. "Baby, do you have a big broom?"

"Yes, but why do you need a broom?" I enquired.

"I'm going to have to kill it!" He said with the voice of a commander.

"Please don't kill it, Joe. It hasn't done anything to deserve that," I begged.

"Then why did you call me up here, if not to kill it then?"

"Joe, can't you just put it in the bucket and take it outside please? Mind you, I guess I should probably call animal control, as releasing it outside would probably be rather irresponsible, and it could be somebody's pet. God knows who would want it as a pet though," I concluded.

"Baby, I know you are into this saving life thing, but this spider needs to die." Before I had said one more word, in he went, shutting the door behind him. I felt terribly guilty and just asked God to forgive me. There was a great deal of loud banging, crashing and expletives yelled that night. It literally sounded like Al Capone was conducting a mass *murder* in my bedroom. Well I guess there was a killing going on - some female spider lost her mate, or somebody lost his or her very furry pet that evening.

"Right," shouted my brave soldier. "Close your eyes whilst I bring it out," he instructed. Joe looked ghastly and I cannot imagine there was much of a desire for him to continue his romantic date that night. There was not much relaxed sleeping from my side either. I could not get the image of that darn creature out of my mind. I hate to kill things and I wish that I did not have this stupid phobia. For two days, I sat in there feeling grossed out and cruel.

I heard an authoritative knock on my front door. A myriad of nervous thoughts went through my mind. I wondered if it was the spider's owner coming to accuse me of slaughtering her beloved pet, or my neighbors complaining about the noise the other night. I also wondered if it was Joe's love interest coming to slap me for ruining her intimate date.

"I'm sorry Dr. Overton, but you are going to have to move and we will transfer you to another apartment. The hurricane has damaged the building and your chimney needs repair. We have to move you this week."

I was almost relieved to see the manager and as much as I dislike moving, and had really loved that apartment with its sunken living room, fireplace and of course, the glass patio area; the image of that hairy arachnid freaked me out and a move was maybe a blessing in disguise. Within a couple of days, I had moved to the other side of the apartment complex. It was gorgeous. The property owners put in a new kitchen, bathrooms, hard wood floors and all new appliances. I enjoyed an open wooden patio looking out onto trees and a river with deer and nature within feet. It was simply stunning. I could not have been happier and life was great.

After a few months, we all watched the news with horror. Hurricane Sandy was on her way and with mandatory evacuation in place, everybody was preparing for the worst-case scenario. Many around me were elderly and refused to leave their homes. The younger men and women all left for inland states or higher ground, but I chose to remain in my home so that I was on hand to help the elderly people. I filled up my bath and basins plus pots and pans with water. I went to the store and bought bottled water, canned food and other non-perishables for the elders and myself. I had candles and a gas cooker, so I knew that even in the worst-case scenario, I would be able to boil water to keep warm and cook basic food to ride out the storm. I went to each of the old people's homes and pulled their furniture away from windows so that their items would not convert into dangerous torpedoes with the wind. I filled up his or her bathtubs as I had my own and I made sure that everybody was safe. I got out my ropes in case I needed to pull deer to safety. I had to do that during the last hurricane to rescue an injured doe. I was ready for hurricane Sandy and wondered why everybody was freaking out. I mean, how bad can a storm really be? I was about to find out.

Did you watch the news that week? If you did, you have the visual for what we endured. If you did not catch the news or see pictures afterwards, try to imagine the story of *Noah's Arc* or the *Perfect Storm* movie with George Clooney and you will be on track.

I had rescued a cat, who I had named, Zach. I found him on Zachary lane, hence that seemed as good a name as any other did. He had lived in a dumpster apparently for over a year, where a fox had tried to kill him. A friend told me all about him and I went to rescue him and bring him home. He was so thin, had multiple injuries from the fox attack and had not only been declawed; but injured very badly, with an obvious botched up job to hack into his toes. After several weeks of trial an error with food and several baths to rid him of fleas and ticks, he was better than ever before in his life. We bonded solidly and he was like my shadow.

With the storm approaching, I tried to get him to hunker down, but he refused to leave the kitchen. He sat on the ground staring under the cooker. Hold that thought, as we will be returning to Zach in a moment or two.

The storm arrived and it was actually quite frightening. Naturally, the electricity went out and it was not only dark, but also very cold as it was now winter. Within a couple of days, we had no landlines or cell phone coverage. The after effects lasted for close to three weeks. Those of us, who could get out, stood staring at the wreckage. Trees had fallen down everywhere and there was no way that traffic could get in or out for over a week. A day or so later, paramedics were trying to get to a boy whose oxygen machine had failed. They asked me to help them get to the boy and carry him to safety. We clambered over fallen trees to reach him and between six of us, we were able to get him to the ambulance. What we could not carry that week, we dragged.

I spent days cooking for the neighbors and did my best to help everybody keep warm and safe. I could not get my truck out, but in hindsight, it did not really matter. There was no gas to pump, thus, there was no need to waste fuel. Eventually, rationed gas was available but the lines were long. Some of my neighbors needed prescriptions and I must have walked the two miles or more to the pharmacy several times a day. It was exhausting and stressful for everybody.

Nighttime was like a scene from an old black and white movie. All I had were candles to give me light. One evening, I had some neighbors over keeping warm, but Zachy still would not leave the kitchen. Day and night, he kept watch. The question was what was he watching? Please God not a spider I prayed. We all sat on my leather couch chatting, when we suddenly heard Zachy dashing about. I had not seen this much activity from him in days. In fact, he had not even touched his food, which was not like him at all. Then we heard squeaking. One friend said, "*Ahhhh*, Zach is playing with his toy mouse."

"Zach doesn't have a toy mouse," I said with a nervous tone in my voice.

"*Uh oh*," said another. We all chorused, "*Uh oh*," too.

One friend turned on the flashlight to see more accurately. Sure enough, Zachy now had a new title. He was to be officially known from that day forwards as *Sir Zachariah, Mouser of the Realm.*

Before I even had the chance to save it, Zachy killed it. He was so proud of himself and proceeded to bring his hard earned gift to me, to admire – Well, the body at least. He had unceremoniously decapitated it. The remains of the mouse were thrown out of the window, much to the disgust of its captor, who was clearly upset because he had not had enough time to gloat over his triumphant victory. The evening ended in prayer whilst Zachy sulked in the corner.

Two days later, Zachy was back on mouse patrol. That same night another one had become his victim. The difference between this one and its mate was the time it took Zachy to kill it. I guess he knew what would be its demise and so he cruelly enjoyed toying with it before his final jaw stopping decapitation. God love him, he was performing an important service and I had not the heart to be mad with him. Besides, I would rather have him catch it, than have it running over me whilst I was trying to sleep.

The following day the neighborhood cockroaches (hundreds of them) decided to leave the filthy apartment upstairs for a much nicer environment below – in my home. It was horrific, but at least I did not see a spider!

Eventually, life got back to normal. We found a large hole in the wall behind the cooker, which management filled, thus ending Zach's moussing days in the kitchen. He proved to be a very bad cockroach hunter - in fact, they scared him (I was not too impressed myself either). The exterminator killed all the roaches within a few weeks, and yes, it was gross. The power returned, trees were removed and everybody could go back to work with gas in their tanks. After damage assessment, Governor Christie was able to ensure the citizens could begin renovation and restoration and the majority of people agreed that he had done a fantastic job to warn and protect us.

Conclusion

It never ceases to amaze me how unprepared the public is during emergencies. Disaster can strike at any moment, some with advanced warning and others out of the clear blue sky. Here are a few essential items to have close to you should the unimaginable happen today.

An emergency bag packed with essential items including:

- Mirror - communication is important
- Medication
- First aid kit

- Bottled water
- Candles - strategically placed around the home
- Matches and lighter
- Pans of water - boil water for heat
- Cash
- Spare clothes
- Sanitary pads
- Canned nonperishable food
- Can opener
- Shovel
- Radio
- Batteries
- Toys for children
- Books
- Reflective vest
- Gasoline
- Blankets
- Pillows
- Pest spray
- Gun and ammunition
- Knives
- Trash sacks
- Cleaning products
- Documents and credit cards in waterproof bag
- Emergency exit plan from every room (known and rehearsed by all)

Lesson 34: Citizenship

It had taken me over a decade to become a proud citizen of the United States of America. I use the word, "Proud," because that is exactly how I feel. I believe that this country is the finest and most powerful in the world. Yes, it has its difficulties, and yes, there are things that are not necessarily ideal; but one has opportunities here, if one is prepared to work hard.

The United States of America is still the premier country that others dream of being able to visit and reside. One can travel north, within hours, from the deserts of Arizona, Texas and New Mexico to the plains of Wyoming, Montana and the Dakotas. One can go east from the glamour, sandy beaches and rain forests of California, Oregon and Washington State, to Maine and the financial and political hub of New York to New Jersey, Washington DC, Maryland, and the Carolinas to Florida. One can see alligators, wolves, bears, buffalos and a whole host of other exotic creatures, and one can go from a checkout girl to Hollywood star in the blink of an eye. This is the home of the free.

Immigrants undoubtedly know far more about the United States than its own natural born citizens. Immigrants have to study the history and politics of this great nation and by the time we take the naturalization exam, we are well prepared and well versed. I find it quite horrifying to see how the vast majority of the people here have absolutely no clue about the history of the USA, or indeed any idea about who currently governs this land. I find it unfathomable that you can live here and still claim ignorance as to who is making policy decisions that affect your life. Nevertheless, when we swear our *Oath of Allegiance* we should be accountable for these declarations.

An officer led me into a small room to take my naturalization test in 2010. Having served in various chambers and worked alongside senators and congressional representatives, I was confident this test would be a breeze. Thankfully, I passed with one hundred percent and then waited for an hour or so to take my oath at the swearing in ceremony, where I would become a naturalized citizen of the United States of America.

The naturalization ceremony was a solemn and meaningful event where we were required to dress in a dignified and respectful manner. It took place in a United States federal court in New Jersey, which demanded respect as representatives of the federal government of the United States of America. At the beginning of the ceremony, the clerk of courts entered the courtroom and asked everyone present to rise for the judge. Following this, everyone present recited the *Pledge of Allegiance* and sang the *National Anthem* of the United States. After the congratulatory speech from the president, welcoming all new U.S. citizens to the country, every candidate recited the *Oath of Allegiance*. We received our naturalization certificate and forms to take to the postal service in order to apply for a U.S. passport. I felt humbled and honored that day.

Conclusion

I am a proud citizen of the United States of America and I hold a dual passport with the United Kingdom. However, I cannot end this chapter without paying the utmost respect possible to the true founders and fathers of this great nation.

There are 566 federally recognized Native American Indian Nations in the United States. The majority of these are located in Alaska while the remainders are located in thirty-three other states. More than two hundred tribal languages exist today. These languages and cultural traditions are extremely important as more than four million Americans self-identify as either American Indian or Alaska Native. These nations are sovereign, meaning they have the right to govern themselves. This sovereignty includes the right to establish their own form of government, enact legislation and establish law enforcement and court systems, among other things.

If you would like to watch relevant films or read some interesting and powerful books and articles about the Native American Indians, I would suggest *Bury My Heart at Wounded Knee* by Dee Brown. Howard Zinn offers a perspective on the role of the US government in its treatment of Indian tribes, particularly in the eighteen hundreds in his book *A People's History of the United States.* Visit: www.richheape.com/index.htm to buy many award-winning videos including: *Don't Get Sick After June, Our Spirits Don't Speak English, The Trail of Tears: Cherokee Legacy, Black Indian An American Story, Native American Healing in the 21st Century, How to Trace your Native American Heritage, Walela: Live in Concert, Tales of Wonder I and II, Romance of A Vanishing Race.*

Lesson 35: Across the pond

The history of the airplane has completely altered the way we travel and planes are undoubtedly an invaluable part of life in developed countries. I, for one, am very grateful to God for presenting man with this way of moving around earth. It has meant that I could conduct business with ease and see my beloved son in either England or America.

Since moving to the United States of America in 1999, I have been back to England only once in 2006, partly due to immigration law. I felt like a fish out of water in the United Kingdom after years away. The driving on the opposite side of the road, in of itself, was a major challenge. I noticed that England was beginning to change in the dynamics of its culture, and after living on Native American Indian reservations, the quaint cobbled narrow streets seemed foreign to me. I had wanted to travel up north to visit our family graves but even the best-laid plans are not always possible. My mentor Jeff Boxen was suffering with terrible grief after the tragic death of his wife of forty-six years. He was distraught without her, and I could not bring myself to put his sadness, or my son's need to spend time with me, below my trip to pay respects to mum and dad or to meet dignitaries. Besides, as they had always taught me, one should not take trips down memory lane; the past is gone, the door is shut – keep moving forwards.

My son was dating a young girl who was emotionally disturbed and instead of a happy time together, the entire trip was disturbed with her insanity and suicidal threats. Thankfully, this relationship did not last too long after I had left, and the pain she caused him was a learning lesson that he will never forget.

Despite Jeff Boxen's mourning for his wife, he wanted to take me to the Ritz for afternoon *high tea*. We had a truly wonderful time, which preceded a delicious dinner at an exclusive Chinese restaurant in Kensington Park. We strolled there from his hotel passing some homeless people along the way. They were crouched in a shop doorway trying to keep warm with one of the skinniest looking mongrels I had ever seen. After we had eaten from a superb menu of delicious dishes, Jeff wanted to take me back to our hotel rooms via taxicab. I felt guilty having eaten such luxurious food, knowing that we had passed people who had obviously fallen upon difficult times. I boxed up some food and insisted we walk back the same route we had come. I was so pleased to see those people and I sat down with them and shared my food. I remembered to bring a snack for the dog. I noticed he was injured. As her owners ate, I tended to the injury as best I could. I will never forget the look on Jeff's face. He did not say a word to me about it until several months later.

"Dearest Chris," he wrote. "When I watched you feeding those homeless people, I felt guilty. You see I have ignored such people all my life, almost afraid that if I talked to them, their negativity would brush off on me somehow. I felt ashamed of myself when I saw how willing you were to treat them like royalty and sit on the dirty floor. Your beautiful dress was ruined. When you ripped your clothes without hesitation to bandage that dog's leg, I could not wrap my head around your great compassion. Truly, you emulate the love of God and I admire you more than you will ever know. That day, I ceased to be your mentor Chris -you became mine." I felt humbled beyond words.

My son Geoff had visited me several times in America and we had shared happy times together. Not many young people can say that they have stayed on a Native American Indian reservation, or visited Washington State, New Jersey and New York. Of course, the ideal situation would have been that I did not get the meningitis, but it is what it was, and life dealt me cards that I had to handle as best I could.

Geoff knew that my life was to be different from most people and I often told him that when God spares you from death, one has to just have faith and obey. He is a truly amazing young man, full of compassion and humor. We love our children of course, but I can honestly say that I really enjoy spending time with my son. He is the kind of person that anyone would be proud to call a friend and he is loyal to his last breath.

One trip that I will always remember consisted of a boat tour around

Manhattan in New York. We had the choice of taking it on a slow ferry or rushing about on the *Beast.* Geoff chose the thrill of the faster boat. We sat at the front and screamed as the boat raced around. It was so much fun and we laughed the entire time as we held each other's hands, and felt our clothes getting wetter and wetter by the minute. It is always very painful to wave goodbye at the airport and there is not one moment of the day when I am not thinking about and praying for him.

I wish I could give him the world and protect him from all harm. I want his life to be wonderful and happy. I want him spared from any harm or sadness. I wish I were rich so that he did not ever have to worry about money and I pray that God will bless him abundantly and make his life extra special. I understand that he is God's son and I know that God created him with a specific purpose to fulfill. I pray that he does obey God and have a meaningful life that brings him satisfaction and grace.

Conclusion

I will never forget the day my son was born. Labor began just before nine-thirty that Monday morning on November 28, 1988. He was born December 1. There was a midwife strike at the hospital and a number of us were waddling around with our waters broken wondering who was going to deliver our children. I was particularly anxious as my other babies had died and I dreaded something going terribly wrong.

My midwife, Sarah, stood by my bed holding a book. This was her first delivery and she said she needed to have the manual to jog her memory. Eventually she went and asked a doctor to come and help her. Geoff needed forceps to pull him out of my body. I saw staff grabbing my son and taking him to an incubator. His skin was blue and he was not breathing. Yes, I all but freaked out. Thank God, he began to cry and for now, we knew he was healthy and a good weight. I lay in my bed watching him sleep. He was, and is the most beautiful human being in my eyes.

Pregnancy and birth is an experience that is impossible to describe to men. To this day, I can still remember Geoff moving in my womb. It felt like butterflies in his early months of growth. By the eight month, his kicks were nothing short of painful and on a couple of occasions I had to go to hospital to get him dislodged from under my rib cage. On the day he chose to turn from the breech positon to head down in my womb for a smooth delivery, we could have sold tickets for the show. It took hours for him to reposition himself comfortably and a few of us sat watching arms and legs, elbows and knees sticking out in the process. It was hilarious to witness, as well as fascinating to me.

It is awe inspiring to contemplate that an egg and a sperm have joined after sex and the miracle of that union has kick-started the process of the transformation of an embryo to a newborn baby. I often think about the process of conception and birth. As a woman, you are not aware of these changes although your hormones wreak havoc on you physically and emotionally. It is not until the baby begins to kick and move that you sense the power of God within your body. When I was able to see him through a scan, I was amazed. Labor and birth is a journey that mother and child experience together. How does one describe the feeling of pushing a baby out of your body into the physical world outside the womb?

If God were to ask me, "Of all the things you have seen, heard and experienced on earth, which would be the greatest?" My answer with no hesitation would be, "The sight of my son on the day he was born, and the cry that he made when he took his first breath."

As it says in Psalm 127:3-5, "Behold, children are a heritage from the Lord, the fruit of the womb a reward. Like arrows in the hand of a warrior are the children of one's youth. Blessed is the man who fills his quiver with them! He shall not be put to shame when he speaks with his enemies in the gate."

I love Psalm 139 where we acknowledge God in the process of pregnancy by saying, "For you formed my inward parts; you knitted me together in my mother's womb. I praise you, for I am fearfully and wonderfully made. Wonderful are your works; my soul knows it very well. My frame was not hidden from you, when I was being made in secret, intricately woven in the depths of the earth. Your eyes saw my unformed substance; in your book were written, every one of them, the days that were formed for me, when as yet there was none of them."

Saint John tells us, "When a woman is giving birth, she has sorrow because her hour has come, but when she has delivered the baby, she no longer remembers the anguish, for joy that a human being has been born into the world."

After the death of our other children, finally God had blessed us with a healthy baby boy. He was a beautiful gift and we named him Geoffrey Anthony Charles Wallace.

I share this story with you in my conclusion to inspire those of you who may have suffered several miscarriages. Several times people told me to forget the idea of being a mother because it was felt that my body was incapable of producing a healthy child. During my prayer time alone with God, he reassured me that he had a baby boy for me. Despite the sarcasm that I endured from neighbors and family, I remained focused. I refused to listen to the naysayers who felt that I was either cursed or inept. I ignored the nasty jabs that I should keep my legs closed and stop getting pregnant. I refused to listen to other women who suggested I should divorce my husband so he could marry a fertile woman. Yes, people were that rude to my face.

Therefore, to conclude, I declare to you right now - one way or another, whether naturally, artificially, via surrogacy, through adoption or by engaging in mission work, if you feel your destiny is to be a mother, then a mother you will surely be by God's good grace. Amen!

Lesson 36: "Action!"

I am like an enthusiastic tourist when it comes to taking photographs. In other words, I am constantly recording everything I see. My biological parents were both artists who could paint in such a way, that their pictures looked like photographs. If my life depended upon painting a masterpiece, I would die fast. I just cannot do it. However, I do have their eye for composition and I enjoy photography and filmmaking. I am self-taught. I have never attended a single photography class in my life, nor have I attended college to learn filmmaking. The talent was naturally there, and it was just a matter of practice to make perfect.

I love to capture unusual images and I will always try to find a way to make the finished product multi layered with each subject. For instance, at my place of worship, we have magnificent statues of Saints Peter and Paul, at the back of the Basilica. When I take pictures of the congregation at various important occasions, I take them over the shoulder of the statues, which create the impression that I am watching over the shoulder of the sculpture of Saint Paul as he is watching the massive congregation. It gives a sense of depth and is certainly more interesting than just pointing, focusing and clicking in an absent-minded manner.

Nobody was more thrilled than I was when we could buy the cell phone with the addition of the camera and recording device built in. In addition to being able to chat with people, I could now take photos and video. The messages of hope, compassion and leadership took on a completely new dimension when I could put slides together and set them to music. Social media then gave me a great outlet to post these videos and teach.

I was one of the first people in my community to have a cell phone. It was like a huge black suitcase and certainly not easy to cart around with me. It beat the pagers though. I hated it when my office would *bleep* me. I would have to pull over and find a phone box. I felt like the *bees knees* with that new cell phone. My friends would *oo* and *ahh* when they saw it and I felt sophisticated. When I was a child, I would watch the sci-fi channels and imagine owning a minute device that could communicate effectively over huge terrain. Over the last fifty years of my life, the cell phones have gone from suitcases to handheld devices to tiny instruments that can fit behind the ear and nestle discreetly in a pocket. "*Woo hoo*," was my comment to that discovery!

When I worked at the Chamber of Commerce in Wyoming, we sat in a meeting one-day discussing re-branding the Chamber. I suggested that we make a film that would include members with their products and services. I enlisted the help of my friend Dan who was a great filmmaker and my close friend Kathy from Bresnan Communications to help launch and air it across its national network. We called the project, "Civic Pride."

I wrote questions that I felt would best represent each company and dignitary. I invited leaders to our office and placed them in front of a green screen. As my filmmaking friend recorded, I asked each person various key questions about their company. We taped for two whole days and nights much to the horror of those assigned for the later hours. We edited for two further days. My assistant and friend Kathy was flabbergasted to discover that I did eat for several days. When it dawned on her that I had not slept either she had no clue as to how I was able to function. "You're not human Chrissy!" she would declare on a regular basis.

Several days later, we had the interviews and images recorded. I wanted to market this film to the best of our ability and suggested we organize the premier as a red carpet event. Everybody laughed at me and sarcastically pointed out that this was cowboy and coal mining country and that nobody would support such an event. I disagreed. With no funding available there was no money in the budget for such an endeavor and without investment, it would be impossible to stage a prestigious event. I got my president to agree that if I could get the funding and organize the entire event with no disruption to our daily responsibilities, we could stage this opening party.

I had formed a close-knit relationship with the senior management teams at the railroad, coalmines and power plants in the state. To date, they had declined to support the Chamber of Commerce. As their new chief of staff for the agriculture, energy and natural resources committee in the county, I had won their respect by organizing tours and forums, where they had the opportunity as subject matter experts to discuss their needs and vision. Their mutual respect equated to guaranteed investment for our organization. This significant funding helped us to address concerning issues and enabled me to compile legislative agendas for congress outlining our solutions to coal mining concerns including mercury removal, carbon capture and sequestration.

I had met with each leader prior to shooting the film and had asked them to provide material for their segments. When I showed them the completed film, they were astonished and impressed with how Dan had managed to put such a compelling and exciting film together for the county. I discussed my marketing ideas with them and with no exception, everybody, including the general hospital wanted to utilize this film as their major recruiting tool. I expressed our wish to celebrate this film at a premier party but explained that without funding, this would not be possible. Within a few hours, we had several thousands of dollars in cash, a hotel willing to gift us their magnificent premises for free, a florist willing to donate table decorations, an orchestra and bag pipers who would play in the valet parking area.

It was a wonderful evening. The women wore evening dresses and most men wore tuxedos. The food was delicious, the music outstanding, the staff attentive and the film a huge success with a standing ovation. Members of Congress flew in and those who could not leave Capitol Hill sent their representatives. Overall, I was so proud of Dan who did not have to advertise his filming services again that year. His gift as a filmmaker was recognized and rewarded. I was thrilled that our county and our Chamber of Commerce was recognized and respected.

Amir sat next to me beaming from one ear to the other as he wiped tears away from his cheek. He leaned across the table, took my hand gently in his and whispered, "Jaan, I'm so proud of you. This film is your legacy to the county. I love you babe." Although congress, the mines, railroad, power plants and Bresnan Communications honored us with several awards that night, my reward came from the mouth of my sweetheart and in helping to put our Chamber of Commerce back on the radar under the capable hands of President Julie Simon – a remarkable woman whom I deeply respect. After the red carpet premier, *Civic Pride* aired several times a day for a year, in six states. It won multiple awards and acted as a major recruitment tool for some of the bigger companies.

I truly appreciate the gift of film and understand its potential. Film gives your audience the ability to see where you are and lose themselves in their imagination as they watch from the comfort of their couches. We all love to go to the movies. We love the drama, the comedy, the passion and romance, the action, the music, the costumes and the animation. We cheer for our heroes and *boo* at the villains. We marvel as others dive deep into the ocean, leap off mountains, and walk through fire. With the advancement of green screen, we can truly become absorbed in a world that few will ever get to explore in person.

The great Walt Disney said, "If you can dream it, you can do it." That is the key to filmmaking and to leading a successful, happy life. Our lives are like a movie where we are the star, director, producer, editor, cinematographer, planner and so forth.

I suggested to you earlier that you learn to live in the present and resist focusing on the future. You might recall that I advised you that it was perfectly feasible to have forward thinking goals as long as they remained fluid. This is the same for a film. As a writer, director and producer I am fully aware that I have to have a concept of what I wish to portray in the final project and I have to have a general outline of what I wish to say. Ideas can seem brilliant on paper and yet when you try to film them, or live them, they seem foolish. It is the same with our plans, goals, dreams and wishes. One minute we are convinced that we want this particular person, job, or car. We cannot imagine that there is anything better than what we have decided we want. We focus and engage in all kinds of techniques including storyboards, visualization, hypnosis, manifestation cards and goodness knows what else. The filming begins and by some complete fluke, it appears; you begin to get exactly what you had hoped would land on your lap. However, much to your dismay, the person or the job turns out to be a disappointment. They were wonderful in theory and yet, inadequate in reality. Upon this realization, you go back to the drawing board. In other words, we are what we think and we are what we focus on.

As Frank Capra said, "There are no rules in filmmaking - only sins. And the cardinal sin is dullness." I have not met a single person over the last fifty years of my life who was boring. Every single man, woman and child has a story to tell which will teach others the wisdom that they have acquired thus far. As the great film director, Steven Spielberg so eloquently said, "People have forgotten how to tell a story. Stories do not have middle or an end any more. They usually have a beginning that never stops beginning."

Our lives are stories; stories that our future generations *will* want to know about. We all delve into our family history to unearth tales of great grandparents who emigrated or survived horrors and injustice. Robert Bresson once said, "My movie is born first in my head, dies on paper; is resuscitated by the living persons and real objects I use, which are killed on film but, placed in a certain order and projected on to a screen, come to life again like flowers in water."

Ed Wood said; "Filmmaking is not about the tiny details. It's about the big picture."

It is easy to feel overwhelmed with the little problems that crop up from time to time. However, as with a film, our lives, when taken in their entirety, produce a story that is fascinating; the story of a mission that every one of us was created to do. A movie requires a leading man or woman. In your epic, God chose you to be the star. You were the perfect choice!

Never think that your life is unimportant. Even an extra on a set is vital to the overall success of a film. There will be times in life when you play the lead role and others where you are merely the support character. There will be times when the script suddenly changes one day and the genre of your movie (life) goes from comedy to drama. That is what makes the movie of your life exciting and there is only one thing that God asks you to do as Woody Allen so eloquently describes, "Eighty percent of success is turning up."

Plain and simple - life just requires you to turn up!

Conclusion

We have the technology today to produce our own simple films. Please learn how to use your cell phones to make records of your life and the lives of those you love. Please do not assume that your loved one is going to be around for an indefinite period. Life is unpredictable and the story of everybody's life is an important thread in the tapestry of life.

Go to your older relatives and sit with them. Ask those questions such as, "Where were you born? Where were your parents born? What did your parents do? What was going on in history during your early years? What did you enjoy learning at school? What is the family talent? Who was your hero and why? What was the saddest moment of your life? What was the happiest moment of your life? How did you meet your spouse? What do you love about your children? Where was the most exciting place you ever visited? What is your favorite book? What is your favorite piece of music?" In addition, "If you were to offer three pieces of advice to the younger generation, what would those three things consist of?"

You can see where I am going with this. When a loved one dies, it is even sadder when we begin to forget what they sounded and looked like. It is even worse when the younger generation has no idea about where they have come from. The history of a family is crucial. I deeply regret that I did not know how to professionally film until only a few years ago. I wish now that I could have filmed my grandparents and parents, not to mention others around me whose essence I can hardly recall today.

We owe it to society to record each other's stories. The book that you are reading right now is for my descendants in order for them to know at least the story of one of their ancestors. I continue to have presence through them, just as my ancestors continue to somewhat exist through me.

Lesson 37: Humanitarian

I have had the profound honor to sit on many committees around the world and I am patron of several charities in India. My interest lies in humanitarian concerns particularly with orphans, wildlife and hospice and in foundations that support our youth in mastering skills to help them find suitable employment. I have founded several projects myself. These projects support victims of domestic violence including men, women, children and their pets. I began these projects in 1996 and I am thrilled to see how many organizations around the world have been supported by this simple and yet highly effective gift which is known as the *Dignity Pack*.

Women who have fled domestic violence receive the *Dignity Packs* at shelters. When a woman escapes from a horrific situation, she does so with very little baggage. Sometimes, a woman must leave unexpectedly and has no time to gather essential items. I introduced this program to America through in Zonta International in Wyoming and it has spread across the country.

Contained within the Dignity Pack are items including:

- Toothbrush
- Hairbrush and comb
- Shampoo and conditioner
- Shower cap
- Cue tips
- Cozy socks
- Photo frame with plastic cover
- Sanitary pads and tampons
- Cuddly bear

- Soap
- Mouthwash
- Talcum powder
- Body lotion
- Deodorant
- Paper and pen
- Note paper and envelopes
- Stamps
- Bible

People donate these items or we purchase them from a local dollar store for about twenty-five dollars. One might ask why we would put a photo frame, cozy socks and a cuddly bear in them. When a person first arrives at a shelter, they are traumatized and on high alert. The socks begin to give a feeling of comfort and the bear is something that she can hold as she sleeps. It makes her feel safe in a childlike way. Oftentimes, a woman will grab some pictures when she leaves the violent scene, minus frames if she has to stuff them into a bag. The frame allows her to put a favorite picture by her side. Please note that we do not put a frame with glass in the packs. Nothing is included that can be used as a weapon against self or others.

This has been a welcomed gift to shelters, who are oftentimes struggling to survive with the limited financial resources available. Most of them are non-profit and depend heavily on outside donations and grants. This is a great community project, which brings others together to help conquer the adverse effects of abuse and neglect. Some people go and shop for the items, whilst others put the packs together. Knowing that you have been able to offer some semblance of comfort to another is a wonderful feeling.

When a man or woman is contemplating leaving a violent relationship, they will hesitate if there are children or pets in their care. Abusers will often punish the abused by using the family pets as a manipulative tool. A victim of violence knows that he or she cannot take her pet to most shelters, which forces them to remain in the violent home, rather than give their pet away. I have founded a project to help in this situation known as the *Peaceful Pets* project. I initiated this to ensure that pets from an abusive household can be temporarily re-homed and ideally introduced during counselling. The pets are highly beneficial in the rehabilitation process of children in particular, who trust their furry or feathered friends. Children tell their pets secrets that they do not feel able to share with an adult.

This is a difficult project to implement in most areas due to lack of funding, room and all the legal dynamics. I am still hopeful that this will be a viable project by authorities. Having ones pet with you gives comfort and peace. No animal or creature deserves abuse or neglect by the very humans it trusts. Special care to protect those who are particularly vulnerable in our society is my prayer.

Conclusion

Domestic violence is terrifying and abused men or women are unaware of the laws that protect them. The best advice that I can offer is to consult with the police. I found them to be very kind and helpful. Call attorneys in your area as many of them are prepared to give you free introductory advice. Ask for advice from a trusted friend. I was amazed (in my own situation) how many men and women had survived a violent attack themselves and it was helpful to talk with them. Contact your local woman's shelter.

Discreetly pack a bag that includes your medication, important files and items such as your passport, driving license, phone, contacts and bankcards. When you leave, these will protect you and act as one less thing to have to cancel or worry about if stolen.

Finally, if your community or group would like further information on community projects to help the abused, you are most welcome to connect with me.

Lesson 38: Burglary

Of all the lessons I have discussed to this point, (or will write about hereafter) lesson thirty-eight was the toughest one of them all. It is by far the hardest one for me to talk about, for reliving it brings back a feeling of great sadness. In hindsight, I can see the good that has come from it, and yet I wish that I had not experienced such a horrific moment in my life. I find I have to brace myself to write about this period, yet I pray that you will find some inspiration from the candidness of my words.

As the title suggests, I was the victim of burglary (and so much more). If you have read this book from page one, you will have no doubt drawn a conclusion as to what kind of a person I am. I am strong, resilient and loving with a determined spirit that can endure a great deal (more than most). God guides me. God protects me and like you, my Guardian Angel is with me every step of the way. I will be concealing the name of my attacker because I wish to protect his family, who I dearly respect, love and cherish. I also have no desire to cause a diplomatic eruption. Officials from his country in Africa have expressed their condolences with an apology that I have accepted. It is not their fault that one of their citizens is deranged and evil.

I had met this man in 2011, but we did not speak until 2012. He was a pastor and he came from a very high profile family abroad. In fact, in his country, he was the equivalent of a prince. He was well educated, eloquent and charming. At first, I was happy to meet a man of God who I could sit and discuss the Bible. He was very knowledgeable and we had some fascinating discussions on the Word. He was equally intrigued to meet a woman who loved the Lord as much as I did (do) and who knew scripture by heart and in detail. We dated, (very briefly) but I quickly came to realize that in addition to an obnoxious sense of entitlement, he had a serious alcohol addiction with a warrant out for his arrest due to multiple unpaid DUI tickets, plus a wandering eye for the ladies.

He would come into my home and ask me to cook him food, which he said was, "Delicious." After he had eaten it, he would systematically go into my bathroom, put his fingers down his throat and vomit up the food in the basin, over the walls and on the floor. I tried very hard to be patient and calm when he said this was a sickness. However, I knew that he was doing this deliberately, for why you would vomit on somebody's walls when there is a toilet in the room.

He would criticize everything about me, because he said that he could see great potential in me, but felt I needed a strong hand from a man of God. He would call and describe things that God had told him to tell me, and he decided one day that I was to be his future wife. At events, he would wander off and observe me from a distance. He would then come back and debrief with sarcastic innuendos. At church, he would insist I sit where he wanted me, which was normally far away from the eyes of other men. When I would go and sit at the front of the church with the other women, he would come and sit next to me and insist I move to the back. When I refused, he would storm out of the church in disgust. He caused uncomfortable scenes at church, so I ceased going to any place of worship where he was the celebrant or congregant.

He was living with an older woman who hosted some of our Bible classes. They lived next door to me, so he was fully aware of all my movements. He would know who came and when I left. She had taken him in when his home burned down and he was on the streets. This dignified woman provided him with everything he needed and was actually a very influential leader in her own right, so they had a mutual respect for one another, despite her own family disliking him intensely and begging her to throw him out of her home. At Bible study, I would see how disrespectful he was to her though, yet she never batted an eyelid. No doubt because my father had been a very strong influence in my life, I knew not to challenge a pastor.

One day after church, he followed me into my home and said, "God has told me that you and I are to get married Christine."

"Pastor, until God tells me himself that you are to be my husband, my answer will be no thank you."

"You would turn down a prince?" he gasped. "What is wrong with you?" he said in disbelief. "I will undoubtedly be the next president of my county and you would be the first lady and a princess."

"With the greatest respect to you and your country, you know my family background, so being a princess is not important to me. You have been out of your country for years and forgive me, but I do not think I would be assuming such a high-ranking positon if I were you. If I were one of your fellow citizens, I would want a leader who is from my country today, not a defector. If you feel sure that I am the one for you, you will have to give me time to pray and I will have to research your country in depth to decide if I wish to live there and help lead it. I will do absolutely nothing without God's command."

"You're being foolish Christine. I am offering you a loving family (he was right about that) and a prestigious position. There is no need for you to talk to others. My word is enough. I love you and you will learn to love me," and with that he tried to kiss me. I pulled away and he stormed out of my home in utter rage.

I questioned myself once or twice, especially when I saw women doting over him with absolute adoration. A few men respected him (others blatantly avoided him) and women went out of their way to flirt. I reflected on this and wondered if I was being ungrateful. I said to myself, was the regal man of God who our Lord wanted me to marry? Why had God put him in my life? Why did I feel afraid whenever he sat next to me?

When my son visited at Christmas that year, this man met him. He told my son that he was a prince and explained that he intended to run to be the president of his country where his father had been a king. He asked Geoff to bless our forthcoming marriage and failed to tell him that I had said, "No thank you." My son disliked him intensely and did not feel that he was the man God intended for me. He found him arrogant and obnoxious. A few days after my son had returned to England, I held a Bible study class in my home. Several of the churchwomen came, along with this man. During the study, he wanted to use the restroom. On his way back, he stopped and stared into my bedroom gasping. He was visibly shaken up and we asked him if he was ok. He nodded. As soon as everybody had left, he turned to me and said, "Did you know that you have an angel in your bedroom?"

"Well it doesn't surprise me," I replied. "We all have a Guardian Angel, don't we? I have always felt that God's legions of angels are around to protect me from harm. Perhaps it was Archangel Michael."

"Your bedroom is a very powerful place," he said with fear in his voice. "I sense you are being protected by God himself."

I looked at him and said, "Did the angel say anything to you?"

"Yes," he replied. "It pointed at me and said, 'You are going to go to prison!'"

"Whoa," I managed to say.

He looked at me and sarcastically laughed. "I must have being seeing things, why would one of God's angels say that to me. I am a man of God!" He had told me on one occasion that his sister had gone to a medicine man in Africa who refused to advise her with this man being outside. He had told her that this man was powerful and had the ability to walk through doors and hurt anybody who tried to harm him.

He cautioned me never to make him angry, for he had the ability to inflict harm on anybody who threatened him. He was of the firm belief that God moved through him with great strength and power, even to the point of protecting him during their civil war. He mentioned several occasions when he should have died, but the gun would not engage.

This man walked back to the entrance of my bedroom and stared inside. He turned and looked at me as if he had seen a ghost and then ran out of the apartment. I sat in my bedroom that night and prayed. If this man had indeed seen an angel who warned him of an impending prison sentence, why had it come to him in my bedroom? If this was one of his crazy ways to manipulate me, then this all had to stop right now!

I saw him the next day on my way out. He told me that he and this woman were moving to another county and asked me to help them pack and move boxes, as I was young and strong. I was relieved to know they were moving away and was eager to help in that process.

The next few days were spent boxing up their things. I opened one closet door in their home to find some of my personal belongings in it.

"What on earth are my things doing in your closet?" I asked in shock. "I thought they were lost and you told me that I was losing my mind!" I was even more furious to discover that most of the things were broken and he just yelled at me that these things were evil and he was doing me a favor.

"Would you like to rationally explain to me how my Bible from childhood is evil?" I angrily enquired. He never did answer that question and as I went through my beloved books, CD's, movies and gifts, I had no alternative but to throw most of them away because they were ruined.

That exact same day, I received notice informing me that this man and woman could not enter my apartment, due to an eviction notice after the discovery of the worst infestation of bed bugs that this complex had ever seen. They knew how clean and beautiful my home was, thus they did not want these people coming in and ruining it, which would cause them to have to fumigate the entire building at great expense. I completely understood and thanked them for warning me. When I confronted this man about the infestation, he went berserk. After I showed him my letter, he was furious to such a degree that I was frankly nervous. He then turned to me and said, "I don't have time for this. I have been up all night and I had to get another pastor to come here. I told you that I was in the Special Forces as a sniper and intelligence officer and that I go on missions with little notice. You see this silver case?" I nodded my head. "Inside are my papers and a gun. They want me to go to Iraq this week."

To this day, I do not know whether that is true or not. It sounded insane; the ranting of a man with a very serious mental affliction. I felt shaken up and I was relieved when they had moved away. I finally felt relaxed walking in and out of my home again. I had told him that I did not want to marry him, or continue any kind of communication whatsoever. He just stood and laughed at me.

Things began to move around in my home, and Zachy was unusually skittish. After the closet incident where I had found my things in that man's home, I was wary. I could not imagine that he had come into my home, so I was worrying about why I could not find things. I did not become overly nervous until I noticed things in my bedroom missing or moved to other parts of the apartment. I went to the complex office and asked if their maintenance people had entered without my permission. They insisted that nobody had been in, so I called the police and gave a statement. The property managers agreed to change my locks.

The next day I went out to find my truck moved from its usual place. I walked all over the complex and found it repositioned in an entirely different area to my home. When I went to look at it, the side panels were missing. Forensics later confirmed that oil was in the gas tank, rendering it destroyed. I was the only one with a key to that truck (at least that is what I thought). The police came and took a statement. I went in to my home to get the spare key, only to find that it was not there anymore. When we had opened up the truck, we found blood in the back and I later discovered that this man had taken the truck duck hunting. Forensics confirmed that the blood was from a bird and not a human. I called him to ask if he had taken my truck and he said he had "Borrowed it," but had not damaged it. I was furious and asked him how he had been able to get into the truck without keys. He calmly said that I had lent them to him, which I flatly denied. When I told him that I was going to report this theft to the police, he laughed at me.

I was beginning to feel extremely nervous and I was very upset about the truck. As with all my possessions, I had taken great care of it and to lose it in this way was heartbreaking. The insurance company was professional and helpful and within days, they had given me money to go and get a new car. Within two days of driving my new car, I began to receive phone calls from this man. He left several messages, which included voice mails saying, "Now that you have a new car, you can go and visit your grave." I kept every message and called the police, who advised me to change my number and keep an account of all his messages.

It was now the month of May. This was a long holiday weekend and I typically did my shopping on Saturday evenings. I was sitting on the couch reading my Bible, when suddenly he crashed through my door, catching me off guard. He ran into my bedroom and I tried to grab my phone. He ran back out again with things under his arm, came right up to my face, and evilly sneered, "If I can't have you, nobody can. You have broken my heart by refusing me and if you don't get out of America within five days, I will permanently disable you!"

"Are you threatening me?" I asked.

"Yes I am. I'm threatening you and I'm promising you!" he yelled and then ran out.

After he had left, I remembered that he had taken specific things from my bedroom including my purse, Bible, medication, money and my gun. I do not know how he knew about my gun. I can only assume that he had come into my home when I was out, which probably explains the things I had noticed moved, or missing weeks before. I still had no idea how he had the old and new keys to my apartment. There were times during our earlier Bible studies that he would go into the kitchen to get water. This is where I always kept my spare keys and I can only assume that he took them to make copies. I called 911. The police took me to the police department to give a statement and after speaking to the judge, who issued a restraining order; I was taken back home. The police assured me that they would go and arrest him.

I felt nervous that night as I sat praying that the police would catch and imprison him. I lived in an apartment building, which had a community entrance. Thus, every time the outer door opened, I found myself holding my breath (literally) and listening for his footsteps. With the back of my apartment facing the dark woods, it was easy for him to hide amongst the trees. It would have been equally easy for him to conceal himself before climbing up the railings to my patio doors. He often wore black clothes and with his dark skin and the pitch dark of night, I knew he could see me, even when I could not see him. I wanted to close the curtains across the patio windows, but I worried that by doing so, I would not see him if he climbed on to my patio. It was a catch twenty-two situation. In the end, I sat on my living room floor, prayed and meditated all night.

I wanted to attend church the following morning so I called the police department who informed me that this man was now in jail with a ten thousand dollar bail. The day before, I had gone to the police department in one of their squad cars, so I had not even looked at mine. As I walked towards my car (and much to my horror), I saw deeply ingrained along the sides, words that are too graphic to repeat. The one who had done this systematically smashed the windows, tires and lights. As you can probably imagine, I was completely shaken up. If this has ever happened to you, (and I pray to God it never does) it is shocking and quite frightening. Regardless of the insurance papers and deductibles, (which in my case was two thousand dollars with this new vandalism) just the thought that somebody has deliberately gone out of their way to hurt you, is mind blowing. Never in my life had anybody done such things to me. I am a very loving and giving woman with caring and compassionate friends and colleagues. Things like this do not happen to people like me; at least that is what I used to think.

Neighbors came out and looked at my car with the same look of horror I was feeling. Seeing police cars coming to their quiet neighborhood, made people very uneasy. This quiet community had never had vandalism problems, least of all mad men and killers.

I tried to calm myself and think like a strategic leader rather than a nervous victim. I called my insurance company to inform them of the vandalism. I followed that up with a call to the police department and then to a towing company that my insurance agent had instructed me to notify. Within minutes, the police officer was there to support me. He was wonderful and tried to reassure me that this nightmare would soon be behind me.

The man from the tow company was very reluctant to switch on the car to move it to the ramp. "How do I know there isn't a bomb under it?" he asked with a very concerned expression on his face. The men and women from the complex all nodded in agreement and I could not blame them either. I could see nobody was going to help so I asked everybody to stand back as I put the key in the ignition and turned. It would not start and a few days later, the specialist report confirmed that oil was in the tank, rendering it to be incapable of restoration. It was tough to lose two vehicles within a couple of weeks.

I went back into my home, sat down and briefly wept before chastising myself for displaying weakness. I knew that this so-called man of God was in jail, so I mustered up the energy to walk to the shops to buy food and refill my prescription. That was when the reality hit home. He had taken my purse with the money and credit cards. I called the bank, cancelled my cards and reordered new ones. I found enough loose change lying around that I could at least get my pills and after a six mile round trip walk, I came back home, sat and prayed to be protected. I spent the next few days planning my next move.

I will never forget the phone call to notify me that this man was out of jail with his bail paid. I sat frozen to the spot and I cannot even begin to tell you what went through my mind. "Frozen to the spot," is a common expression and yet, most of us have no concept of what it really means or feels like. I do now. Your whole body ceases to move and it almost feels like your heart stops beating. You become hypervigilant and it is cripplingly lonely.

I sat thinking about what my father would have told me to do, if he were there and I knew that he would have advised me to be strategic and to protect myself in any way I deemed necessary. I had thirty large blue barrels of clothes and supplies, which I was collecting to send to my mission projects in Africa and India. I decided to use them as a barricade. They were very heavy and I thought they would protect my entranceways. I dragged some and pushed others with all my might to block the back and front doors. I even put some underneath each window, which I felt would at least slow down an attack. Now you might be wondering why I did that. I sensed I was in danger and I was correct in that evaluation. None of my friends knew this was happening, as I had not wanted any of them to be in danger. I concluded that this would be over soon and so I just needed to be tactically calm. The police told me that there would be a court date in a few days and all I had to do was to get by until then. They assured me that they were keeping watch and advised me to be vigilant. Being candid, it was a horrible situation.

I was afraid to leave my home because I knew he was out there with my gun. At his own admission, he was a trained military Special Forces sniper who had killed without remorse. It was not until after all of this was over that I learned from his son and sister, that he had beaten his children and ex-wife in the past. He had even hit a woman from one of his churches, who had called the police, but later dropped the charge. Nobody had prosecuted him. It was apparent that we had a violent man who was a public figure, living in our neighborhood.

It was now June 4, 2013. With the barrels moved into place and the curtains drawn across some of the windows so he could not see me, I crawled to bed like a hunted animal. It was horrible! I awoke at eleven thirty that night to sense there was somebody in my bedroom. I turned to find a person standing over my bed with something in his hand. I murmured, "Who's there?" He leaned forward. The hallway light was on and when I turned to see who it was; I saw it was this man. He was standing there in his black clerical clothes.

I tried to grab my knife, which was under my pillow, but it was not there anymore. I yelled aloud and he ran. I ran after him and just before he made it to my front door, he turned around and looked at me with the most *evil* look that I had ever seen in my life. That look stopped me dead in my tracks. I ran back to my bedroom, grabbed my phone and dialed 911. The police were there very quickly and the dispatcher stayed on the phone with me until they arrived. I was terrified! I was almost too scared to walk down the hallway, but I knew I had to, or how would the officers get in. As they arrived, we noticed that the door was slightly ajar and the barrels dislodged. Why had I not heard that? I had changed the locks, and yet he had still managed to break in. We simply could not understand then or now how he had keys to open it.

The dispatcher instructed me to open the door for the police to enter. They came in to interview me and searched the home thoroughly. Just before we left for the police department, we found a pair of shoes by the patio doors. I told them that they were not mine and when I looked at them closely, I knew they were his, because he had a way of breaking down the backs of them when he walked. They put the shoes in an evidence bag. Walking out to the police car was nerve wracking. I literally could not stop shaking, as I knew this man was out there. Four officers shielded me and the area was teeming with police officers. It looked like a scene from an action movie with flashing lights and armed cops running around the vicinity. As I was getting into a squad car, I remembered Zachy and I realized that I had not seen him. I got out again with the intention of going back in to my home to check that he was ok. The officers told me that he was hiding under the bed. "I have to go and see for myself," I cried.

"Ma'am, we have got to get you to safety. Trust me, your cat is safe we promise," the officers reassured me.

I met with the victims advocate at the station and she was very kind. Every single person there was wonderful and treated me very well. They assured me that they would work together to catch this man and that I needed to remain calm and write a concise witness report detailing everything I knew about this man including where he lived. I did as they had asked and with God's help, I managed to write a detailed statement.

The police brought me back home at two o'clock in the morning. The officers went in first to secure it and then left with an assurance that they were patrolling the complex and that I was safe to sleep. I sat down and admittedly, I cried. Zachy jumped up onto my knee and although he was obviously nervous, he remained there.

People often ask me what was going through my mind that night as I sat wondering what was happening outside. Frankly, I was feeling intense fear combined with a sense of deep sadness. I used to love my home and particularly my bedroom. I had worked *very* hard and used a month's commission to treat myself to a stunning king sized four-poster bed, which I loved so much. Now when I glanced at it, I could not see anything but that man leaning over me as I slept and I knew that I would never be able to sleep in it again. Can you imagine what would have happened if I had stayed asleep? What goes through the mind of a man as he creeps into a woman's home and bedroom, removes his shoes, takes the knife from under the couches and her pillow and proceeds to do – do what? What was he planning to do to me? Was he going to rape me? Was he planning to suffocate me? With my knife in his hand, was his intention to stab me to death? However, he did not, could not, kill me because I am certain my Guardian Angel was right there by my side and he had already warned this man months before, that he was going to go to prison.

I could not get that evil look he had given me out of my head. It resembled the worst satanic movie ever made. I could not sleep, as my home (which had always been my beautiful sanctuary) felt invaded. Every minute dragged by and so I decided to read my Bible and meditate for comfort and strength. Two hours later, at four-thirty, I heard the outer door open. Knowing the police were still outside, I assumed it was one of the officers. The Holy Spirit warned me that it was he. My heart began to race and I scanned the room for a protective weapon. It was then that I discovered that the knives I had placed under my couch were all missing. As he dislodged the door, I wanted to believe it was my imagination. That kind of thing happens in movies, not in real life, or so I thought. However, this was not a movie; it was reality. He *had* come back and I doubted the police even knew.

"Father God!" I prayed. "Please Lord, have mercy on me. Help me Lord!"

As he crept into my home, I yelled, "Stop!" As he ran, I chased after him, but he got away before I could grab him. Now before you think that was either a brave thing to do or just plain foolish, I will be candid with you. If I had of caught him, I do not know what I would have done. I am not going to sit here and pretend to be some brave hero. The truth is I did not know what I was doing. Most people run *away* from danger and yet, I have no idea why I ran *after* him. We believe that he came back to the house to get his shoes. Those shoes would contradict any alibi he might later offer.

I called 911 and the police ran in immediately. They had been outside all along and so, yes, this man had even snuck passed them. This time they advised me to go to a public place like the hospital or a mall until the court hearing a few hours later, but I told them that I was not prepared to do that for fear innocent people might be hurt. In the end, they agreed to take me to the police department.

A couple of hours later, I called a taxicab (I still had no car) and went to the court hearing. There had been an administrative error and the clerk told me to go home and wait for their notice. I felt very skittish at the courthouse and I told the security officers what was happening. They reassured me that I would be safe. Couples and attorneys were preparing for divorce proceedings and I sat in the corner with my back against a wall, as I wanted to be in a positon to watch who came in and out.

I arrived home to find the police, who told me that I needed to go into protection. My property owners were also there. As much as they cared for me, they insisted that I had to leave in order for nobody to be injured. I asked the police how long I needed to hide before the Grand Jury hearing and they explained it could be several weeks or even months.

I sat facing a dilemma. I had to move immediately. I had a home full of furniture, no car to transport anything and nobody close to me who knew what I was experiencing. I called two friends that I thought I could trust. One was a pastor and the other a business colleague. Pastor came with a truck and packed up all of my beautiful furniture, which I told him to give it away to people in need. I knew that I would never be able to be around any of that furniture again, for it was a crime scene as far as I was concerned. He kindly took all of my mission barrels as well and over the next few months, he sent them to humanitarian projects in Africa. The other man offered to put my personal things into safe storage and promised me faithfully that he would protect them as his own. These were my clothes, documents, books, CD's, awards, certificates, bedding, pots and pans and most importantly, gifts from my son, Amir and my parents. In other words, the things I held onto had significant sentimental value as well as legal, financial and professional importance.

I was to go to the shelter for battered women, but when they said I could not take my cat, I refused to leave without him. Therefor I went to an undisclosed location where I could take Zachy with me. I filled a trash sack with medication, phone, computer, essential files and documents, purse, two pictures of my son, cat food, litter and tray, a couple of dresses, plus my Bible and commentaries. How ironic that everything I had ever told victims of domestic violence to grab in the *Dignity Pack* program, were now a part of my life. Here I was in that same crazy, frightening, horrific situation.

Several weeks later, I appeared before the Grand Jury. I had not slept well, nor had I eaten much. I was weak and frankly, traumatized. I had no decent clothes in which to appear. I literally had nothing with me from my home and I was washing my clothes in the basin with a bar of soap. Hour upon hour, I sat in that room numb one minute and jumpy every time I heard footsteps the next. I was afraid to be inside and cautioned about going out. I had spent most of the time reading my Bible and praying, and the rest crying. I fully admit that I was quite simply a wreck knowing that man was still loose and I felt ashamed that I was in such a weakened position.

There were twenty-three jurors that day in the courtroom and I was a witness for the county who were prosecuting the man for five counts of crimes against the State of New Jersey, including burglary. I tried to be very concise and calm when giving evidence during those hours. With each count, I waited outside the courtroom whilst the jurors discussed all the evidence presented from the police department and me. Half way through, a male juror admitted that he knew this man personally and proceedings halted to remove him from the room. The judge discussed the situation and allowed the proceedings to continue without the juror.

I tried very hard to remain focused, but it was difficult when I saw the visible effects of my story on the jurors. Some of the women were weeping and the men had clenched fists. When the police officer was to testify, he touched my hand and smiled at me before going in to the courtroom. When he came out, he told me that unfortunately men like this often get away with things, especially if it is their first offense, which he personally found disgusting. Even the County Prosecutor warned me that as this was this man's first crime, and given whom he was, the likelihood of a prison sentence was not promising. I went back to the secure room that had been home to me for the last few weeks and waited to hear the verdict. The Grand Jury indicted that man of five counts, including three for burglary. As he had not stabbed or raped me, there could not be a count for attempted murder.

This man was being sheltered, so it was felt that if I left New Jersey, he would reemerge. Several weeks later, this man was arrested. He served eight weeks in jail before pleading guilty to all the charges. In exchange for a plea bargain, he was sentenced to two separate three years of probation to run consecutively, ordered to take a mental health evaluation and ordered to attend drug and alcohol rehabilitation.

Meanwhile, I had no home, no car, no job, no money, no furniture, no personal items and no peace of mind. Yes folks, you read correctly! It seems that me being a U.S. citizen with a completely clean record, is not as influential as a pastor (and prince) with diplomatic advantages.

To this day, I have to assume (pray) he is walking around New Jersey streets and not hiding out in the bushes where I am currently living, even more enraged and deranged waiting to pounce on me. I have to assume (trust in the law) he is attending probation and rehabilitation. I have to trust that if he breaks the rules of his probation he will go to prison and I have to hope that at the end of his probation they will deport him back to Africa. His people can deal with him and I would hope that his behavior as a convicted felon would ensure he does not become their next president, or God help them! I also have to assume that he is not terrorizing other innocent women as he has done with his former wife, children and me.

I can only imagine the sermons this man gives in church and I genuinely worry about what he might do next. The next woman may not be as fortunate as I was and her family may end up attending her funeral, God forbid.

Conclusion

God showed me his mercy that night, and saved my life. Earlier in the year, my Guardian Angel warned this man that God knew he was planning to hurt me. As one of his sheep, he would not allow me to die until it was the ordained moment.

Here are a few wonderful verses that speak to God's protecting angels.

Matthew 18:10 "Be careful. Don't think these little children are worth nothing. I tell you that they have angels in heaven who are always with my Father in heaven."

Psalm 91:11 "For he will command his angels concerning you to guard you in all your ways."

Hebrews 1:14 "Are not the angels all ministering spirits, servants sent out in the service of God for the assistance of those who are to inherit salvation?"

Matthew 18:10 "Then the devil left him, and behold, angels came and were ministering to him."

Lesson 39: Depression

There is a stigma attached to depression and an even worse one when somebody dares to (think about, or actually does) commit suicide. I was once asked if I had ever considered taking my own life after the attack and my answer was, "No, but I did pray to be allowed to go home." I hoped God would have mercy on my soul and allow me to go to sleep. I imagined him then taking me to heaven in that peaceful state. I was exhausted with feeling like prey.

When the beloved actor Robin Williams committed suicide, the world mourned deeply and everybody was both shocked and stunned that there had been nobody to help him with his depression and drug addiction. The media speculated as to what could have triggered the tragic decision to take his life. Was it the drugs and alcohol? Was it the early stages of Parkinson disease? Was it a financial crisis? Could it have been mania or some other mental affliction? Many debated as to whether he was either brave or a coward for slitting his wrists and hanging himself in the bedroom. The truth is, nobody will ever know. He allegedly neither left a note explaining his decision, nor told anybody who is prepared to reiterate that conversation. Frankly, it is none of our business.

I have been through a great deal of challenge in my life and I have faced very sad and difficult times like many of you. That is not to seek pity, but just an obvious observation. I do not regret any of my life, for having been to the gates of heaven, I fully understand that life on earth is to learn the lessons of grace, humility, forgiveness and love for all beings. I know God created me for a purpose and that my life was not a mistake. God has shown me his great and glorious mercy and I attribute my faith to being able to walk through each situation looking to him, and trusting in him that this is for my greatest good.

During those weeks in which I hid waiting for justice, I felt so afraid and it was as if I was in the darkest and deepest hole imaginable. In fact,

I was not falling into a hole; I was pathetically sitting at the very bottom of it. There was nothing else below me. I felt somewhat separated from everybody and everything and it was very, very, very tough. I had next to nothing to wear, to wash with, to eat or to call my own. Evil was all around and if God had said to me, "My child, you can come home now!" I would have said, "Amen!"

The devil was laughing his behind off watching me. Oh, what a pathetic creature I must have looked! I am sure he mockingly said, "Let's see if her precious Lord will save her now!"

I am not going to kid you; I was not even brave enough to take my own life. I dislike pain and there is not a painless or easy way to die. I also could not bring myself to commit such an act, knowing that another human being would have to find my decomposed body and deal with it. I could not do that to my beloved son either, for what had he ever done to deserve the horror of knowing his mother had committed suicide because a man had driven her to a state of almost hopelessness from fear and loss. I could not let Zachy down, for he needed looking after. I could not let all of my teachers and students down. I was supposed to be their rock. Stumbling was one thing, quitting was not an option. I could not give up on my father God either. I knew that although this was a glimpse of hell for me, he was there with me. Not for one second did I think otherwise. He had sent angels to watch over me and I knew that my Guardian Angel was sitting right next to me, with his wings wrapped tightly around me.

God touched my heart and told me to read Psalm 91 (NIV)

"He who dwells in the secret place of the Most High
shall abide under the shadow of the Almighty.
I will say of the Lord, "He is my refuge and my fortress;
My God, in Him I will trust."
Surely He shall deliver you from the snare of the fowler
And from the perilous pestilence.
He shall cover you with His feathers,
And under His wings you shall take refuge;

His truth shall be your shield and buckler.
You shall not be afraid of the terror by night,
Nor of the arrow that flies by day,
Nor of the pestilence that walks in darkness,
Nor of the destruction, that lays waste at noonday.
A thousand may fall at your side,
And ten thousand at your right hand;
But it shall not come near you.
Only with your eyes shall you look,
And see the reward of the wicked.
Because you have made the LORD, who is my refuge,
Even the Most High, your dwelling place,
No evil shall befall you,
Nor shall any plague come near your dwelling;
For He shall give His angels charge over you,
To keep you in all your ways.
In their hands, they shall bear you up,
Lest you dash your foot against a stone.
You shall tread upon the lion and the cobra,
The young lion and the serpent you shall trample underfoot.
"Because he has set his love upon me, therefore I will deliver him;
I will set him on high, because he has known my name.
He shall call upon me, and I will answer him;
I will be with him in trouble;
I will deliver him and honor him.
With long life, I will satisfy him,
And show him my salvation."

I read and re-read that Psalm many times, before I went into meditation. Now, more than ever before, I was thankful for all those precious years of meditation training. I visualized my teacher Lama Surya Das, and I began to follow how he had taught me to breathe and relax my mind and body. I meditated upon God. I allowed goodness and love to flow through me. I meditated upon our Lord Jesus and thought about his life, precious teachings and my sincere love for him. I simply dissolved into the grace and mercy of our Savior.

When I went to the Grand Jury, I was still very upset. However, the mere fact that I had even been able to leave that room and go to testify, was a miracle in of itself. I can admit this today. When I stood at the courtroom door on that jury day, I took a deep breath and said, "Lord, stay close to me." I honestly imagined that my testimony would ensure that this man went to prison, thus protecting other women from injury. Had I have known then that he would receive leniency, not deported, but rather, permitted to walk around the streets of New Jersey and USA, I may have thought twice about appearing. I console myself by saying that if he stalks or injures another woman, being a convicted felon, the woman (if she survives) will receive justice.

After Grand Jury, I prayed for clarification as to what God wanted me to do. I felt like I was being given a glimpse into what Jesus had somewhat experienced in the desert for those forty days and forty nights and those desperate hours in the garden of Gethsemane. I realized that nothing could ever truly harm me if I kept my eyes on him and continued my life in humility, with love and kindness for all. That, "All,' included me. I knew that I had to get up with his strength, polish my armor and be the soldier that I had promised to be for him. I stood up, looked in the mirror and sang the hymn, "Onward Christian soldiers," by Sabine Baring-Gould, which was written in 1865.

Onward, Christian soldiers, marching as to war,
with the cross of Jesus going on before.
Christ, the royal Master, leads against the foe;
Forward into battle see His banners go!

Refrain:
Onward, Christian soldiers, marching as to war,
With the cross of Jesus going on before.

At the sign of triumph, Satan's host doth flee;
on then, Christian soldiers, on to victory!
Hell's foundations quiver at the shout of praise;
Brothers, lift your voices, loud your anthems raise.

Like a mighty army moves the church of God;
Brothers, we are treading where the saints have trod.
We are not divided, all one body we,
one in hope and doctrine, one in charity.

Crowns and thrones may perish, kingdoms rise and wane,
but the church of Jesus constant will remain.
Gates of hell can never 'gainst that church prevail;
We have Christ's own promise, and that cannot fail.

Onward then, ye people, join our happy throng,
Blend with ours your voices in the triumph song.
Glory, laud, and honor unto Christ the King,
This through countless ages men and angels sing.

Conclusion

Life is a truly wonderful gift and an opportunity to see the magnificent glory of God's amazing creation. Today, more than ever before in history, we have the capability within seconds, to talk to others around the world and to share wisdom and knowledge beyond our wildest comprehension. However, it also comes with unexpected challenges, when you least expect them.

From my experience, if I could give you some wisdom that I know would sustain and lead you out of the darkest hole imaginable it would be to read your Bible, and know it inside out and upside down. The Word is the finest life manual that you will ever read or need. Every single situation that can possibly ever arise has the answer and advice contained within its precious pages.

God knew that we would all need this wisdom map and encouragement. If we try to walk through life without it, it is like attempting to travel from one side of the world to the other with no compass or map, no knowledge of languages spoken and limited financial means. When we go on an important trip, (and frankly, there is none more important than the journey of life) we do not leave our maps at home. Neither do we remove the manufacturer's manual from the glove compartment in our cars. Speaking for myself, there have been times when my truck has made strange noises, or a light has popped up on my dashboard in the middle of goodness knows where and I have dived into the manual to try to work out what is possibly wrong.

The same can be said for life my friends. Even during those difficult days, I knew to bring the Word with me, and thank God that I did. I found strength and comfort in reading how others had faced hellish situations, but by faith, found the courage to persevere and triumph over adversity. I hope that my book has inspired you to know the Word more fully. I am the living example of Christ's love in the life of a sinner. God has never let me down and goodness knows I have found myself in some tight spots over the last fifty years.

I pray that you and I meet one day. I want you to see his glory in my eyes and hear his loving words through my voice and testimony. I wish to hold your hand and tell you that he knows your problems and pains and I hope that I get to pray with you and ask him to come into your heart right now and show you how to walk the rest of this journey with strength and purpose and most importantly; with love, forgiveness and humility. You are a perfect image of him; and he loves you in a way you will never fully understand.

Finally, nobody can destroy you when you turn to him in your darkest and most painful hours. I learned through this entire trauma, that God is watching over us. My Guardian Angel had told my attacker months before that he was about to face imprisonment and that his dastardly deeds would be forever etched on his book of life. We all have a book of life, which is why I pray for the strength and compassion to work through the process of forgiveness with him, just as I had with the man who had raped me as a child, and with those who had betrayed me over the years in various ways.

As Jesus said, "Father, forgive them for they know not what they do." Moreover, we say in our prayers, "Forgive us our trespasses, as we forgive those who trespass against us."

Lesson 40: Friendship

Here I was homeless, carless, jobless, penniless, and destitute in my 48th year. Suffice to say, I was no longer in protective hiding and that man was still on the loose, but God only knew where. The country prosecutor and the police department all advised me to leave the state.

The insurance company had given me some money that I used to stay in a motel for a week and to rent a car for a few days. I had some very serious decisions to make and so I sat down and prayed. I wondered if I should go back to England, but decided that this was not a good idea. Apart from anything else, I felt too ashamed to face what seemed like a barrage of questions that I had no energy to answer. Besides, I was now a U. S citizen and felt that if anybody was to leave, it should be him as he was not even a legal resident. I wondered seriously if I should go to India and work as a missionary for a while or ask one of the many ambassadors I knew to let me stay in their country until such time I was feeling safer.

God has blessed me throughout life with many amazing men and women who love me unconditionally. I knew how upset and angry they would be to hear of recent events. It was customary for us to speak regularly and yet, I had not spoken to any of them for months, as I did not wish for them to be injured. One such very dear friend was an elderly retired reserve U.S. army general who is an exceptional entrepreneur and specialist in intelligence and transportation. Marc and I had been working together for years in the iron ore and metallurgical coal exporting business, and I trusted and respected him very highly. He lived in Florida and I had visited him a couple of times on business. It was normal for us to speak several times a week and to email every day. With recent events, I had neither called him nor emailed.

I needed to reach out to somebody trustworthy and inwardly knew there was nobody more courageous and decent than him. To say that he was massively relieved to hear from me would be a gross understatement.

I recalled the events of the last few weeks. Marc was beside himself with sadness, concern and rage. He interrupted me mid-sentence, "Chrissy, honey, can you drive?"

I told him that I could. "Then come down here right now!" He replied. "You will be safe here and if that son of a bitch comes anywhere near you, he will have to face me!" he yelled. "You can stay here for as long as you need to Chrissy."

"I have Zachy, Marc. Is that OK?"

"Of course Zachy is welcome," he reassured. "Do you have enough money to get here?" He asked. I told him that I did, but said that I did not wish to drag him into my situation. He would not take no for an answer. I stayed in Virginia for one night and Georgia the next. Within three days, Zachy and I were in sunny Florida.

It is impossible to be unhappy in central Florida. The sun shines every day and everybody is excited to be on vacation. I felt so welcomed, loved and safe. Admittedly, I still had problems falling asleep and I still felt very uncomfortable going in and out of the home, but with time, I grew to feel more at ease. I knew that I had to begin to make rational and wise decisions.

When the outrageous news came through that this man was on parole, any thoughts about returning to New Jersey were gone. That was a tough pill to swallow. Although it felt unjust, it was a fact that I simply had to accept. I knew on a spiritual level that God had plans for me and that this whole nightmare would serve to glorify him in a way that perhaps staying there would not have accomplished. I consoled myself that everything dear to me in a material sense, was in storage and I planned to retrieve them within the next few weeks. I was repeatedly reassured they were all safe in storage and that this was a gift from my colleague.

Zachy and I found comfort sleeping on Marc's couch. He shared everything he had with me, including his car and resources. He encouraged me to get a job and when it was too much for me yet; he accepted that and was patient and kind. Nobody could pray for a better friend and nobody could have treated me with more love, kindness, generosity and dignity. Never once, did he put me in a situation that ever made me feel uncomfortable and my recovery and safety was his number one priority.

Marc was a devout Roman Catholic. I often told him that when he went to heaven, God would bless him for his kindness towards me. As it says in the Gospel of Saint Matthew, chapter twenty-five, "When the Son of man comes in his glory, escorted by all the angels, then he will take his seat on his throne of glory. All nations will be assembled before him and he will separate people one from another as the shepherd separates sheep from goats. He will place the sheep on his right hand and the goats on his left. Then the King will say to those on his right hand, 'Come, you whom my Father has blessed, take as your heritage the kingdom prepared for you since the foundation of the world. For I was hungry and you gave me food, I was thirsty and you gave me drink, I was a stranger and you made me welcome, lacking clothes and you clothed me, sick and you visited me, in prison and you came to see me.'"

Conclusion

Friends are more valuable than all the gold that exists in the world, and far more precious than any diamond or jewel. When you find a faithful and loving brother or sister of God, you will not have to ask them to talk about their faith, or justify their belief system. You will merely watch how they treat the humblest person or creature they meet.

Friends like Marc are the ones that Jesus tried to exemplify in his teachings. By unselfishly welcoming a wretched waif and her stray cat, he showed mercy to them that surely demonstrates the glory of God. This compassionate generosity will undeniably earn him a very special place in one of God's rooms in his mansion. May God bless him in ways I cannot imagine! Amen.

Lesson 41: Mother Mary

I have studied theology to post-doctoral level and unlike many; I have been to the gates of heaven and returned. The Holy Spirit resides within me. Every word I utter and every act I undertake, he is the center of my attention. He is love and it is with love that I try to serve him as best as I can. I have been on a faithful journey, which has been a long, exhausting and yet spiritually fulfilling walk so far.

I accompanied Marc to the Basilica of the National Shrine of Mary, Queen of the Universe, in Orlando. I had visited it before and had felt a wonderful sense of peace. It was lovely to be back in the church filled with love, kindness and serenity that is home to tens of thousands of visitors each year. The music, led under the directorship of Dr. William Picher, was simply magnificent. Whatever image you have in your mind of heavenly chorus, the Basilica choir is the angels personified.

Since my last visit several years before, I had studied the Catholic faith and had even begun to pray and meditate using a rosary that had been a gift. Sitting in the Basilica in 2013, I listened to a stunning homily on the *Lord's Prayer* from the accomplished and most humbly eloquent Monsignor Juanito Figura, who was on sabbatical from the Philippines. His teaching moved me deeply and it was obvious to me then that he had a strong Catholic faith with clear insight into scripture. I went into the chapel a few weeks later and asked God to show me what Monsignor had that I was lacking in my life. I spoke and then I listened, just as I had done since I was a little child. Two hours or so passed by.

I heard him tenderly say to me, "My mother."

I turned around thinking somebody was in there with me; it was that audible. Seeing nobody human in the room I shrugged my shoulders and concluded that I either had misheard or was daydreaming.

"My mother," I heard again. I looked all around, but I was the only one sitting in there. "Christina, he has my mother." I stopped dead in my tracks. The only one who ever calls me by this name is God, with the occasional client who misheard me. "Father," I said. "Speak to me. I am listening."

"Mary is my mother, Christina. Mary is in his heart."

Within, I began to hear, "My soul magnifies the Lord, and my spirit rejoices in God my Savior; because He has regarded the lowliness of His handmaid. For behold, henceforth all generations shall call me blessed, because He who is mighty has done great things for me, and holy is His name. And His mercy is from generation to generation on those who fear Him. He has shown might with His arm. He has scattered the proud in the conceit of their heart. He has put down the mighty from their thrones, and has exalted the lowly. He has filled the hungry with good things, and the rich He has sent away empty. He has given help to Israel, his servant, mindful of His mercy, Even as he spoke to our fathers, to Abraham and to his posterity forever."

Regardless of whether you are used to hearing the Holy Spirit speaking to you or not, this was shocking to me. I did not know that version of the *Magnificat* at all. I was accustomed to a different version that said, "My soul doth magnify the Lord, and my spirit hath rejoiced in God my Savior. For he hath regarded the low estate of his handmaiden. For, behold, from henceforth all generations shall call me blessed. For he that is mighty hath done to me great things; and holy is his name. And his mercy is on them that fear him from generation to generation. He hath shewed strength with his arm; he hath scattered the proud in the imagination of their hearts. He hath put down the mighty from their seats, and exalted them of low degree. He hath filled the hungry with good things; and the rich he hath sent empty away. He hath helped his servant Israel, in remembrance of his mercy; as he spake to our fathers, to Abraham, and to his seed forever."

I was quite literally trembling, for God was there with me in that chapel. No, I did not hear Mary speaking to me; it was he. I felt an overwhelming feeling of adoration and love in his voice for her. I felt ashamed of myself. I had never really given her the respect that I had even given to my own mother on earth. How dare I shrug my shoulders and not contemplate her holiness. Out of every single woman that ever was or is or will be; God *chose* Mary to be the woman who gave birth to his Son Jesus. Yet I had looked upon her as a historical figure.

Most non-Catholics are discouraged from seeing Mary as a saint or as a significant person to pray for, pray with and ask to intercede for us. Yet, we say within our hearts to those who have passed away (like a parent) "Mum, put a good word in for me up there please," and people fondly smile. However, if we do the same with our Lord's mother, people have a tendency to freak out.

Who was it that gave birth to the Messiah and raised him from infant to man? It was of course Mary his mother. I felt terrible shame. I love God with all my heart; that is no secret. I love him to live for him, and I love him that I would gladly die for him. Yet, I fell short because I did not give his mother the honor and the respect she deserves.

In my quest to understand what my priest had radiated from his heart, I met the mother of Christ. God urged me to come closer to the church and to immerse myself in the practices of the Catholic faith.

"Thank you Father," I humbly said. "Please forgive me. Please have mercy upon me oh Lord," I prayed. I walked out of the chapel and heeded the call to become a Roman Catholic. The Basilica was not a parish church, so I went to the Incarnation Catholic Church in Orlando. The priest was Father Doc Holiday. The church was formally Episcopalian before its congregation, priests, deacons and bishops all converted to Catholicism the year before. My theology degrees, forty-eight years of faith and clear understanding of doctrine and catechism assured the priest and bishops during my long interview that I was an excellent candidate for confirmation.

Father Holiday asked me to take confession before my ceremony. I chose to do this sacred act of confession and reconciliation with my priest. I am aware that Christians of other faiths take issue with this practice. Regardless of what one might say; I have asked for God's forgiveness many times throughout my life and yet in my human weakness, I have never felt absolved. The sin has continued to linger within me and after the whole attack issue; I was still full of rage and fear. I examined my conscience and prayed most humbly before going to see my priest.

When I went to Monsignor, I felt very nervous. I figured forty-eight years of sins were going to take a long time to confess. He was very kind to me and encouraged me to repent wholly. The Basilica does not have a closed confessional right now, which may seem disconcerting to those who prefer to confess with anonymity. However, father looked down and actively listened to my confession in a holy way. I could feel God was with us in that room and I knew that I was praying with a wise and precious man of God who had received his authority to forgive me. I felt safe to pour out my heart and confess everything that I could remember. I knew that I had wounded God with my sins and I needed to return to communion with him. I felt sorrow and guilt for the anger I was feeling and asked him to remove these sinful thoughts. I confessed and promised to forgive and agreed to whatever reparation was required.

Father gently asked me if I had said everything I needed to express. I nodded. He looked up and began to discuss my sins with the best advice anybody had ever given to me. We prayed for the absolution of my sins. My reparation is obviously a private matter between God, my priest and me. When I walked out of there, my shoulders felt unburdened and my slate felt completely clean. It was then that I realized the deeper meaning of what I was about to do with my conversion. I also understood the significance of the gift father and all priests offer us.

Jesus taught his disciples (the first priests) to receive his instructions, to gift us this blessing of being a physical presence in the process of forgiveness. I believe that a holy and contrite man of God, who lives his faith in full obedience to God, is a precious gift to us in one of the most difficult aspects of human life. It is difficult to unburden a sinful nature that wants so much to follow God's laws, but fails. I can only speak for myself. Confession has been one of the most precious gifts in my life. I am much closer to God now than ever before.

In preparation for confirmation, I was to choose a confirmation name from a list of saints or angels. Frankly, I felt unworthy of a holy person's name and decided to call myself "Mercy," as this exemplified the character trait I wished to emulate and receive in my life.

It was an honor to be the only candidate confirmed on that wonderful day and many were there to support me from the Basilica, including Marc as my sponsor. Later that day we reviewed the photographs of the ceremony. We were astonished to observe, (with no trick of lighting or sun shining through) there had been a magnificent blaze of golden light shining around the altar for several seconds as I took my vows. I felt blessed and humbled beyond words. Christine Mercy Overton walked out of that ceremony to begin another new chapter in her life.

Conclusion

Even if you are not comfortable praying for Mary today or ever, I ask you to please at least see her as the mother of Jesus Christ. Please give her the respect she deserves. She is not some *historical figure* that we should argue glibly over, but the precious (pure and untainted) woman who God chose to be his mother on earth and with whom he has taken back to him in heaven. It took me forty-eight years to realize this fact. Now that I have, I feel a deeper belonging and devotion to God and a more reverend respect for all he deems is holy.

Mary was not just a regular mother, but also our heavenly Mother who is the sanctuary and repose of the Holy Trinity and she is in the divine dwelling place.

Lesson 42: "Goodbye Jeff!"

I was devastated to receive the news from my mentor of over thirty years that he had stomach cancer. Jeff Boxen was the ultimate positive thinker and so I felt strongly that he would recover with the help of chemotherapy and radiation. It was a shocking revelation to discover that the opposite was happening and that in fact, the treatment was not working.

"Chrissy, please give me some advice," Jeff asked me a few days before Christmas 2013. He had been in hospital for several days and was feeling vulnerable.

"Jeff," I softly said. "This may be your last holiday with your family. I pray it's not, but we have to be realistic."

"Yes, you are right," he said.

"It's very important that you spend this time with all your family and you must tell each one that you love them and are proud of them. Trust me; this is a gift they will always cherish."

"I don't have a cent to buy them a gift," he said sadly.

"Jeff, the greatest gift you can give to them is your time and your love. Think about when Joan was dying (his wife) and how precious it was to just sit and hold her hand. There is nothing you can buy that is that important and now, more than ever, your family needs to cling together with faith."

"Yes," he agreed. "I am going to recover though and I will come to see you," he said with his usual optimistic attitude. We prayed and chatted some more before he was too tired to speak.

"Jeff," I said finally.

"Yes Chrissy," he replied.

"I love you," I said with as much compassion as possible. "I want you to know that you are so precious to me and that no matter what, I will see you in heaven, whether you get there before me or not!"

"I love you too my dearest sweetheart," he acknowledged. "You and I were destined to meet and I look up to and respect you so highly. There are not many people like Dr. Overton in this world and I can say she was my best friend!"

I wrote upbeat letters to him several times a day, with the hope that I could instill some semblance of peace within his troubled heart. He remained positive and hopeful throughout the treatments and I found his attitude so inspirational and brave. Unexpectedly, I received a text message to say that he had sadly passed away and as I sat, desperately trying to process that tragic news, I learned a friend of mine in Florida had also died that day. This news did not truly affect me until the following morning when I had unconsciously picked up my phone to call him, only to realize that our illuminating conversations of the last thirty years were a thing of the past. I was on the internet searching for flights to England, when I received another text message from his daughter. Jeff had been cremated that morning and she apologized for the bluntness of this news. It felt so final and I miss him every day.

I have talked about Jeff a great deal in my book and in the *forward;* I included the testimonial he wrote on professional sites. He was so proud of me and we shared a unique bond that even death cannot snatch. I know that he can see me as I am writing this book and I am certain he is beaming with happiness. He had always wanted me to write a book and even suggested we co-author a book of inspirational quotes. I pray that his soul rests in peace, and I look forward to seeing him later in heaven.

Conclusion

I am dedicated to being a mentor and I feel blessed to have many students around the world. Our younger generation looks to us for guidance, wisdom and answers to questions about things that concern them. It is our duty as elders to impart this knowledge with careful thought and loving words. If we want a more stable, peaceful and positive world, then those of us who have lived here for a few decades must teach those who are vulnerable the skills to survive and thrive here.

As Mother Teresa often said, "At the end of life we will not be judged by how many diplomas we have received; how much money we have made or how many great things we have done. We will be judged by 'I was hungry, and you gave me something to eat, I was naked and you clothed me. I was homeless, and you took me in.'"

The main thing I learned from Jeff Boxen was to look at everybody and say, "What can I say or do to make your day better in some way?" Moreover, if all else fails; smile a smile of genuine warmth. Nobody can resist it when your lips turn up at the edges and your eyes reflect alertness. That was the number one key to his success. From the very first moment I met him, he walked confidently and exuded a magical power with his huge smile from ear to ear and twinkling eyes that said, "I'm so happy to meet you!"

Lesson 43: Serving God

It is a great honor to serve as a lay Eucharistic minister. I assist the priest in administering Holy Communion to the many thousands who visit the Basilica each year. "Eucharist," in the Catholic Church, refers to both the celebration of the Mass, that is, the Eucharistic Liturgy, and to the bread and wine which are transubstantiated (changed in substance) into the body and blood of Jesus Christ. The term "Holy Communion," refers only to the latter. Thus, the terms "Eucharist," and "Holy Communion," are not interchangeable.

The priest distributes Holy Communion with one or more assistant ministers, depending on the size of the congregation. There are two types of assistants: ordained ministers, and non-ordained lay ministers. An "Ordinary Minister of Holy Communion," is an ordained bishop, priest, or deacon. The term "Ordinary," refers to the fact that ordained ministers are the ones who would ordinarily assist in the distribution of Holy Communion. However, the shortage of ordained ministers has led to the need to enlist laypersons in this ministry. An "Extraordinary Minister of Holy Communion," is a Catholic layperson who assists in the distribution of Holy Communion, either during the Mass, or afterwards, such as to the housebound.

I also serve as a lector at the Basilica. This ministry is dedicated to God's living word as proclaimed by the lector. One way to proclaim his Word in Scripture is through structured verse speaking - simple in concept and dynamic in application. By building the reading line by line from the beginning and maintaining a flow of thought to the end, the life contained within a scriptural reading (or any liturgical proclamation) can be enhanced by the lector applying the elements or tools of this structural format. This was something for which I had been trained from childhood and I use both my public speaking and musical background to enhance the ministry that brings the Bible alive to listeners. Proclaimed in this way, sacred Scripture becomes a form of spoken music (powerful or gentle - always respectful) whereby the printed word is lifted off the page and proclaimed as a living, dynamic and timeless form of praise to glorify and celebrate the Word of the Lord.

Discovering which of your gifts best enhances your church, is a very important element of life. Most churches depend upon the talents and volunteer spirit within its congregation to reach out to the community and serve them on a daily basis. Each member of the congregation is able to bring their individual strengths and interests to the body of the church, temple, synagogue and so forth.

Whereas some people have the gift of singing and thus enjoy being members of the church choir, others are content to work behind the scenes with ushering or visiting the sick. A wise church will have orientation for new members to reveal their ministries and from this, an individual can pray about which they are best suited.

I have worked extensively with churches of all different sizes and types over the last ten years or so. Some of the ministries I've introduced or helped reorganize include; altar services and care, arts and environment, children's liturgy, music, ministry to the sick, readers, ushers, bereavement, gift shop, hospitality, marriage enrichment, men's club, young adult, feeding the homeless, food pantry, and prison visiting. In the vast majority of cases, there is always at least one area that every person has an interest or aptitude in, which will undoubtedly enhance the positive running of their place of worship.

When I went through Christian Bible College, I learned a great deal about ministry and theology to the doctoral level. One of the most amazing and perplexing features was when it came time for us to take our training out into the mainstream churches. We were encouraged not to discuss the historical-critical methods taught throughout those years of instruction. We had labored over the discrepancies and contradictions discovered in the historical errors and pondered over scriptures (for example, other Gospels and Apocalypses) that were at one time considered canonical but that ultimately did not become part of the Bible. In fact, we discovered a good number of the books of the Bible are pseudonymous (for example, written in the name of an apostle by someone else) that we do not have the original copies of any of the biblical books but rather only copies made centuries later, all of which have been altered. My professors concluded that it was far clearer to keep the message uniformed and safe; thus, we were encouraged to shelve our instruction and teach the basics.

Throughout my spiritual life, I have always felt that it was not my job to keep anybody from freaking out, but to be with him or her and offer a comforting presence during grief or crisis. As a teacher, it is my job to help my students read and comprehend the Word in such a way that they can apply it to every situation that they might encounter. I encourage them all to join their church's Bible study groups and to seek the wisdom of their religious leader.

Conclusion

We are all encouraged to serve others in life. It is a wonderful feeling to use your gifts to help others in need. The only caution to this observation is to advise you to keep your ego in check. In other words, it is excellent to step forwards and serve at church for instance, but one must be doing tit to serve God and not to be center stage for applause and recognition. John, the Baptist told his students "He must increase; I must decrease."

Lesson 44: "It's all gone?"

Over the years, I have pondered over the lesson Jesus taught his disciples about picking up their crosses and leaving everything behind. I am by no means materialistic, but like many of you, I have enjoyed the comforts of having a car to drive and modest clothes to cover my back. Admittedly, there were things in the storage unit up in New Jersey that had significance to me; not least withstanding bank statements, photographs, clothes, and cd's, videos, business documents, awards, certificates and gifts from friends and family.

It had been tough to leave those things behind when I went into hiding after the burglary, but I was constantly reassured that they were safe and secure. I was excited to think that of the reunion between my belongings and I, especially the school projects that my son had so proudly made for me when he was a little boy and a video of my mum. I am sure that if you were a parent or grandparent, you would feel the same way. It is adorable to see the face of one's child when they hand you their works of art to display in your home. Just glancing at these treasures from time to time, gives you a feeling of pure happiness and pride.

By the end of March 2014, I was finally ready to travel up north to retrieve my belongings and I contacted the man who had safely put them away for me. I had to call the police department first in order for them to accompany me to the unit. Everything was organized and I called my friend to inform him of my visit and to thank him so much for his great kindness. "Sure no problem," he said. "I'm really looking forward to seeing you!" He enthusiastically added.

Quite literally, the next day, I received an odd letter from a debt collection agency. I had no clue as to what they were talking about, so I called them. They told me that the storage unit in New Jersey had tried to get payment for the account from my so-called friend; and after investigation, they had found me. They explained that the account remained unpaid. I still had no idea as to what they meant and so I asked them to give me the phone number of the unit. I assured them that if this were correct, I would take care of the payment immediately.

Was I feeling a bit nervous? You bet I was!

The next few minutes were nothing short of shocking. I was in no mood to hear more sad news. The manager of the unit had no clue that the contents were my personal things. He explained that multiple letters were sent to my so-called friend requesting payment, and later to inform him that without it, they would have no choice other than to exercise their legal rights. He apparently ignored their mail and phone calls.

What were the rights you might ask? They were entitled to auction off the entire contents of the storage unit to recoup losses. I know what you are thinking and you would be right. There was an auction in January 2014. Yes, *everything* I owned was gone!

To say that I was devastated would be a huge understatement. At first, I was in complete shock, and I literally begged this man to reassure me that he could trace the whereabouts of my things. Regardless of the price, I wanted to buy back my belongings back and to retrieve the very personal items, which would be of no use to anybody else. I asked him why nobody had contacted me before now. He had no response, other than to keep saying that he was very, very sorry for my loss, and that it was not his problem. He explained to me that sometimes in the past, a buyer did return personal items, including documents and photographs; but not in this case.

I telephoned my so-called friend, who had no idea that I now knew the truth. When I confronted him, he made up a preposterous story of how he had given them his credit card information. He also asked me not to be angry because he was just out of hospital after some thugs had beaten him. I asked him which hospital he had gone to and after our conversation, I called the hospital, police and the storage unit to confirm his story. He had neither been in hospital nor given the unit his credit card information. When I called him back, he said that he had received the letters and calls but just kept repeating that it was not his fault and that I needed to accept this and move on. "Move on?" I yelled. "What do you mean move on? I trusted you with the most important things in my life, and all these months you constantly assured me that my things were safe. My God, you were excited I was coming up there to get them. Is this a sick joke? You should have told me where they were and I would have paid for them myself. You told me not to worry and that this was a gift from you. How dare you! Why did you lie to me in this way?" I shouted.

He hung up the phone without a word. I called him back but he would not pick up. I was indescribably hurt and this final betrayal felt very painful and sad beyond all comprehension.

When Marc returned home, he walked through the door to find me lying on the floor in a fetal position; sobbing my heart out. At first, I could not stop crying to tell him what was wrong. I just kept thinking about how I would never see any of my things again. It would have been easier if they had been destroyed by fire or flood; at least I would not have had to worry about who was reading my private documents or tossing away my pictures, clothes and gifts.

Constantly in my mind, I kept reflecting upon the fact that on May 24' 2013, I had lived in a beautiful home, drove a reliable car and sat on lovely furniture with my sense of safety intact. I lived in a state full of friends and professional possibilities and my life was happy and fulfilling. Twelve days later, it was all gone, with the exception of all my precious and cherished personal belongings. These cherished items were supposedly stored away until such time that I was strong enough to go and bring them to my new home. Now through no fault of my own, they too were all gone. I had absolutely nothing left.

When I had calmed down enough to tell Marc why I was crying, he was beyond enraged. Repeatedly all I could say was, "It's all gone! It's just all gone!"

Conclusion

I pray to God that you never have to go through such a dreadful experience as this in your own lives. Words are inadequate when one tries to express a loss that seems to rip you apart. If I could give you some advice, should the unthinkable happen to you, it would be to:

1. Keep copies of everything that is confidential and important in a safe box stored in the bank.
2. Make sure that every picture is duplicated and safe. It is very easy to fall into a pattern of not storing things when they occur; so please be consistent with doing this.
3. If you have school projects and gifts from your children, photograph them and make sure these are on flash drives.
4. If you have films of family and friends, with events that are cherished memories, keep a copy of these in the bank storage unit. There is *nothing* worse than losing these films and steadily forgetting what your family looked or sounded like; trust me I know and it is a very painful lesson.

Life is unpredictable. If you learn nothing else from my situation, it is that unimaginable things can and do happen. When they do, you are engrossed in the situation and not able to take care of securing your possessions. It does not have to be a flood, hurricane, tornado, and fire; it can be a mad man or a gang that chooses to creep into your home, and take what they desire. Take control of your lives, my friends, and make sure that what you deem to be precious and holy is secure and safe.

Lesson 45: Forgiveness

I had lost *all* of my personal belongings and the realization of this was overwhelming. I was enraged and traumatized and the more I tried to rationalize it, the angrier I became. I knew that if entrusted with a person's valuable items, especially if that man or woman had just experienced a massive shock and threat to their life, I would have protected their things as if they were my own. My sense of integrity would demand that I took the position of a caretaker, and guard those things with my life if necessary. To be flippantly cavalier about such a trusted act of faith and to knowingly disregard my sense of responsibility to such a degree that the injured party has to then deal with losing everything for which they cared; was unfathomable to me.

As my anger began to dissipate, I was able to pray, meditate and reflect. I had to deduce that the man who attacked me and the man who had not protected my things; were both sick. No normal human being would act with such callousness and contempt if they were mentally intact. It was a major wakeup call for me. I realized that from this point forwards; I must have a far greater sense of discernment with whom I permitted to share my personal space and not to necessarily trust another when they claim to have my best interests at heart. That is not to say that you or I should ignore others or keep everybody at a distance; but rather that we must learn to be more careful, vigilant and aware of the red flags of warning that wave at us and shout, "Caution!"

If we learn to listen carefully to others, people do give themselves away with subtle words and innuendos. Their actions can appear to be abnormal, with extreme likes and dislikes or flirtatious behavior that makes you feel uncomfortable. We all dish out sarcasm from time to time, but when another consistently makes crude or crass remarks to ridicule or mock a person harshly, one must conclude that this contemptuously destructive personality is not the kind of friend or companion we need in our lives - as President Barack Obama is famously known to say; "Period!"

It was March 2014. In one hand, I had no home, no car, no job, no money, very few clothes and a life that could easily fit into a suitcase, if I had one to call my own. In my other hand I had God, my Bible, a computer and access to a phone, a strong faith, humor, strength of character, education, love for others, kindness, compassion, passion, determination, Zachy my cat, faithful and supportive friends and one hell of a story to tell!

I was extremely conscious of the negative feelings still inside of me and decided that the only way I was going to be able to move forwards positively was to seek absolution through confession, and begin the process of forgiveness. I understood that the pain I was justifiably feeling, was neither healthy nor conducive to recovery. I also knew that as a God-fearing Christian, if Jesus could show mercy and pardon to those who insulted and crucified him, then I had to find it within myself to forgive those who had so outrageously betrayed me in one way or another.

The forty-day period of Lent was approaching. This was when I always shut myself away from the world and concentrated completely on the strengthening of my faith and relationship with God. Now, probably more than ever, I needed to seek that place and state of serenity. I knew that in order to be wholly holy, I needed to cultivate a calm mind, a contrite heart and a still spirit.

I drove to the Basilica and was delighted to find that it was Monsignor scheduled to hear confessions. His wise advice, no nonsense approach with a firm foundation in Catholic doctrine and psychology always made perfect sense to me. I sat with a humble and contrite heart. I then prayed the Catholic prayer for confession and began to talk to God about how I was feeling. Father was very kind to me and reassured me that my feelings were natural. I received absolution for the anger in my heart and given the perfect penance; seek to forgive and pray for those who had hurt me.

My students often ask me why I feel the need to celebrate the Sacrament of Confession and to explain to them what the true meaning of "Forgiveness," is. An emotionally stable human being seeks to apologize if he knows (or he has been made aware of the fact that) he has harmed another in word, thought or action. Even animals have a sense of knowing when they have let you down and they hang their heads in shame. Seeking forgiveness is therefore an essential ingredient in the process of repairing the damage with the other person and walking forwards together with a clearer understanding of how we are to act from that moment onwards.

Forgiveness, in a sacramental context, refers to the removal of obstacles that lie in the way of intimate union with God and others. Sin destroys or weakens the relationship with God and our neighbor. Forgiveness is thus part of a broader process of reconciliation with God, others, the world, and oneself. Forgiveness has three important elements that are crucial if the process and relationship is to be restored. These apply to every relationship, including the one we have with God.

Repentance: You must be truly sorry for the sin or act that you have committed. There is little point in apologizing for something if you feel that you either have no fault, (rarely true) or if you are saying "I'm sorry," to get something for yourself.

Admission: You must be prepared to transparently admit your wrongdoing, without following it up with a, "But if you hadn't said that, I wouldn't have done this or that." This is your admission of guilt, not theirs. Even though God knows exactly what you have done wrong, by completely opening up and admitting absolutely, one is able to receive complete forgiveness. This wiping the slate clean is always a peaceful relief.

Reparation: You must be resolved to not make this mistake again and to make recompense for the damage that you have caused. We human beings are fragile and foolish sometimes, and it often seems as though we repeatedly (as in addiction or habit) make the exact same mistakes. Thus, we have to decide to be honest and self-disciplined in order to change our behavior and seek the necessary help to overcome our weaknesses.

Conclusion

I had to sit and re-evaluate my entire perspective on this situation. The county prosecutor had advised against seeing the man who attacked me; thus, I could not tell him to his face what his heinous act had done to me. By not seeing him face to face, I was also not able to apologize for whatever it was that I did wrong that made him so determined to end my life. He had pled guilty to the charges, which freed him from a prison sentence for now. He had served eight weeks in jail. Probation meant several years of evaluation, including alcohol and drug testing. I prayed this would help him to recover. If God had wanted his punishment to be more severe, it was not to be by sending him to prison for a few years. Who knows if he sits and thinks about what he did to me. That is none of my business. I do know that he will relive what he did and how it affected me when he dies and I will witness the event upon my judgment.

I realized that I had to let this go somehow; or at least to continue with my life as best I could, without the fear and anger which was hurting me. Yes, this man was clearly a disturbed soul who was obviously hurting far more inside than he could ever hurt the likes of me. I realized that I was only responsible for my own feelings in this matter and I chose to bring myself to a place of peace with God's mercy and grace.

As for the other man who had blatantly lied to me, I honestly could not wrap my head around his irresponsible and disgraceful behavior. He never apologized for his callous disregard of my precious possessions. Every word uttered to me was a complete fabrication. Investigation on him unearthed a criminal background in theft, fraud, deception and drug abuse. He also had a history of mental instability.

After weeks of dedicated fasting, prayer and meditation, I was able to forgive them all by the end of Lent. I realized that the storage manager was only doing his job and that neither of the other two was mentally healthy and therefor they had no ability to behave in a rational way. I have not forgotten their cruelty as that is a process that will take me time. However, I can say I have forgiven them, even though they have not asked me to do so. Forgiveness does not require that they ever do, but I wanted to release that pain and I wanted God to forgive me for all my wrongdoings then and forever.

Thus to forgive is an essential component to recovery and when accomplished, the burden is lifted and you feel sheer joy and relief.

Lesson 46: A new me!

Having made a good confession, which had freed me from all the anger I was feeling, I was ready to enter in to the season of Lent with a renewed spirit of grace and determination. In the Catholic Church, the year is divided into liturgical seasons based on significant events in the life and earthly ministry of Jesus Christ, as well as the great mysteries of our faith. The Church Year begins with Advent, which is celebrated as four weeks of preparation before Christmas. Catholics are required to live liturgically by actually entering into the Church year. Easter, where we celebrate the resurrection of Christ, is preceded by Lent, a season of self-examination, fasting and penance in preparation for our Easter day observance. The Catholic Church places much emphasis on the importance of Christ's victory of death, that an Easter season of fifty days is celebrated, culminating in the great feast of Pentecost.

My parents had always raised me to practice several observances during the period of Lent, which included abstaining from certain foods and behaviors. In their place, I attended church more frequently. I reflected upon this time and decided that I needed to make some major changes; not just for Lent, but for the rest of my life.

I was a smoker of cigarettes. In fact, I had smoked since I was a very young child. It helped me to go to the toilet more easily after the sexual abuse to my rectum. Without the stimulant, I struggled to defecate without sever pain or bleeding. Admittedly, I was never a heavy smoker. I had one in the morning and one in the evening and occasionally one or two during the day. I had tried to quit however in the past, but this only led to me not being able to go to the toilet for several days at a time rendering me very ill as you can imagine.

A friend had recently introduced me to the new vapor sticks, which had the nicotine I needed to stimulate my body to release, but was minus all the poisons of a normal cigarette. Marc bought me one, and I took to it like a duck to water. Within two days, that wretched smoker's cough was gone and my body reacted well to it. The mere thought of a cigarette repulsed me after that and it was a tremendous thrill to be cigarette free after forty plus years as an addict.

I was fifty pounds overweight and regardless of my upbringing and genetics, it was time to evaluate my diet and implement some major changes. I resolved to quit eating potatoes, pasta, and bread or wheat products. These starchy, high carbohydrates added to my bowel problems and caused extreme bleeding and pain. I had never been a carbonated drink fan, but I certainly knew that I needed to drink more water. I began to walk three miles a day, which was later replaced with swimming eighty to a hundred laps of the club pool each afternoon. Within five months, I had dropped those fifty pounds, and not only did I look good; I felt great!

People were amazed with my transformation and constantly asked me to reveal the secret to my success. I told them that I drank a low carb, high protein shake for breakfast, with a cup of tea. I would eat lean meat and salad with a piece of fruit for lunch. Dinner consisted of lean meat with vegetables or egg and cheese salad. If I got a case of the *munchies*, I would eat a low carb fiber bar at night. I never felt hungry and I was able to establish a nutritious diet that I would be able to maintain for life. I permitted myself one treat, which was a spoonful of rum and raison ice cream. I kept my carbohydrates to twenty units per day and weighed myself each morning. I had never felt healthier before in my life and my mind was absolutely clear – perfect for meditation.

I went to Mass every day during Lent, with the exception of one. I spent those forty days and nights in prayer, meditation and spiritual renewal. In addition to studying the Bible, I read several books by His Holiness Pope Francis and the late Archbishop Fulton Sheen. I reflected upon my life, and in particular, the devastating losses of the last few months. I understood that there was a spiritual reason for this complete cleansing of my life and although the pill was hard to swallow, I resolved to move on with a positive frame of mind.

Back in 1989, when I had gone to the gates of heaven, God warned me that my life on earth would not always be pain-free. He told me quite categorically that I was returning to earth to spread the Gospel and comfort the suffering. He made it very clear to me that I was to be a "Spiritual Ambassador," for him and that I was not to be bogged down in the usual humdrum of life. He had stated before my return to life, that should it look like I was walking in the wrong direction, He would immediately stop me. Therefore, I took these losses as a sign that I had obviously been walking in the complete opposite direction than where my Lord wanted me to go and that he had actually blessed me by bringing my life back on track.

I sat during Mass one morning thinking about my purpose on earth. I was to read the scriptures during the holy days of Easter and I knew that there would be several thousand people at each service. It occurred to me that perhaps God wanted me to use my voice for his glory, and so I asked him to reveal his purpose to me. As I walked out of the Basilica after Mass, God prompted me to go into the meditation garden, where the *Stations of the Cross* appeared almost out of nowhere. In all my years as a Christian, I had never taken the time to study them. For Roman Catholics throughout the world, the *Stations of the Cross* are synonymous with Lent, Holy Week and, especially, Good Friday. This devotion is known as the *Way of the Cross* the *Via Cruces* and the *Via Dolorosa*. It commemorates fourteen key events of Christ's crucifixion including His final walk through the streets of Jerusalem, carrying the cross. Performing the devotion meant walking the entire route, stopping to pray and reflect at each station.

I. Jesus is condemned to death

II. Jesus is made to carry His cross

III. Jesus falls the first time

IV. Jesus meets His sorrowful mother

V. Simon of Cyrene helps Jesus carry His cross

VI. Veronica wipes the faces of Jesus

VII. Jesus falls the second time

VIII. The women of Jerusalem weep over Jesus

IX. Jesus falls the third time

X. Jesus is stripped of His garments

XI. Jesus is nailed to the cross

XII. Jesus is raised upon the cross and dies

XIII. Jesus is taken down form the cross and placed in the arms of His mother

XIV. Jesus is laid in the sepulcher

We cannot imagine this kind of murder in the western world. Most of us would like to visualize a loving, peaceful and humane death, which is preceded by a fair trial with an unbiased jury. We debate our capital punishment laws to offer the person condemned to execution a swift death without unnecessary suffering. My students often say, "We aren't that barbaric today!" Yet, in the Middle East right now, people are being beheaded and crucified. These barbaric executions are just as prevalent today as they were some 2000 years ago when we butchered our Messiah.

I watched the movie, *The Passion of the Christ* by Director Mel Gibson, when released in 2004. The first time I went to see it, I found the scenes to be too brutal and walked out of the theatre. When I was asked why I had left, I made the stupid comment of saying, "We all know the story and I knew how it ended." I cringe when I recall those foolish words. The truth of the matter was that I hated violence and I could not bear to stand watching others in pain. I love God so much and to see his son suffering in such a way was too much for me to internalize with such graphic images. Mr. Gibson's portrayal was just too gory for me back then.

After walking around the *Stations of the Cross*, some ten years after the release of the movie, I was determined to go back to Marc's home and watch it from start to finish. I knew that this film would be tough to view, but I realized that it was far tougher for his loved ones to stand there and actually witness this horror firsthand.

Contemplate

At the age of thirty-six, Jesus was condemned to death. At the time, crucifixion was the cruelest death there was and reserved for the most heinous criminals and crimes.

Pilate ordered a flogging before his crucifixion. Therefore, Jesus' hands were manacled to a metal ring atop of the scourging post, rendering him unable to move. Two legionaries stood behind him on both sides and another to the side holding an abacus to track the number of lashes inflicted. The other two grasped wooden-handled flagrums, from which extended three leather lines. There were no gaps between the lashes. They had been instructed to break Jesus, but not to kill him at that point, as Pilate wanted to see him publically humiliated on the cross. After the lashing, Jesus was led back to prison, where the Roman soldiers draped a dirty purple cloak over his bleeding naked body. They knew that this material would stick to his body as the blood began to dry. They gave him a pseudo scepter made of reed and jeered at his claim to be their King.

The company of soldiers turned sadistic. They cut and wove a crown of inch long curving thorns, which was tightly fitted onto Jesus' head. It dug deep into the skin, brushed up against the nerves and banged into the bones causing blood to pour down his face. Some of the men beat him whilst others spat in his face. A few cruelly knelt and mocked him whilst others snatched the scepter and beat his head with it causing the thorns to imbed even more deeply into his skull.

Jesus was to be nailed to the cross by his hands and feet. Each nail was six to eight inches long and they were driven into his wrist and not into his palms as is commonly portrayed. There is a tendon in the wrist that extends to the shoulder. The Roman guards knew that when the nails were being hammered into the wrist, that tendon would tear and break; forcing Jesus to use his back muscles to support himself so that he could breathe. Both of his feet were nailed together. Thus, he was forced to support himself on the single nail that impaled his feet to the cross. Jesus could not support himself with his legs because of the pain, so he was forced to alternate between arching his back, then using his legs, just to continue to breath. Imagine the struggle, the pain, the suffering and the courage. This gruesome torture lasted for three hours.

Before his crucifixion, the guards ripped off the purple cloak from his flesh, but left the crown of thorns to penetrate deeply into our Lord's skull. He was forced to carry a six feet long, seventy pounds plank made of unfinished wood on his shoulders to the execution site known as Golgotha, which sat on a low rise near the city. However, with the beating and blood loss, he lacked the strength to carry this beam and after stumbling, a man named Simon came forward to help him, whilst the crowd laughed and cried out in evil excitement. This was the same crowd who days before had shouted "Hosanna to the king!" Now they screamed, "Crucify him!"

Once crucified, Jesus stopped bleeding. He had no more blood to bleed out, so only water poured from his wounds. Jesus said in exhaustion that he was thirsty, so the Roman killers, who sat and mocked him by casting lots for his possessions, offered him a sponge which had been soaked in sour wine, knowing that it would sting his lips. All the while, he could clearly see and hear the festivities of Passover and yet nobody could or did do a thing to help him.

Two other criminals were crucified that day and they hung on either side of Jesus. One mocked him whilst the other, (who recognized that he was the Messiah) asked to be remembered in heaven. The onlookers included Jesus' mother Mary and his faithful follower Mary of Magdalene. Also standing there was his beloved disciple John. Despite the agony, Jesus said to them both, "Woman, behold you son," as he looked at John and to John he said, "Behold your mother."

The evil was beyond our imagination and yet, despite the jeering and spitting, the torture and the blasphemous disregard for our King, he still said to our God, his father, "Forgive them, for they know not what they do."

After he had drunk the wine, he took his last breath and declared, "It is finished!"

Joseph and Nicodemus removed Jesus' body from the cross. They placed him inside a new tomb (which was their custom) and his body was to remain in there for twelve months. After a year, the bones would be removed and placed elsewhere. A stone, (which weighed hundreds of pounds) covered the entrance and guards kept watch.

Three days later, Jesus' mother, Mary, went to the tomb with the intention of anointing his body with oils. She could not have moved the stone herself and there was nobody to help her because Jesus' disciples had fled in fear and other people were still celebrating the feast. When she arrived there, the stone, (which had been blocking the entrance) was moved away and there were no guards there either. Upon entering, she discovered that the body of Jesus was not in there, although his burial clothes were lying on the slab.

During the course of the next forty days, the Lord appeared twelve times to his disciples and hundreds of other witnesses saw him on a mountain proving to them that although he had died, he had risen from the dead. Many witnessed his ascension to heaven where he sits on the right hand side of his father.

I would highly recommend you just sit for a few minutes and contemplate what you have just read. It *is* profound and I would honestly encourage you to watch Mel Gibson's portrayal of this horrific and yet crucial event in our Lord's life. It is the cornerstone of our faith. Without his death, resurrection and ascension to heaven, we would not be in a position to face eternal life though his sacrificial blood.

I shared this remarkable account to help you and I gain perspective. I realized in April 2014, that although my losses were very real and raw, in comparison to his magnificent and miraculous life giving teachings, which were followed by the most horrific acts of barbarism and death imaginable; my troubles seemed almost insignificant.

I also began to reflect upon all those people being persecuted for their faith in the Middle East today. No doubt, like me, you sat watching the news with horror at the sight of people being murdered by the extreme Islamic radical terrorist organizations. As they held up each child as a barricade against gunfire, I could not imagine what those poor little ones were feeling. Nor could I comprehend the suffering of thousands of people stranded on that mountain knowing that if they went down to the ground, they would be butchered, and if they stayed on the summit, they would starve or die through dehydration and disease. Watching our citizens slowly and cruelly beheaded with small knives before our eyes and realizing that people were facing crucifixion for their faith was (is) inconceivable.

The western mentality tends to lean towards the "This happens in other people's neighborhoods and not in ours." However, the reality is, we are at war, and there are many who hate both Americans and Christians and want us all dead! As Christians, we must stand up for our faith, not cower to those who hate everything that is the foundation of our religion, and love for Christ.

Is your faith in him strong? If held at gun or knifepoint, would you denounce your allegiance to God? Would you buckle under the pressure, or would you praise God with your very last breath? Are you pretending not to even have a faith or religion (other than to look to nature) because you think it will keep you under the radar?

These are important questions for you to reflect upon with honesty. One never knows if, or when, others who do not share our faith will confront us. If you are a Christian who is very public about his or her faith, as I am, you have to know that those who hate Christ are going to attack you. The strength of our faith today needs to be as strong and dedicated as it was when his disciples followed Jesus 2000 years ago.

Have you ever considered the strength of their faith? Matthew suffered martyrdom in Ethiopia and was killed by a sword wound. Mark died in Alexandria, Egypt, after being dragged by horses through the streets until he was dead. Luke was hanged in Greece as a result of his tremendous preaching to the lost. John faced martyrdom when he was boiled in huge basin of boiling oil during a wave of persecution in Rome. However, he was miraculously delivered from death.

The apostle John was later freed and returned to serve as Bishop of Edessa in modern Turkey. He died as an old man, the only apostle to die peacefully. Peter was crucified upside down on an x-shaped cross.

According to church tradition, it was because he told his tormentors that he felt unworthy to die in the same way that Jesus Christ had died. James was thrown over a hundred feet down from the southeast pinnacle of the Temple when he refused to deny his faith in Christ. When they discovered that he survived the fall, his enemies beat James to death with a fuller's club. James, son of Zebedee, was beheaded at Jerusalem

Thomas was stabbed with a spear in India during one of his missionary trips to establish the church in the Sub-continent. Jude was killed with arrows when he refused to deny his faith in Christ. Matthias, the apostle chosen to replace the traitor Judas Iscariot, was stoned and then beheaded. The apostle Paul was tortured and then beheaded by the evil Emperor Nero at Rome in A.D. 67. Bartholomew was flayed to death by a whip. Andrew was crucified on an x-shaped cross in Patras, Greece. After being whipped severely by seven soldiers they tied his body to the cross with cords to prolong his agony. His followers reported that, when he was led toward the cross, Andrew saluted it in these words: "I have long desired and expected this happy hour."

Conclusion

I asked myself two questions during Lent. Firstly, is my faith strong enough to endure extreme hardship and if I was asked to deny my Christian faith in exchange for my life, would I denounce and renounce him or would I boldly stand and proclaim, "He is my Savior. Do with me as you wish. I will not deny my Lord!" I had three answers that never wavered: Yes, No and Yes.

When the great chief Crazy Horse went into battle, he proclaimed, "It's a good day to die!" What does this really mean? It means that none of us has the remotest idea of when God is going to call us home, so we must live each moment as if it were our last – one day it will be. We must be consistently brave and stand up boldly for our beliefs. We should have a flexible plan, with the understanding that God may nudge us on to different paths, where He will guide us to safer pastures and peace.

Lastly, we must continue to pray earnestly for mercy, tolerance, compassion and peace for all men, women and children who are facing imprisonment, torture and persecution for their religious beliefs and ethnicity. We cannot ignore these atrocities because this war on religion is no longer on distant shores, but right here in our communities today.

It is indeed a good day to die and it is an important day to live!

Lesson 47: Gospel of John

I had never considered recording the Bible before, but after each Mass where I had read the scriptures, literally dozens of people would come up to me and ask me where they could find a copy of my reading the Word. On Easter Sunday, 2014, a priest from another diocese could not wait until the end of Mass to speak to me. I was sitting by the side of the altar waiting to go and lead the prayers, when I felt a tapping on my shoulder. It was this priest with tears in his eyes. He thanked me for the passion of my reading and said that he felt very strongly that I should produce a CD of one of the Gospels. As he left the altar and returned to his seat amongst thousands of other members of the congregation, I smiled and inwardly said to God, "If you want me to do this Lord, please show me how."

On June 17 2014, God spoke to me. He told me I was to read the entire Gospel of John on June 20. I sat in prayer and made notes on the messages that He was giving me. I was to open a telephone conference line, design a flier and market this event on my Facebook page.

Was I daunted by this instruction? Yes, a little bit, but I had complete faith that God ordained this. It took three hours and ten minutes to read the entire Gospel to the hundreds of listeners. It was humbling to receive their positive feedback, which included a request for a copy of the recording. God told me that I needed to make a professional recording. I had already made two motivational films utilizing the Basilica choir as the musical soundtrack and so I went to speak to their musical director, Dr. William Picher, about the possibility of working with him on a recording project. Dr. Bill is a wonderfully talented musician with a certain amount of recording experience, and we spoke at length about the ins and outs of such a project. I felt strongly that Dr. Bill and I could come together to produce a wonderful CD that would honor God and bring others closer to him, through listening to the Bible spoken in a gentle and soothing way.

I chose to read and record the Gospel according to Saint John, as it is a beautifully written and contains stories about the life of Jesus that are not widely known, unless actively studied. This book has twenty-one chapters and between each one, Dr. Bill composed *musical bridges*, as I like to call them, taking the listener from one chapter to the next. We enlisted Dr. Bill's son, Michael, who is an upcoming film producer and director to help make a promotional film to help us raise the funds to complete the project and we planned to digitally master, duplicate and release the CD just in time for the Christmas holidays.

Conclusion

Recording the CD was a process that flowed smoothly and seamlessly and it was blatantly obvious to me that this was very much a "God-driven," project. I often had to stop and contemplate the magnitude of this recording which had come to me at a time in my life where I had nothing much to offer anybody in terms of material items.

When we are children, we rarely have the money or aptitude to give lavish gifts to our loved ones. However, those who understand the sentiment cherish even a colored picture gifted via innocence. Sometimes in life, we have limited resources and some of us may feel like we cannot contribute to society as much as we would wish. My grandmother once said to me, "Dear, even if you have no money to give, you have something that is far more precious to God."

"What's that granny?" I asked.

"It's your heart," she replied. "You're so young, and yet you have one of the kindest hearts I have ever known. I pray you never lose that gentle caring for people," she replied.

"Is it good to be kind?" I asked her.

"Yes dear," she replied. "A kind heart is worth more than gold because it is pure and holy." I did not understand what she was trying to teach me back then, but as I have matured, I have come to realize that loving others with an unconditional kindness with word and deed is very important.

The burglary and auction had rendered me pitifully poor. Nevertheless, even those men had not taken away my capacity to love others and worship my Lord. This humble CD of the Gospel of John was a gift to the baby Jesus from my heart and it is my gift to whomever purchase it and listens to the story of our Lord and savior.

The English poet Christina Rossetti bases "In the Bleak Midwinter," in 1872, in response to a request from the magazine Scribner's Monthly for a Christmas poem. Published posthumously in Rossetti's *Poetic Works* in 1904, the poem became a Christmas carol after it appeared in *The English Hymnal* in 1906 with a setting by Gustav Holst.

The last verse of the Hymn and a sentiment I live my life by is:

"What can I give him, Poor as I am?
If I were a shepherd, I would bring a lamb.
If I were a wise man, I would do my part.
Yet what I can, I give him - Give my heart."

Lesson 48: My story...

If I had a dollar for every time somebody had told me I should write a book about my life, I would be rich now. I had always resisted writing one because quite honestly, I had been conditioned to keeping many events secret and besides I could not imagine anybody being that interested in me to read it. My students and friends all contradicted my excuses by saying, "Are you crazy? Your life is so amazing and inspirational. People need to read about your walk with God and learn how he blesses you every day."

As I contemplated undertaking an autobiography project, I began to feel concerned about my ability to meet the strict editorial standards. Some suggested I work with a ghostwriter if I was going to be that paranoid about my literacy abilities. I resisted that idea, as I did not want anybody else writing my story or changing the way I expressed myself. I write in the same way that I speak and although I knew that meant I would probably never win the Library of Congress Literacy Award, it would at least be authentically and originally mine.

I was sincerely concerned about appearing to betray the trust of certain people who had shared my journey in life. Part of me wanted my son to know who I was and I pondered over that for a very long time – years in fact. Students and friends who were inspired by my life, felt that many people going through similar situations to the ones that I had experienced, would gain strength and clarity from my ability to bounce back after tragedy had struck.

Satan was whispering to me constantly that everybody would read my book and mockingly conclude that I was a complete failure in life. Nevertheless, as I told my friends, "I am not a failure. It may be a contradiction, but I am successful at finding what doesn't work! Furthermore, I walk with Christ and I am obedient to his command. My life is to love others and not to concern myself with selfish desire or need."

I decided in June 2014 that if this was what God wanted me to do on this new track he had placed me on; he needed to show me in his usual obvious way. Literally, two hours later, unexpectedly, Nicole Osbun from Balboa Press, a division of Hay House Inc., called me. After a long discussion, Nicole agreed to give me six weeks to write my book and then to get it published. I was a bit scared and intimidated on one hand and excited and determined on the other. " Lord," I said on bended knee. "If you want me to write this book, then I need you to please help me. I want this to glorify you in every way."

Conclusion

We are not all meant to be world famous authors. Most of us are very humble, with basic writing skills. Some of us are engineers, others are doctors, and yet as diverse as the world is today, we do all have one thing in common: a story to tell. That story could be from five years of life to 105 years of adventures. Whatever the time span, we all have plenty of highs, lows, loves and losses to share.

The best advice that I can give to anybody who feels that they have a book inside of them is to pray about it first. The next important thing is to ask, "What is my motive?" If the idea is to become rich and famous, you might become deflated and miserable if your book does not even sell a few hundred copies. The best approach is to write your book with the expectation of just touching one person's heart. That could be your child or a friend. It is important to express your wisdom in such a way that another being can learn from you. If more read your work, then that is nice, but it should not be your main objective.

It has taken me five decades of living and six weeks of writing to produce, "50 things I've learned from 50 years of life: Five Decades of "Ah-Ha!" Life Learning Lessons."

Everybody was amazed with the speed at which this book was written, but it was obvious to us all that God wanted this book published and in the hands of all those who needed to hear its wisdom. Thus, I take no credit for the wonderful messages of hope contained in this book. Even I have read it from start to finish and said, "Wow God, you are magnificent! You have clearly protected me and shaped my life in ways I could never have imagined. All the glory goes to you Lord. Hallelujah. Amen!"

Lesson 49: "Thank you!"

Before you start worrying that this chapter is going to be a very long and boring list of names, be at peace. I am going to write about this from a completely different perspective. It is an important lesson that I learned from a very early age and is the gift of, "Gratitude."

When I was about ten years old, I overheard my parents discussing the financial plight of my elderly aunt and uncle. I was too young to understand what they were saying and to this day, I cannot recall the exact situation. Nevertheless, I vividly remember them concluding that their situation was very troubling.

Less than a week later we were about to take our annual vacation to the south of England. My aunt, who was also my godmother, came to wish us a wonderful trip. She pulled me to the side and wanted to give me some spending money. To a nine-year-old child, the five-pound note was a fortune. Having heard that she and Uncle Marc were in dire financial trouble, but not wanting to admit that I had eves dropped on the conversation, I tried to avoid accepting the money. Besides, I had concluded, we were well off and I did not need this gift, however kind the intent. I was too immature to know how to handle the protocol of accepting or declining this financial gift and instead of saying "Thank you," and accepting it; I mumbled something to the effect of "Thank you, but I don't need it," and ran away. Naturally, I was seen to be very rude, ungrateful, spoilt and obnoxious and my aunt made her anger known to my parents. My parents were mortified and that was the only time in my childhood that my mother spanked me - very hard. I accepted that punishment in silence. When my parents demanded to know why I had been so rude, I refused to explain.

The tone of that four-week vacation was just horrible and I can remember it to this day. I felt sick to my stomach every time the subject was mentioned; which was often. It was not until a family friend came to stay with us for a few days, that the truth was revealed to my mother and father. Mary Heely, or "Heahops," as I called her, (I still have no clue why I named her that) was a wonderful person who my parents had known since childhood. She was the housemistress to Sarah, the Duchess of York, and Prince Andrew's former wife. We all have one person, usually a woman, who thought the sun rose and set for us. In their eyes, we were perfect and they battled for us when others had long gone and given up. Heahops was that person for me and I was very sad when she passed away a few years later.

Heahops was not a big fan of my sister. She felt that if any child should be accused of being rude, obnoxious, spoilt and ungrateful it should be my sister and not me. My sister would frequently shout and slam doors and every day was one of tantrums and outbursts of tears. Secretly, I was afraid of her during my childhood years because she could be very unkind bless her. On one occasion, she deliberately pushed me off our garden swing. I landed on the brick wall and my upper teeth were broken. On another day, she dragged me to the shops with an umbrella lodged under the upper roof of my mouth. She did not like me and that was rather obvious for I was never permitted (apart from once) to enter her bedroom or touch any of her belongings. I will say though that when she married, I was invited to be her bridesmaid and she was my son's Godmother. God knows I tried.

Heahops sat me down after dinner one night. Earlier, as the food was being served, my mother had reminded me to say, "Thank you." My sister chimed in with, "She doesn't know how to say that," with a sarcastic tone in her voice. I could not take it one more minute and ran away from the table. I was immediately brought back and required to sit and eat the dinner in silence. Food does not taste good when it has tears all over it and I was so miserable. My sister laughed at me the entire time. Afterwards, Heahops took me outside. I could not look at her because I knew that I was in trouble and I felt ashamed. I should not have eves dropped on my parents' conversation so I knew that if I confessed that I had listened in, I would be in even more trouble. Yet by not saying anything, I had offended everybody.

I tried not to cry, but I could not stop that child's tears from falling. I told her everything, for I figured it could not get much worse for me. After all nobody was talking to me, except with sarcastic remarks and sighs every time I walked passed them. I kept being sent to bed for refusing to eat my food and I was wetting my bed every night.

As I reiterated the story to my beloved Heahops, I looked up to see her crying. Instead of being angry with me, she wrapped her arms around me and hugged me so tenderly that I cried even more tears than before. She comforted me and told me that she would smooth over the situation with my mother and father. I plucked up the courage to ask, "Did I do the right thing by not taking the money?"

"Yes and no dear," she replied.

"I don't understand. How can it be right and wrong?" I asked.

"Because when somebody wants you to have something of theirs, you must accept it and say, 'Thank you,' for if they did not want to give it you, they wouldn't, darling." She was such a wise woman who knew how to explain things to me that made perfect sense. That was it; I should have just said, "Thank you."

I knew that Heahops had spoken to my parents, because within a few minutes they came out to where I was sitting. I can still see the expression on their faces in my mind. I had my apology rehearsed, however, before I could say a word mum and dad did the apologizing for all of us. A few years later as I sat nursing mum in her final days of life, she recalled this day by saying that it was one of the worst days of her life. She had felt so guilty and ashamed for how they had treated me. When she remembered that day and the one at boarding school, she said it always filled her with deep remorse. I reassured her kindly that I had learned a great deal from those horrible experiences and that I was grateful to have learned the gift of "Apology," that summer.

When we got back to the north of England, I plucked up the nerve to go to my aunty Joan after church and tell her the truth. She was angry with my parents, but grateful for my courage. She offered me the five pounds again and I accepted it with a very big, "Thank you so much! I will use it wisely." I was walking down the street a few weeks later when mum and I passed an old homeless man. I felt so sorry for him and I pulled that money out of my pocket and gave it to him. I never told my parents in case they would be angry with me. However, I felt he needed it far more than I did.

Teaching our children (from an early age) the etiquette of "Please," "Thank you" and "I'm sorry," is a very important lesson, which will carry them into adulthood with confidence, dignity and humbleness. We all dislike seeing children and young adults who have no concept of manners and walk about either having tantrums or with a sense of entitlement. I do not blame the younger generation for their lack of manners. I hold parents completely responsible for failing in their duty to prepare their children for the adult world.

It is never too late to learn and so here are a few thoughts of my own on how to say "Thank you," in a way that is sincere and meaningful.

1. The person you are thanking should understand that you mean what you say rather than trotting out words from a sense of obligation. Your tone should be even and you should avoid mumbling.
2. The words you use should reflect what the person did to help you. For instance, "Thank you so much for helping me with my project. I wouldn't have been able to finish it without your advice."
3. If you do not feel like the other person helped you, do not say it. The tone in your voice will tell them that you are not being honest.
4. When somebody helps us, we should realize that he or she has sacrificed his or her time or resources and a thank you recognizing that fact is important. You might say, "Thank you so much for letting me stay at your home last night. I know it was a busy time for you and it was not easy to have a houseguest. I really appreciate that you took me in anyway."
5. Using the appropriate body language is also important. You should maintain eye contact, face your body toward them, keep

your arms open, touch the person if it is appropriate (which might simply include a light touch on his or her arm) or in a professional setting a handshake is sufficient.

6. You should show emotion especially if the person has influenced your life in a big way. You do not have to cry, but let your face show how touched you are by that person's help.
7. Face to face apologies are always the best, rather than text or email.
8. Phone calls are more difficult because you cannot see the other person over the phone. It is harder to communicate your true feelings but it is better than not expressing your gratitude. Go to a quiet place before calling them. Speak clearly and slowly and only concentrate on this call. In other words, do not call somebody when you are driving or doing housework for instance. You want the person to know that they have your undivided attention.
9. Make sure that the recipient is able to speak to you. Be aware of time differences and avoid calling first thing in the morning or last thing at night.
10. Make sure your body language is open which I know sounds strange when you are using a phone to communicate, but your stance does affect the tone in your voice. If you are lying down to make the call then you will sound too casual and the sincerity will be lost.
11. To make the gratitude feel more personal use their name. For instance, "Thanks, Dave!" is much nicer than just a plain old, "Thanks!"
12. My favorite way to thank people is the good old-fashioned thank you card. These are great for professors, teachers or wedding guests for their generous gifts. I take a great deal of time to choose my cards and I err on the side of formality when I am not too familiar with how they will accept it.

Conclusion

We have so much to be grateful for in life and so many people who help us along the way with their gifts, time and talent. Learning to not only recognize when somebody has gone out of their way to help us, but to understand the best way of acknowledging this with finesse and class, is such an important character trait and gift in of itself.

In these modern times, we frequently send emails and texts to each other and simply assume that what comes through the mail boxes on our street corners are bills, election advertisements and junk. I maybe old fashioned, but I love to receive cards and hand written "Thank you," notes. Just knowing that somebody has bought me a card, written it with love, licked the stamp and envelope and gone to the post office to mail it, gives me a thrill.

Teach your children and grandchildren to have the correct etiquette of saying "Thank you," and then your child will not have to sit with their "Heahops," and shed tears about how they messed up with their five-pound holiday gift. It is up to us adults to teach our children these lessons and not to assume that they will learn them later on in life.

Please teach this to them today!

Lesson 50: "What's next?"

Welcome to the final chapter and lesson of my life to date. I wrote this book for four reasons. Firstly, God commanded me to share his teachings from east to west and from north to south and this begins that process.

Secondly, I wanted my precious son and descendants to have the story of my life, or at least the first five decades of it. Little is written about those family members who came before me, which is a calamity in my opinion. At least future generations can read my book and know the wonderful story of one of his or her relatives' walk with God. My son, Geoff, has undoubtedly paid the biggest price for his mother's obedience to God in fulfilling her responsibilities on earth. I could not be prouder of him and I could not love anybody on earth more than I do Geoff. May God protect and guide him and our descendants with his favor, grace and continued blessings.

Thirdly, I wanted to inspire others to lead happier and more fulfilled lives. As I walk forwards, my intention (if it is his will) is to expand upon the lessons contained within this autobiography and use them as a platform to help you live your lives more profoundly than you ever dared, hoped or dreamed was possible.

Fourthly, I wanted to verbalize and share with those people who have played an important role in my life, that I am a stronger and happier person for all they taught me along the road called, "Life." A few of those fellow human beings brought plates with dishes containing tough lessons for my consumption. They were difficult to swallow and harder to digest especially when the, "It is better to have loved and lost, than not to have loved at all," meant more often than not accepting the role of the perceived loser.

I am grateful to the many men and women who have helped me to understand the process of professional prowess, achievement and relationship building. They taught me to never give up or make excuses for failure, but rather to set realistic strategic goals, which would stretch me beyond the limits of leadership responsibility. I am grateful to the many people who have shown me love, kindness, respect, tenderness and compassion, not least withstanding permitting me to offer these same traits in return. To each person that has crossed my path; I would like to say sincerely that I am grateful for their precious time, friendship and kindness. I was never an easy person to live with (my life is unconventional, faith based and service with love to others driven) and I realize that I made some mistakes, which unfortunately I cannot retract. I ask forgiveness for any wrongdoings against anybody, and I pray that God blesses them in ways I cannot imagine.

We have covered some very diverse topics in this book including adoption, miscarriage, divorce, disease, death, spirituality, violence, politics, ministry, mentoring, business strategy, film and photography. I trust that you have found inspiration within some of these lessons and that you have gained some knowledge and great tips to implement within your own lives.

I am going to end this book on an upbeat note and look forward to sharing many other wonderful lessons in the future. I do hope that we meet; perhaps at a book signing or an inspirational keynote speech event.

My grandmother taught me a little song by Susan B. Warner written in 1868 that I have carried with me over the last five decades. "Jesus bids us shine," has always inspired me to shine like a huge lighthouse beacon. This light does not shine to warn you of danger; but rather to lovingly reflect the message of, "If you need a soft place to rest your weary bones, come here. This house (my being) is where Christ resides and love is the watchword and comforting blanket that is ready to envelop you with love and unconditional compassion!"

"Jesus bids us shine, with a pure clear light.
Like a little candle burning in the night.
In this world of darkness, we must surely shine.
You in your small corner and I in mine."

In the Matthew's Gospel, we are told, "You are the light of the world. A city set on a hill cannot be hidden; nor does anyone light a lamp and put it under a basket, but on the lampstand, and it gives light to all who are in the house. Let your light shine before men in such a way that they may see your good works, and glorify your father who is in heaven."

Conclusion

Life is not a solo performance. One can live peacefully as a hermit for part of it, but even the recluse becomes forlorn if he does not interact with fellow human beings from time to time. We are social creatures by nature. Together we produce an elaborate tapestry called, "Creation."

If I may humbly give you advice, it would be to respect and love others with every fiber of your being. Be generous with it and envelop others with a feeling of sincere warmth and kindness. May there never be a single creature or human being that meets you, sees you, or hears about you that leave without knowing that there is at least one person on this planet who genuinely cares about them, and who is interested to know what they can do to help you in the name of our heavenly Father.

I would also like to encourage you to take courage and not run from discomfort or to settle for superficial relationships. Learning how to love others deeply requires you to place yourself in situations that are troublesome at times. Never permit yourself to squash anger at injustice, exploitation and oppression. Rather, you should fight for justice, equality and peace. I pray that God blesses you with tears to shed for all those who suffer from pain, rejection, starvation and war. I pray that instead of turning away, you will turn towards and offer your hand to comfort them and change their pain into joy.

Finally, I pray God blesses you with the exact same thing he has given to me – foolishness to think that you can make a difference in the world; so that you will do the things that, others tell you are impossible.

The grace of our Lord Jesus Christ and the love of God and the fellowship of the Holy Spirit, be with you all, evermore. Amen.

Sources

"Onward Christian soldiers"
Public domain. Written by Sabine Baring-Gould 1865.

"Jesus bids us shine."
Public domain. Written by Susan. B. Warner, 1868

"In the bleak mid-winter."
Public domain. Written by Christina Rossetti 1872, 1904

Cover photograph by Michael Cairns of Wet Orange Studio.
5247-B International Drive Orlando, FL 32809 Telephone 321.287.6266
or email Michael@wetorangestudio.com.BJ